The Concept of Sustainability and Its Application to Labor Market Policy

Claudia Lubk

The Concept of Sustainability and Its Application to Labor Market Policy

A Discussion of Political Feasibility, Implementation, and Measurability

Springer Gabler

Claudia Lubk
Martin-Luther-Universität Halle-Wittenberg
Germany

Brandenburg University of Technology Cottbus-Senftenberg, 2016

ISBN 978-3-658-16382-2 ISBN 978-3-658-16383-9 (eBook)
DOI 10.1007/978-3-658-16383-9

Library of Congress Control Number: 2016956812

Springer Gabler

Printed on acid-free paper

This Springer Gabler imprint is published by Springer Nature
The registered company is Springer Fachmedien Wiesbaden GmbH
The registered company address is: Abraham-Lincoln-Str. 46, 65189 Wiesbaden, Germany

Danksagung

Die Verantwortung für eine wissenschaftliche A
Sie bedarf jedoch der Unterstützung, um erfolgr
Zeit der Forschung und des Schreibens dieser D
len Personen begleitet. Ich danke meinem Dokt
der mich bei der Themenfindung unterstützte un
ram Berger, dem ich für die Übernahme des Zw
stuhlleiter die Freiheit, meinen Forschungsinter
für konstruktive Gespräche zur Verfügung. Pro
Lehrstuhl ein sehr konstruktives, forschungsbe
Arbeit abschließen konnte und viele neue Impu
Kollegen an der BTU Cottbus, namentlich er
Pitsoulis, Birgit Verworn, Ute Krüger, Samah A
ich neben wissenschaftlich anregenden Diskuss
Erinnerungen. Auch meine Kollegen an der M
allem in der Endphase dieser Arbeit unterstützt
die über die berufliche Zusammenarbeit hinaus z

Schließlich hat meine Familie mit ihrer Unters
on überhaupt erst ermöglicht. Meinen Eltern
für all ihre Hilfe auf meinem bisherigen Leb
ausforderung und das Sorgen für mein körpe
Geduld und ihre wertvolle Unterstützung bein
die Endphase dieser Arbeit. Der größte Dank
jede Phase der Begeisterung, aber auch jede
lebt. Er hat mich motiviert und unterstützt, i
immer wieder ermuntert, diese Arbeit abz
forscher Anton und Helene, die die wunderb
Arbeiten sind, wäre die Zeit, die ich mit dies
annähernd so bereichernd gewesen.

Abstract

Sustainability as a guiding principle shall, according to international and national agreements, be mainstreamed into all aspects of political and everyday life. As labor market policy is an important policy field that interacts with many other policies, it should be sustainable. So far, the transfer between sustainability and labor market policy is discussed only marginally, and a generally accepted definition of sustainable labor market policy is lacking. This work aims at analyzing the transferal between the guiding principle and the policy field. The two are discussed separately to elaborate the most important aspects necessary to make the transition towards sustainable labor market policy. In addition, specific attention is given to the political feasibility of measures to implement sustainable policies, and challenges for the realization of the sustainability concept are considered. Based on this analysis, a working definition of sustainable labor market policy is developed. This definition is then applied to indicators that can be used to evaluate the sustainability of labor market policy measures and programs, thus merging three fields of research: labor market policy, sustainability, and evaluation.

Kurzfassung

Nachhaltigkeit als Leitmotiv soll nach internationalen und nationalen Beschlüssen in alle Bereiche des täglichen Lebens integriert werden. Arbeitsmarktpolitik als ein wichtiger und einflussreicher Politikbereich sollte demnach nachhaltig gestaltet werden. Bisher wurde der Zusammenhang zwischen Nachhaltigkeit und Arbeitsmarktpolitik nur am Rande diskutiert, und es existiert keine allgemein anerkannte Definition nachhaltiger Arbeitsmarktpolitik. Die vorliegende Arbeit widmet sich diesem Zusammenhang zwischen den beiden Bereichen. Beide werden zuerst getrennt diskutiert, um die relevanten Aspekte für den Transfer zur nachhaltigen Arbeitsmarktpolitik herauszuarbeiten. Besonderes Augenmerk wird dabei auf die politische Umsetzbarkeit der Maßnahmen gelegt, und Herausforderungen für die Realisierung des theoretischen Konzeptes werden betrachtet. Basierend auf dieser Analyse wird eine Arbeitsdefinition für nachhaltige Arbeitsmarktpolitik entwickelt. Diese wird dann auf Indikatoren, die zur Evaluation nachhaltiger Arbeitsmarktpolitikmaßnahmen eingesetzt werden können, angewendet. Damit werden die drei Bereiche Arbeitsmarktpolitik, Nachhaltigkeit und Evaluation miteinander verbunden.

Contents

Claudia Lubk

The Concept of Sustainability and Its Application to Labor Market Policy

A Discussion of Political Feasibility, Implementation, and Measurability

Springer Gabler

Claudia Lubk
Martin-Luther-Universität Halle-Wittenberg
Germany

Brandenburg University of Technology Cottbus-Senftenberg, 2016

ISBN 978-3-658-16382-2 ISBN 978-3-658-16383-9 (eBook)
DOI 10.1007/978-3-658-16383-9

Library of Congress Control Number: 2016956812

Springer Gabler

Printed on acid-free paper

This Springer Gabler imprint is published by Springer Nature
The registered company is Springer Fachmedien Wiesbaden GmbH
The registered company address is: Abraham-Lincoln-Str. 46, 65189 Wiesbaden, Germany

Danksagung

Die Verantwortung für eine wissenschaftliche Arbeit liegt in den Händen des Autors. Sie bedarf jedoch der Unterstützung, um erfolgreich abgeschlossen zu werden. In der Zeit der Forschung und des Schreibens dieser Dissertationsschrift wurde ich von vielen Personen begleitet. Ich danke meinem Doktorvater Professor Wolfgang Cezanne, der mich bei der Themenfindung unterstützte und die Arbeit betreute. Professor Wolfram Berger, dem ich für die Übernahme des Zweitgutachtens danke, ließ mir als Lehrstuhlleiter die Freiheit, meinen Forschungsinteressen nachzugehen und stand jederzeit für konstruktive Gespräche zur Verfügung. Professor Ulrich Blum bot mir an seinem Lehrstuhl ein sehr konstruktives, forschungsbegeistertes Umfeld, in dem ich meine Arbeit abschließen konnte und viele neue Impulse bekam. Meinen wissenschaftlichen Kollegen an der BTU Cottbus, namentlich erwähnt seien Lars Weber, Athanassios Pitsoulis, Birgit Verworn, Ute Krüger, Samah Abu Assab und Doreen Weber, verdanke ich neben wissenschaftlich anregenden Diskussionen auch viele wunderbare persönliche Erinnerungen. Auch meine Kollegen an der MLU Halle-Wittenberg haben mich vor allem in der Endphase dieser Arbeit unterstützt. Ein großer Dank gilt Isabelle Jänchen, die über die berufliche Zusammenarbeit hinaus zu einer guten Freundin wurde.

Schließlich hat meine Familie mit ihrer Unterstützung die Erstellung dieser Dissertation überhaupt erst ermöglicht. Meinen Eltern Waltraut und Rainer danke ich herzlich für all ihre Hilfe auf meinem bisherigen Lebensweg, für geistige Anregung und Herausforderung und das Sorgen für mein körperliches Wohl, aber auch ihre unendliche Geduld und ihre wertvolle Unterstützung beim Schaffen von zeitlichen Freiräumen für die Endphase dieser Arbeit. Der größte Dank gebührt aber meinem Mann Axel. Er hat jede Phase der Begeisterung, aber auch jede Zeit des Zweifels mit mir gemeinsam erlebt. Er hat mich motiviert und unterstützt, in den richtigen Momenten abgelenkt und immer wieder ermuntert, diese Arbeit abzuschließen. Ohne ihn und unsere Miniforscher Anton und Helene, die die wunderbarste Ablenkung vom wissenschaftlichen Arbeiten sind, wäre die Zeit, die ich mit dieser Forschungsarbeit verbracht habe, nicht annähernd so bereichernd gewesen.

List of Tables

List of Figures

List of Abbreviations

BAUM	Bundesdeutscher Arbeitskreis für Umweltbewusstes Management (German committee for ecologically aware management)
BMU	Bundesministerium für Umwelt, Naturschutz und Reaktorsicherheit (Federal Ministry for the Environment, Nature Conservation and Nuclear Safety)
BMWA	Bundesministerium für Wirtschaft und Arbeit (Federal Ministry for Economy and Labor)
CAN Europe	Climate Action Network Europe
CGE	Computable General Equilibrium Model
CS	Corporate Sustainability
CSDI	Composite Sustainable Development Index
CSPI	Composite Sustainability Performance Index
CSR	Corporate Social Responsibility
DeGEval	Deutsche Gesellschaft für Evaluation (German Society for Evaluation)
DESTATIS	German Federal Statistical Office
DIW	Deutsches Institut für Wirtschaftsforschung (German Institute for Economic Research)
DJSI	Dow Jones Sustainability Index
DVFA	Deutsche Vereinigung für Finanzanalyse und Asset Management (German Association for Financial Analyses and Asset Management
ECB	European Central Bank
EDP	Ecological Domestic Product
EEB	European Environmental Bureau
EF	Ecological Footprint
EI	Education Index
EMAS	Eco-Management and Audit Scheme
EPE	European Partners for the Environment
ESAW	European Statistics on Accidents at Work
ESD	Education for Sustainable Development
ESF	European Social Fund
ESDN	European Sustainable Development Network

ETUC	European Trade Union Confederation
EUROSIF	European Sustainable Investment Forum
EU SDS	European Unions' Sustainable Development Strategy
EYSI	Expected Years of Schooling Index
FNG	Forum Nachhaltige Geldanlagen (Forum for Sustainable Investments)
FoEE	Friends of the Earth Europe
GVA	Gross Value Added
GDP	Gross Domestic Product
GNI	Gross National Income
HDI	Human Development Index
HGF	Helmholtz-Gemeinschaft Deutscher Forschungsgesellschaften (Helmholtz Community of German Research Centers)
HPI	Happy Planet Index
HR	Human Resources
IAB	Institut für Arbeitsmarkt- und Berufsforschung (Institute for Employment Research)
II	Income Index
IISD	International Institute for Sustainable Development
ILO	International Labour Organization
IMF	International Monetary Fund
ISEW	Index of Sustainable Economic Welfare
IZA	Forschungsinstitut zur Zukunft der Arbeit (Institute for the Study of Labor)
LEI	Life Expectancy Index
LInx	Life Cycle Index
LMP	Labor Market Policy
LPI	Living Planet Index
MCE	Multicriteria Evaluation
MEW	Measure of Economic Welfare
MYSI	Mean Years of Schooling Index
NABU	Naturschutzbund Deutschland (German Society for Nature Conservation)
NGO	Non-Governmental Organization

NRA	Natural Resource Accounting
NRU	Natural Rate of Unemployment
PPP	Purchasing Power Parity
PSR	Pressure-State-Response
QWL	Quality of Work Life
R&D	Research and Development
REAM	Rapid Evaluation and Assessment Method
RTE	Real-Time Evaluations
RNE	Rat für Nachhaltige Entwicklung (German Council for Sustainable Development)
SDG	Sustainable Development Goals
SEEA	System of integrated Environmental and Economic Accounting
SOEP	Socio-Economic Panel
SPI	Sustainability Performance Index
SPI	Social Progress Indicator
SRU	Sachverständigenrat für Umweltfragen (German Council of Environmental Advisors)
UN	United Nations
UNCED	United Nations Conference on Environment and Development
UNCHE	United Nations Conference on the Human Environment
UNCSD	United Nations Conference on Sustainable Development (Rio 20+)
UN DESA	United Nations Department of Economic and Social Affairs
UNDP	United Nations Development Programme
UNESCO	United Nations Educational, Scientific and Cultural Organization
UNFCCC	United Nations Framework Convention on Climate Change
UNSDSN	United Nations Sustainable Development Solutions Network
WCED	World Commission on Environment and Development
WGBU	Wissenschaftlicher Beirat der Bundesregierung "Globale Umweltveränderungen" (German Advisory Council on Global Change)
WSSD	World Summit on Sustainable Development

1. Introduction

In a more and more connected and complex world, where distances are often considered as relative and transportation- and transaction costs seem to sink due to technical developments, the awareness of global ecological, social and economic challenges is considerable. News of natural disasters spread quickly and is covered in international media; economic crises are usually not limited to one region but are international, if not global; and most people are confronted with poverty and social inequality on a regular basis, either because they have to experience them themselves or because information about those topics is abundant.

Therefore, it seems apparent that concepts like sustainability, which comprises ecological, social and economic concerns and puts them in a framework that works on a global level, is an adequate option for a globally accepted guiding principle. If this is the case, it is necessary to integrate the concept into political decisions and measures, especially those that concern a large number of individuals and an important aspect of those individuals' lives. In the case of Germany, there are currently more than 800.000 persons taking part in labor market policy measures (BUNDESAGENTUR FÜR ARBEIT 2015), more than 0.4% of the german GDP is spent on active, more than 1% of GDP on passive labor market policy measures (KLUVE 2013). The percentages in other countries are similar. In general, labor market policy receives a considerable amount of total public spending. As a political field with a large impact on the micro- but also the macro level, the guiding principle of sustainability, if it is to be realized, must also be integrated in labor market policy and the according measures.

This work assesses how sustainability and the labor market are connected and how current indicators used to evaluate sustainability or labor market policy measures consider the connection between the two aspects. So far, to the author's best knowledge, the connection between the labor market and sustainability has not been made in more than a passing mention. For example, there is no clear definition of sustainable labor market policy. Consequently, research to evaluate policy measures must first find a suitable definition. To do so, a thorough understanding of sustainability and its aspects is necessary.

Chapter 2 therefore discusses the definitions, characteristics and dimensions of sustainability.

Chapter 3 then moves on to examine the realization of sustainability. It considers past achievements and moves on to the description of strategies for sustainable development to provide a basis for the following discussion of the political feasibility of an implementation of the concept. Challenges for the implementation in society, but also on a political and international level are analyzed with the help of economic concepts.

One main point of this work is the application of sustainability to labor market policy. Chapter 4 examines the labor market. General characteristics of labor market policy and the measures used to intervene in the market are discussed and connected with the dimensions of sustainability. A definition of sustainable labor market policy is developed.

Chapter 5 is a methodical chapter regarding the use and building of indicators. Indicators for sustainable development are discussed, with an emphasis on german indicator systems, but on the international level. The measurement of wellbeing is then used as an example for the building of indicators.

As evaluation is one of the main areas of application for indicators, chapter 6 gives an overview over the tasks and proceedings of an evaluation. It provides necessary information about the requirements for indicators that can be used in assessments.

In chapter 7, an indicator set for the evaluation of the aspect of sustainability in labor market policy is developed. This set comprises macroeconomic as well as microeconomic aspects and assesses the indicators according to the sustainability criteria developed in the chapters before.

2. Sustainability

Watching the news or reading newspapers on any given day leads to being confronted with one word over and over again: sustainability. Sustainability or sustainable development has become a commonly used and rather familiar slogan. It is used by politicians, researchers and journalists, but is also increasingly found in regular conversations.

A 2009 survey of the Bertelsmann foundation (BERTELSMANN STIFTUNG 2009) found that 62% of young Austrians and Germans interviewed had already thought about questions associated with sustainability.[1] Another representative survey conducted in 2010 by the Federal Environment Ministry of Germany (BMU) and the German Counsel on Sustainable Development showed that the degree of familiarity with the concept of sustainability increased more than threefold within a few years. In 2000, only 13% of the interviewees had heard of the principle sustainable development; this percentage increased to 43% in 2010 (RAT FÜR NACHHALTIGE ENTWICKLUNG 2010; BMU, UMWELTBUNDESAMT 2010)[2].

A simple search of the web via Google yields more than 200 million hits for "sustainable development" and more than 100 million hits for "sustainability"[3]. Even assuming a large number of double hits, irrelevant pages and outdated results, those numbers are impressive. Anyone watching the news or reading newspapers cannot escape the term either. Sustainability clearly is not a concept known only to a handful of scientists in their ivory tower.

It being such a widely known concept, one has to wonder whether everyone has the same understanding of the term and whether there is a commonly known exact definition. The examples cited above, the web links containing the term, the news shows and newspaper articles, the interviewees asked about their knowledge about sustainable development – are they talking about the same concept? On closer observance, they do not have much in common. They come from different areas – the performance of companies, insurance issues, sports, museums, politics and environment, just to name

---

1 The question asked was: „Have you ever considered whether your way of living might harm other people, future generations or nature?" Detailed analysis revealed that the likeliness for a positive answer increased with the level of education.

2 The question asked was: „Sustainable Development is sometimes appears as a general principle for environment protection. Have you or have you not heard of this principle?"

3 http://www.google.de; searched September 2013.

a few. They are used in different contexts and with different emphasis. So either people are talking about different concepts with the same name; or sustainability is a very comprehensive concept with a definition that allows for a generous application in various contexts. Of course it is also possible that the term is often used incorrectly and is not suitable for the situations it is applied to. While this latter possibility raises an interesting research question – whether a possibly widespread erroneous and misleading use of an accepted and positively connoted concept is coincidental or intentional – it will be discarded for the purpose of this work, as the inaccurate use of catchphrases belongs to a different field of research.

If it was the option of different concepts sharing the same name, research on the topic would have to differentiate between the different forms of sustainability, and their respective definition and application. It would then have to decide which of the definitions is applicable for researching labor market policy. This option has to be kept in mind, as it is possible that the people using the term "sustainability" have different definitions or concepts in mind when doing so. The relevant question would then be whether the different ideas about sustainability that people intend to convey are due to the fact that there is no such thing as the one true definition of sustainability, or whether they originate in an inadequate knowledge of this one true definition.

As the following sections will show, most "official" definitions (i.e., those used by researchers, public and political institutions) stem from a common origin, which contradicts the theory that there is no one basic concept of sustainability. At the same time, this fact does not preclude the hypothesis of the different concepts people have in mind when using the terms "sustainability" or "sustainable development". Based on an elementary definition, the concept may have been developed into different directions by different stakeholders. This possibility will be discussed in subsection 2.3.

However, if sustainability is an inclusive concept with a very broad definition which can be applied to many different fields, how does one specify and implement a concept this comprehensive? And is the concept with all its comprehensiveness useful for precise political decisions? Is it useful as a vision and a goal for future development on the global, federal or communal level? Or does its generous applicability lead to an easy realization of its stipulations and is it not useful as a political concept? These questions shall be discussed during the course of this chapter.

2.1 The Evolution of the Concept

Historic roots of the concept of sustainability in Germany are traced back to HANS CARL VON CARLOWITZ, who, in 1713, wrote the "Sylvicultura oeconomica", a guide to arboriculture. He criticized the short term orientation of the economy and describes the ecological limits to growth, all in reference to trees and woods. He only uses the word "nachhaltend" (sustainable) once, but explains his ideas assertively enough to be thought one of the fathers of sustainability in Germany (HABER 2011, pp. 10-11). His basic idea is to use the gains of the woods, not their substance (or, in other words, to use the interest, not the capital), and thereby preserve the resources (GRUNWALD, KOPFMÜLLER 2006).

The term, if not the concept in itself, as it most likely has been common knowledge with people working in agri- or arboriculture for a long time, has not been of specific importance in the following centuries. Its ever-growing importance is mainly due to three occurrences: The first is the publication of the Club of Rome's *The Limits to Growth* in 1972 (MEADOWS ET AL. 1972). This was followed in the 1980s by the Stockholm Conference with the appointment of the World Commission on Environment and Development (WCED), commonly called the Brundtland commission after its Chairman Gro Harlem Brundtland, former prime minister of Norway, and its report "Our common future" in 1987. The third important event was the United Nations Conference on Environment and Development in Rio de Janeiro, commonly known as the Rio Conference, in 1992, the followed by the United Nations Conference on Sustainable Development held in the same place in 2012, therefore called Rio +20.

There have been other steps towards a wide acceptance of the concept, but those three single events are the starting point for many of those. They shall shortly be introduced here, as understanding the origins of the concept and its development is necessary when trying to fully understand it and to develop appropriate and useful indicators or indicator systems to assess its success.

2.1.1 The Limits to Growth

The Limits to Growth was the publication of an important research project that tried to quantify different global development possibilities using computer models and simulations based on the concept of System Dynamics[4]. Its intention was to show the result

4 The idea of System Dynamics is to include interdependence, mutual interaction, information feedback and circular causality in a dynamic model. The models are simulated as "a system of coupled, nonlinear, first-order differential (or integral) equations" (SYSTEM DYNAMICS SOCIETY

of individuals' behaviour on a global level and to discuss mankind's ability to understand, and deal with, the results of their actions. The study was commissioned by the CLUB OF ROME.[5] The publication in 1972 has been widely disputed. It reports the results of simulations of economic and population growth under the constraint of limited resources. The underlying problem to be remedied was described by the authors as follows: "It is the predicament of mankind that man can perceive the problematique, yet, despite his considerable knowledge and skills, he does not understand the origins, significance, and interrelationships of its many components and thus is unable to devise effective responses. This failure occurs in large part because we continue to examine single items in the problematique without understanding that the whole is more than the sum of its parts, that change in one element means change in others" (MEADOWS ET AL. 1972, p. 11).

There have been many different interpretations of the study, ranging from claiming that the authors intended the prediction of the end of the world to seeing it as proving that economic growth cannot continue endlessly on a finite planet. It has been laughed about as a collection of predictions by alarmists and a work of Malthusians trying to repress economic growth. According to the studies' authors, "the intent of the project is to examine the complex of problems troubling men of all nations: poverty in the midst of plenty; degradation of the environment; loss of faith in institutions; uncontrolled urban spread; insecurity of employment; alienation of youth; rejection of traditional values; and inflation and other monetary and economic disruptions" (MEADOWS ET AL. 1972, p. 10). After the analysis of twelve different scenarios predicting possible outcomes of our world within the next century, based on a number of assumptions (RANDERS 2010), the authors came to the following conclusions:

1. "If the present growth trends in world population, industrialization, pollution, food production, and resource depletion continue unchanged, the limits to

---

2013). For an introductive overview see for example the homepage of the System Dynamics Society (http://www.systemdynamics.org/).

5 The CLUB OF ROME describes itself as "an informal association of independent leading personalities from politics, business and science, men and women who are long-term thinkers interested in contributing in a systemic interdisciplinary and holistic manner to a better world. The CLUB OF ROME members share a common concern for the future of humanity and the planet" (CLUB OF ROME 2013). The aims of the Club are defined as follows: "to identify the most crucial problems which will determine the future of humanity through integrated and forward-looking analysis; to evaluate alternative scenarios for the future and to assess risks, choices and opportunities; to develop and propose practical solutions to the challenges identified; to communicate the new insights and knowledge derived from this analysis to decision-makers in the public and private sectors and also to the general public and to stimulate public debate and effective action to improve the prospects for the future" (CLUB OF ROME 2013).

growth on this planet will be reached sometime within the next one hundred years. The most probable result will be a rather sudden and uncontrollable decline in both population and industrial capacity.

2. It is possible to alter these growth trends and to establish a condition of ecological and economic stability that is sustainable far into the future. The state of global equilibrium could be designed so that the basic material needs of each person on earth are satisfied and each person has an equal opportunity to realize his individual human potential.

3. If the world's people decide to strive for this second outcome rather than the first, the sooner they begin working to attain it, the greater will be their chances of success." (MEADOWS ET AL. 1972)

The study's novel approach and its results were widely discussed. One of its most renowned critics stated that "[t]he emergence of the anti-growth school was the latest peak in a long intellectual cycle of pessimism about economic growth that originated with Reverend T.R. Malthus in the early 1800s" (NORDHAUS 1992, p. 1). "The ultimate message was that so many constraints operate on the global economy that there is no way to wriggle out of the straitjacket of resource limitations" (NORDHAUS 1992, p. 3). NORDHAUS' critique is supported by STAVINS (1992), who in a discussion of NORDHAUS' paper *Lethal Model 2*, backs his critical point that exploration, discovery, technological progress and substitution are not or only indirectly included in the model.

This argumentation is also supported by Gunnar MYRDAL, a specialist on developing countries, who criticizes the data that is behind the simulation of the *Limits to Growth*. He points out that especially for developing countries the data is very weak. He also doubts that a global model is helpful in solving regional problems and adds that he considers the most pressing problems to be regional (MYRDAL, 1973 pp. 204-205; OLTMANS, CHOMSKY 1976, pp. 33-39). The critical points are extended to the 1992 update of the *Limits to Growth ("Beyond the Limits")*, which NORDHAUS (1992, p. 5) judges to be nothing but ""Lethal Model 2" with the same cast, plot, lines, and computerized scenery" instead of incorporating the critics notes and statements.

There are also defenders of the study, at least for its general idea, approach and its contribution to raising the public awareness for environmental problems.[6] Newer publica-

6 A collection of published reactions and statements about the *Limits to Growth* by OLTMANS and CHOMSKY cites for example Jan TINBERGEN, who stresses the study's importance in communicating the phenomena it discusses; a point of view supported by Paul A. SAMUELSON, among others; even if both criticize the preciseness and assumptions of the model (OLTMANS, CHOMSKY 1976).

tions checking the predictions of *Limits to Growth* against reality showed that the results were not very far off the mark.[7] The works' defenders also stress that the limits to growth described in the book are not, as is often assumed in discussions, limits of economic growth; instead the term refers to the limited growth of what is now called the *human ecological footprint*, a theory that many contemporary scientists, especially those concerned with sustainable development, support (RANDERS 2010). While the conclusions and statements of the Club of Rome's report were never completely removed from public, political and scientific awareness in the years after its publication, it has been cited and discussed with new force with the growing popularity of the sustainability concept.

2.1.2 The Stockholm Conference and the Brundtland Commission

The United Nations Conference on the Human Environment (UNCHE) took place in June 1972 in Stockholm (therefore often referred to as the Stockholm Conference). It was the first United Nations Conference on environment and is therefore often considered as one of the starting points of international environmental policy.[8] The participants proclaimed that "[t]he protection and improvement of the human environment is a major issue, which affects the well-being of peoples and economic development throughout the word; it is the urgent desire of the peoples of the whole world and the duty of all governments" (UNCHE 1972, p. 2). This might not sound impressive today, but seen in its time this is a very important statement, as environmental policy, or international environmental policy in particular, were not at all mainstream.

The participants of the Stockholm Conference agreed on a number of principles that can be seen as precursors to the principles and measures adopted by later conferences dealing with sustainable development. Those principles stress the fundamental rights of man to freedom and equality as well as adequate conditions of life. However, they call for the protection of the environment for the benefit of present and future generations. They demand, for example, that "[t]he capacity of the earth to produce vital re-

---

7 TURNER, for example, shows that *Limits to Growths* "standard run", which is not one of the extreme scenarios but rather one of the "middle" options, closely matches the actual data (TURNER 2008, pp. 402-410), while SIMMONS (2000) finds that while some predictions of the study were rather correct, others were even overrun.

8 Some of the UN specialized agencies held conferences on the topic before 1972, e.g., the United Nations Educational, Scientific and Cultural Organization (UNESCO), with its *Intergovernmental conference of experts on the scientific basis for rational use and conservation of the resources of the biosphere* in Paris in September 1968, but those were conferences on a scientific rather than on the government level.

newable resources must be maintained and, wherever practicable, restored or improved" (principle 3) and "[t]he non-renewable resources of the earth must be employed in such a way as to guard against the danger of their future exhaustion and to ensure that benefits from such employment are shared by all mankind" (principle 5). They also already include the social and economic dimensions in their principles, thus uniting the three dimensions ecology, economy and social affairs that are to become the basic pillars of later sustainability strategies and principles (UNCHE 1972).

Ultimately, the Stockholm Conference led to the establishment of the United Nations Environment Programme (UNEP) (DRESNER 2008), the United Nations' branch for environmental concerns, in December 1972. Almost a decade later, the next step towards a growing importance of sustainable development as a guiding principle in politics and business was the appointment of the World Commission on Environment and Development (WCED) in December 1983. Its mandate was defined as follows:

> (a) *"To propose long-term environmental strategies for achieving sustainable development to the year 2000 and beyond;*
>
> (b) *To recommend ways in which concern for the environment may be translated into greater co-operation among developing countries and between countries at different stages of economic and social development and lead to the achievement of common and mutually supportive objectives, which take account of the interrelationships between people, resources, environment and development;*
>
> (c) *To consider ways and means by which the international community can deal more effectively with environmental concerns, in the light of the other recommendations in its report;*
>
> (d) *To help to define shared perceptions of long-term environmental issues and of the appropriate efforts needed to deal successfully with the problems of protecting and enhancing the environment, a long-term agenda for action during the coming decades, and aspirational goals for the world community, taking into account the relevant resolutions of the session of a special character of the Governing Council in 1982; (...)* (UN GENERAL ASSEMBLY 1983).

The UN General Assembly was aware of the necessity to not only provide an assessment of the current environmental and developmental situation, but rather a practical guide offering strategies to implement sustainable development. Therefore, the commission's members were chosen from many different political backgrounds – e.g., finance, planning, science, technology or agriculture. This was to ensure that political principles would be observed, thereby simplifying the realization of the commission's findings (WCED 1987b).

The commission's 1987 final report *Our common future* stated clearly that it addressed governments and their agencies and ministries, but also private enterprises. But first and foremost the commission's findings were for the people, particularly the younger generations, directly or through groups, NGOs, the scientific community, and educational institutions; as they would have to understand the concept and have an interest in providing a future for their children (WCED 1987b). Thus being a report by experts on all fields for all human beings whatever their capacity or office, the report was widely accepted. *Our common future* was judged to have made an important contribution to a rising awareness of the importance of sustainable development in decision-makers but also with the general public (WCED 1987a). It contains very probably the most cited definition of sustainable development (cf. subsection 2.2) and is therefore considered something of a starting signal for a deeper engagement with the concept on all levels of society.

2.1.3 The Rio Summit in 1992

The third milestone is the United Nations Conference on Environment and Development (UNCED) in Rio de Janeiro in 1992, also called The Earth Summit. This conference was truly global, 172 Governments participated, 2.400 representatives of NGOs were present; and an additional 17.000 people attended the NGO forum that took place as a parallel event. The resulting documents were the Rio Declaration on Environment and Development; the Statement of Forest Principles; the United Nations Framework Convention on Climate Change and the United Nations Convention on Biological Diversity (UNITED NATIONS, 1997).

The conference reaffirmed its former declaration, adopted at Stockholm in 1972, and stressed the importance of international agreements (UNCED 1992b). In a new declaration, 27 principles were proclaimed. Relevant principles for sustainable development were, among others, the following:

> "Principle 8: "To achieve sustainable development and a higher quality of life for all people, states should reduce and eliminate unsustainable patterns of production and consumption and promote appropriate demographic policies.
>
> Principle 9: States should cooperate to strengthen endogenous capacity-building for sustainable development by improving scientific understanding through exchanges of scientific and technological knowledge, and by enhancing the development, adaptation, diffusion and transfer of technologies, including new and innovative technologies." (UNCED 1992b)

The problem with the resolutions of the Rio Conference was that they do not contain precise and verifiable commitments. The 27 principles proclaimed request international cooperation and protection of the environment, and to achieve a higher quality of life for all people, but do not set any specific goals or timetables. The specification and implementation of concrete actions was left to the individual governments, yielding very diverse results. Most of the principles do sound reasonable at a first reading, but raise questions at the second glance. Who decides which patterns of production are unsustainable and which indicators are used for the decision? If a higher quality of life for all people (including those in countries with an already high standard of living) is to be reached, how is the quality of life to be measured? And is the goal to realize equal quality of life for all people or an improvement of every (or some) individual's current situation? And who decides on the criteria for the measurement, which priorities are to be set and who will pay for the implementation of measures? Is it acceptable to diminish some people's well-being in order to achieve a general improvement of the quality of life? Who controls the implementation of measures, and are there penalties for countries or institutions if they do not adhere to the rules towards a sustainable development? The list of questions can be prolonged almost infinitely. The large number of open questions shows that the goals proclaimed after the Rio summit were too vague, and therefore not entirely helpful in furthering the development of precise measures and milestones to be reached.

The participants of the conference agreed to implement the principle of sustainable development in the 21st century. The so called Agenda 21 was presented, its novelty being an approach that considers ecological, economic and social dimensions as equal. However, it stipulates that in a long-term approach, economic and social activities have to play a subordinate role to the ecological dimension. This was required on the grounds of the boundaries of the ecological dimension that may not be overstepped if the survival of the human race is to be ensured. All members of the EU as well as most OECD-member states implemented national sustainability strategies until 2002, as required by the decisions adopted during the 1992 Rio de Janeiro conference on sustainability (SCHEER 2006, p. 25). Whether the implementation was successful and will succeed in the long run remains to be seen.

The overall success of the conference and its decisions is debatable. Firstly, the idea of international action towards the protection of the environment was by far not embraced by all. Especially developing countries that did not have the problem of too many factories polluting the environment, but rather the opposite, apprehended the utilization of the environmental considerations as excuse to create new trade barriers to slow their development (JOHNSON 2012). Secondly, the development and implementation of measures and strategies towards sustainable development were left in the hands of individual countries and governments. There was no generally binding set of deadlines, which diminished the effectiveness of the conference's results.

Another possible reason for not reaching the goals stated in Rio 1992 are the changing geopolitical realities such as new emerging powers (UN DESA 2012b). In the 2012 publication *Back to Our Common Future* it was acknowledged "that, since 1992, there have been areas of insufficient progress and setbacks in the integration of the three dimensions of sustainable development" (UNITED NATIONS 2012). A group of UN representatives researching the progress in reaching sustainability concluded that the hopes of Rio 1992 were not fulfilled, even if some successes were achieved. They also stated – as has been specified by many others before them (cf., e.g., the BRUNDTLAND report) – that most problems on the road to sustainability cannot be solved independently from others by one single party, thus creating the need for common action (UN DESA 2012b).

2.1.4 After Rio 1992

The Rio conference was followed by a succession of other conferences, namely the International Conference on Population and Development in 1994, the World Summit for Social Development in 1995 and the Kyoto Climate Change Conference in 1997, all but the latter ending without specific contracts[9]. In 2002, the World Summit on Sustainable Development (WSSD), also called the Earth Summit or, in reference to the first Earth Summit in Rio de Janeiro ten years before, colloquially Rio +10, took place in Johannesburg. It is often noted that the United States, as one of the biggest global players not only where pollution, economic power and influence are concerned, were absent from the Summit[10]. The Johannesburg Plan of Implementation listed many commitments, many of them with numeric specification and dates by which these goals were to be reached. For example, the proportion of people suffering from hunger was to be halved by 2015. By 2020 the lives of at least 100 million people living in slums were to be improved. The proportion of people without access to safe drinking

9 The Kyoto Protocol, relevant for sustainable development only with regards to the environmental aspects, contained commitments towards the reduction of greenhouse gases and was ratified by 192 parties, the United States not among them. (UNFCCC 1999)

10 George W. Bush decided to not attend the Johannesburg Summit, sending Colin Powell in his place – the latter only putting in a very short appearance. The gesture was judged to be clear and in line with the US decision not to ratify the Kyoto protocol and Bush Seniors only very short appearance at the Rio conference 10 years prior. This was expected to pose a significant obstacle towards gaining feasible results of the conference (FREEDLAND 2002).

water and basic sanitation was to be halved. Production and consumption were to become sustainable with the help of a 10-year framework of programs. There were also numerous commitments towards an improved management of the natural resource base and health, among other topics. To realize these goals, the commitments also contained measures to establish an institutional framework for sustainable development on the global and national levels (UN DESA 2002). The pledges were ambitious, but their realization was not enforced and even if there is no regular monitoring of the complete list, ten years after the adoption of the goals it can be said that many of the commitments have not been achieved (UN DESA 2012b).

After the limited success of former conferences and meetings, the hopes pinned on the United Nations Conference on Sustainable Development (UNCSD) in Rio de Janeiro in 2012 (also called Rio 20+ as a follow up-conference to the first Rio summit 20 years prior) were not too high. In preparation for the conference, a United Nations project named "sustainable development in the 21st century", better known by its abbreviation SD21, offers an assessment of current studies as well as a vision of sustainable development in the 21st century. The project's objective was to gather knowledge, lessons learned, data collected in recent years and current research results, to offer a substantial and relevant contribution for the UNCSD. It was also expected to contribute to discussions and further research on the topic as a whole (UN DESA 2012b). SD21 research was to be composed of four main elements, namely an assessment of the execution of decisions and strategies from former conferences; modelling long-term scenarios for sustainable development; research on certain areas of sustainable development such as energy or land use; and the design of a long-term vision for sustainable societies which was to be based on the models of ecological economics. This combination of research topics is to be kept in mind as it is structured in a way used for many evaluations and assessments not only in sustainability research.

After Rio 20+, governments, civil society groups, academia and the public had and have very different opinions on the progress made so far and the approach to be taken in the future. Opinions vary greatly on whether the path to be taken is clear, the means are there and the only thing lacking is the political will, or whether the plan and the means are lacking as well. The only thing most groups concerned agree on is that the path taken at the moment is unsustainable (UN DESA 2012b).

2.2 Definition

All discussions of sustainable development were based on the same general idea, on a common guiding principle. But whether everyone involved in the conferences and studies about the topic has the same understanding of the specifications of this guiding principle is arguable. There are a confusing number of definitions around, some of which differ only in wording, others in precision or applicability. Some of the definitions include specifications of single components, others are rather general.

2.2.1 General Definition

It is necessary to differentiate between sustainable development and sustainability. The former is the process of changing society, while the latter describes the end of the process, i.e., a status or a condition (Grunwald, Kopfmüller 2006). Thus, to reach sustainability it is necessary to enable development to be sustainable, making sustainability the long-term goal or vision and sustainable development the path towards the realization of the goal. Most characterizations refer to sustainable development. The definition most others are based on is the definition of the WCED that was published in the BRUNDTLAND report (cf. subsection 2.1.2):

> „*Sustainable development is development that meets the needs of the present without compromising the ability of future generations to meet their own needs. It contains within it two key concepts:*
>
> - *the concept of 'needs', in particular the essential needs of the world's poor, to which overriding priority should be given; and*
> - *the idea of limitations imposed by the state of technology and social organization on the environment's ability to meet present and future needs."* (WCED 1987b, 41/1-3)

The WCED definition has been the basis for many other definitions. Some are simply paraphrases, e.g., EKARDTs “Sustainability or sustainable development means that future generations will be able to live, but also that all members of the current generations do” (EKARDT 2005, p. 25).

Others widen the concept, e.g., ROGALL who defines that “Sustainable Development aims, in addition to international justice for present and future generations, to establish high ecological, economic and social-cultural standards respecting the limits of the environmental space.” (ROGALL 2007, p. 37) or aim to specify it, such as the german NETWORK FOR SUSTAINABLE ECONOMICS who rephrases the definition into “Sustainable development aims to realize adequately high ecological, economic and socio-cultural standards within the limits of the natural capacity of the earth for current and future generations, thus enforcing the principle of intra- and intergenerational justice” (NETZWERK NACHHALTIGE ÖKONOMIE 2012a, p. 2).

Another adaption comes from LUDWIG who demands at least somewhat tolerable living conditions for future generations and the chance for economic development for current generations in developing countries. He describes sustainable development as economic development that aims to regenerate or restore production and living foundations by changing current production and consumption patterns (especially in industrialized countries), thereby creating conditions of a living that can be durable for an indefinite period of time (LUDWIG 2001, p. 3).

What those definitions have in common are the aspects of time (current vs. future generations) and needs. The definitions of ROGALL and the NETWORK FOR SUSTAINABLE ECONOMICS include three areas within which sustainability is to be reached – the ecological, economic and sociocultural dimensions – but also stress that natural limits have to be respected. The hierarchy of importance of the dimensions shall be discussed in subsection 1.7. The differences between the various definitions can be attributed to the complexity, but also the dynamics of reality and the concept (GROBER 2010). But there are other, more methodological, reasons for the differences. The existing definitions of sustainability or sustainable development are either very general or very specific, depending on the context they are made for. As a general principle, certain vagueness in the definition is to be expected, as a rather superficial and unspecific definition can be adapted to any situation and is therefore more likely to be widely accepted. The concurrent need for a specific definition for concrete topics is in stark contrast to the fact that it is impossible to find a useful global definition due to the complexity of the general principle, and the different initial situations and the different needs (GÜNTHER, SCHUH 2000).

2.2.2 Sustainability as a Concept

A definition can only be the starting point for the development of concrete concepts. Sustainability is not a clear vision, presenting a future world with clear images of its design in all areas. Rather, it is a concept, a way of thinking that allows to imagine – and eventually to create – a large number of different future worlds. Therefore, a successful concept of sustainable development must include minimum requirements (what needs to be sustained, developed) as well as showing possible paths to realize the maintenance of the minimum requirements, leaving policy makers and all involved in the development and the execution of measures towards sustainable development freedom to set their own focus points. This guarantees a common denominator globally, while giving flexibility on a national and regional level (UN DESA 2012b). A person or group developing a definition of sustainability (with the intent to use that definition for projects, programs, publications, etc.) might have different objectives – benevolent or not. A political party might plan to maximize votes, companies are more interested in minimizing costs or gaining customer interest and approval, a group of nature and environment protectors will likely focus on environmental protection (TREMMEL 2003), and scientists are possibly looking for an all-encompassing definition applicable for each and every situation or a definition adapted to their specific field of research. While the latter are hopefully rather objective, if maybe either too general or too specific in their definitions, politicians' objectives could lead to definitions that are not helpful at all because they are too vague or aimed at enabling a ruling party to easily reach their self-defined goals and thereby gaining public approval while investing minimum effort and resources. Of course, political definitions can also be helpful and constructive towards realizing sustainable development.

In summary, there are manifold reasons for the different definitions and interpretations of the concept. Possibly the most important reason is that the parties involved have different perspectives, values and prioritizations and their interpretations are therefore based on different angles. This also includes different aims and intended uses and applications for the definitions. Another reason may be the differing perceptions of time frames. For a politician, any period exceeding an election period may be considered long-term, whereas environmentalists may consider such a period as a rather short-term approach.

JACOBS (1991) calls concepts allowing for a large number of competing interpretations "contestable". Sustainability is not the only widely known contestable concept; many political concepts share this property, for example liberty, (social) justice or democracy. Those contestable concepts are easy to agree on but there are many different interpretations and specifications when it is necessary to find a precise definition to implement the concepts. The precision and unambiguousness of a concept can be defined as follows: "A concept is precise if a person who knows the meaning of the concept can decide for every fully described issue whether the concept applies or not" and "a concept is unambiguous if all persons who know the meaning of the concept come to the same decision regarding the application of a fully described issue to the concept" (TREMMEL 2003, pp. 33-36). Following this explanation, the more general definitions such as the one from the Brundtland Commission are not precise, as they raise too many questions about their components; for example about the definition of needs, about the prediction of future needs, about the substitutability of (environmental) goods when assuring the possibility to fulfill future generations' needs, etc. They may be unambiguous, though, because they are vague enough to be clearly suitable and applicable for the issues described.

GÜNTHER and SCHUH describe the correlation between specification and consensus as follows: the higher the consensus, the more general is the principle. If specifications are necessary, for example to formulate measures, the consensus decreases (cf. Figure 1). This complicates the definition of sustainability or sustainable development, as it is necessary to find a precise definition that can be used as a guideline for application within political concepts, but also one that stakeholders from many very different fields can agree on – a task that is most likely impossible. So even if stakeholders were interested in a useful and specific definition of sustainability that everyone could agree to, it is likely that they would not succeed in formulating one. In cases where there is no interest in a serviceable description of the concept – possibly because the term is used as a figurehead meant to prove that its user is up to date and interested in the "good kind" of development, but is not intended to provide advice for actual action – the interest in a very general definition is indisputable anyway.

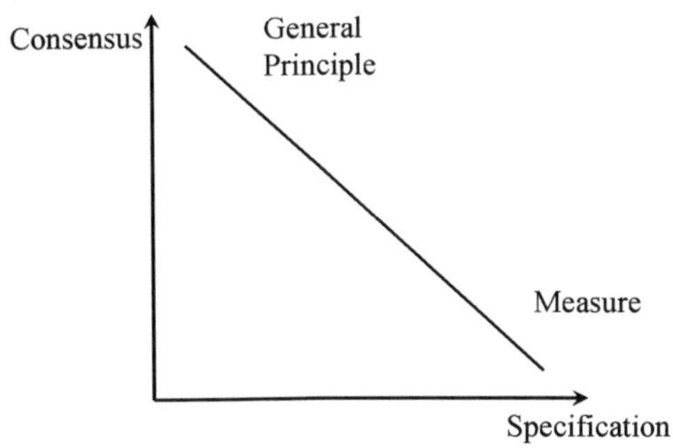

Figure 1: Consensus and specification of definitions
(GÜNTHER, SCHUH 2000, p. 16)

Political objectives and their influence on sustainable development will discussed in more detail in subsection 2.3, as they are relevant in a field that is dependent on politics for its realization.

All in all, the statement that "under the heading of SD [Sustainable Development] a number of (partly) inter-related issues such as environmental exploitation, demographic changes, economic destabilization by financial crisis or poverty are subsumed. Hence, SD rather constitutes a global, political agenda than a theoretical conception" (GUTWALD et al. 2011, p. 2) is a good summary. This view is also supported by

DRESNER (2008), who states that to agree with the concept does not mean to agree with a specific decision, but rather with the underlying values.

As to the acceptance of the concept it seems that it is generally accepted and an indisputable guiding theme for politics (ILLGE, SCHWARZE 2004), even though there are those environmentalists who suspect that a concept such as sustainability that has been as readily and widely accepted by politicians might be meaningless (DRESNER 2008). Politicians who agree on the concept (if disagreeing with regard to its content) are criticized for their disagreement on the political measures and instruments that could bring society closer to a realization of sustainability (DIEFENBACHER 2001). This discord may be one of the reasons for the criticism voiced – understandably, as a well-defined concept that does not lead to useful measures for its realization is of little help outside some ivory towers of science. The ambivalent judgment of the concept shall be discussed in further detail in subsection 2.3.

The discussion about the definition of sustainability or sustainable development helps to identify the relevant criteria for a sustainable development. Important factors mentioned in the definitions are (the observance of) natural restrictions, limitations posed by technology and society, intra- and intergenerational justice as well as the concept of "needs". ANT summarizes the basic ideas as multidimensionality, nonlinearity, integration, balance, participation and pluralism (ANT 2008b). Those crucial points and factors shall be discussed further in the process of this work.

2.3 Intra- and Intergenerational Justice

In its definition of sustainable development, the BRUNDTLAND COMMISSION states that the central guiding principle the concept was to become should ensure the possibility to meet the needs of the present while preserving future generations' ability to meet their own needs. While the concept of *needs,* or rather its definition and application, is very open, this clearly means that the commission sees equality between intragenerational and intergenerational fairness (JÖRISSEN, COENEN 2003). The German Network for Sustainable Economics seconds this interpretation in its own definition "Sustainable development aims to realize adequately high ecological, economic and sociocultural standards within the limits of the natural capacity of the earth for current and future generations, thus enforcing the principle of intra- and intergenerational justice" (NETZWERK NACHHALTIGE ÖKONOMIE 2012a, p. 2). The employment of the terms *fairness* or *justice* in this context is rather unspecific, though, as the parties concerned with sustainability have different ideas about how fairness or justice can be defined in this special case and, eventually, realized.

2.3.1 Justice and Fairness

One of the main problems of the realization and implementation of policies toward sustainability is the concretization of justice. In theory, the case is clear. The OXFORD DICTIONARY explains justice as "just behavior or treatment", "the quality of being fair and reasonable"; the CAMBRIDGE DICTIONARY enhances this explanation by stating that justice means "fairness in the way people are dealt with". As *fairness* is used to explain justice, it obviously is mandatory to understand that term as well. The CAMBRIDGE DICTIONARY helps again by stating that fairness is "the quality of treating people equally or in a way that is right or reasonable" whereas the OXFORD DICTIONARY states that being fair means "treating people equally without favouritism or discrimination".

Those definitions raise more questions than they answer. Treating people equally might be the law in many countries, but treating people equally on a global level when the surrounding circumstances vary greatly is likely an unsurmountable challenge and may lead to even greater inequality. Treating people in a way that is right or reasonable is too unspecific to help with a practical problem. The decision what is right or wrong depends on values, rules and norms of a society, and it is impossible to apply the values and norms of one society to another, thereby ranking one society's values higher than the other's. Seizing the core of treating members of a generation just is almost impossible, especially when considering the framework this is to be realized in. The same living conditions for everyone, even restrictingly assuming that every member of a generation aspires to the same lifestyle, might be realized given an indefinite supply of goods and the possibility to realize the same quality of life for everyone. This would require the means to not only provide the goods necessary, but also the leisure time, family surroundings and environmental conditions, among many other things. As goods are limited and as there are tradeoffs between the working time needed to achieve growth and the leisure time people wish for, between the supply of goods and environmental conditions, etc., the realization of justice by making everyone as well off as the societies with the highest welfare is not viable. This should not hinder the legislative and the executive to aspire to a society with at least more equal chances for everyone within current and future generations, though.

There are those who stated that as in developed countries the basic needs of the population are all but fulfilled, it seems legitimate to concentrate more on the intergenerational than intragenerational justice. Even if there existed an applicable concept of equality, how to realize equality between different generations poses an even bigger challenge: the knowledge about the needs of future generations. Assuming that basic needs are known or can be predicted (with more or less precision), we have no information about their norms, consumption structures, production functions, political structures, etc. (GRUNWALD, KOPFMÜLLER 2006). Realizing intergenerational justice is also hindered by the fact that the persons concerned cannot plead their cause themselves (SRU 2002). This is one of the most important reasons for the lack of consideration of intergenerational justice (cf. subsection 3.3.4).

Neoclassic economic theory included resource questions by representing them as allocation problems. Later on, the intertemporal dimension led to an inclusion of distributive justice between generations into the theoretical economic consideration (HOLSTEIN 2003). The neoclassical option, the handling of justice issues as allocation problem, has the advantage of simplicity. The typical approach towards fair or just allocations is the efficiency criteria, namely the PARETO-efficiency and the CALDOR-HICKS criterion. The first states that any allocation where it is impossible to improve one concerned party's welfare or utility without decreasing another one's is to be considered efficient. As real life rarely provides politicians with situations where, to say it with MILTON FRIEDMAN, there is a free lunch, i.e., where it is possible to improve some peoples' situations without "paying" for it by a decrease in another area, this criterion does not leave a lot of room for improvement. The CALDOR-HICKS criterion describes an allocation as efficient if one party's utility can be improved to such extent that it is (theoretically) possible for them to compensate the others loss. This leaves a bigger range to make policy in, but to rely on this criterion assumes the possibility to measure utility. In addition, there is the open question of compensation and just or fair distribution of the gains.

Another theoretical approach to justice is JOHN RAWLS *theory of justice*, that discusses situations where a person puts "forward conflicting claims to the division of social advantages under conditions of moderate scarcity" (RAWLS 1971, pp. 110-111). He asks whether this person has obligations or duties to third parties such as future generations, and assumes that respecting future generations' needs has to be considered a moral responsibility. The criterion used to measure justice is benefit-based: the non-deteriorating welfare (HOLSTEIN 2003). While non-deteriorating welfare is a comprehensible concept, its implementation poses new problems. In theory, intergenerational justice can be based on an egalitarian approach where future generations must be enabled to enjoy at least the same level of quality of life as current generations. Non-egalitarian approaches only demand that future generations are left with minimum conditions of humane living. Current strategies are based on the egalitarian concept. Research on egalitarian conditions distinguishes between two subcategories, namely strong and weak sustainability, which will be discussed in detail in subsection 1.5 (SRU 2002).

It has to be kept in mind that many economic theories are based on a concept of human nature that assumes absolute rationality in every action of an individual, the so called *homo oeconomicus*. Current studies show, though, that a more balanced conception of human nature would be in order. Experiments prove the assumption of individuals without compassion, without a sense of justice and fairness and without irrationalities wrong (BERGHEIM, BÖCKERS 2010). As this work deals specifically with sustainability in the labor market and sustainable labor market policy, it is necessary to have a closer look at the social aspects of justice. To define and measure the fairness or justness of a certain subject, it is necessary to clarify the following issues:

1. It is necessary to determine the measurability of advantages, disadvantages, chances, etc. This is essential to allocate the corresponding goods/values. Often, preference fulfillment is the measure of choice.
2. The principles of justice have to be chosen. When formulating a strategy for justice, the distributive aims such as equality, sufficiency, etc., have to be chosen and agreed on.
3. Justification has to be provided. This is necessary to ensure objectivity and impartiality.
4. It has to be decided who is to be concerned by the specific definition of justice. All human beings or only a certain group of people? (GUTWALD ET AL. 2011)

These four points are in accordance with the requirements of a successful evaluation, the planning of political strategies and measures or, in fact, the procedures of any strategy, be it scientific, political or corporate.

2.3.2 Calculation

The calculations necessary to specify and quantify justice and fairness have occupied many scientists, commissions and politicians, as concrete numbers are necessary to communicate and, in some cases, get permission to realize, projects. There are different approaches possible, depending on the assumptions made about the requirements of future generations. The assumptions are based on ethical norms and on the time frame considered (KRYSIAK 2007). PFISTER and RENN (1996) state that it is possible to determine the potential that is necessary to enable future generations to gain experiences that are desirable from a present-day point of view to be preserved.

One method of quantification is the balance of generations that aims to quantify a possible gap between revenues and expense employing a long-term approach. The basic idea is an intergenerative budgeting system that takes into account that current national debt has to be repaid with the net tax payments of current and future generations. Net tax payments are defined extensively to include all payments made to the fiscal sector against payments and benefits received by the fiscal sector such as public goods, education and other transfers; this net value is then weighted with estimations of life expectancy and an estimated economic growth rate. This calculation yields, among other indicators, a balance of generations or, in other words, the implicit national debt. If this indicator is negative, the future claims of (future and current) tax payers, given the continuance of the current legal situation, are higher than the sums needed to pay off the debt, thus creating a so called sustainability gap (HAGIST ET AL. 2006).

The German Federal Statistical Office (DESTATIS) also collects data to monitor intergenerational justice, including environmental indicators such as the use of renewable energies or greenhouse emissions, GDP indicators such as government deficit, the investment quota or private and public spending for research and development, as well as educational indicators such as young people's degrees or qualifications (STATISTISCHES BUNDESAMT 2010a). These data give a hint to the state of provision for intergenerational justice, but do not offer an assessment at first glance, as the bundle of indicators does not set any priorities or weightings. The indicator bundle is not useful for an exact calculation. Another approach towards quantification is the requirement of a constant capital stock, defining sustainability as the situation where this capital stock is preserved. The maximum amount of goods that may be consumed during a period can be calculated as

Amount of goods to be consumed

= goods and services produced within period – degradation of capital stock

(PFISTER, RENN 1996, p. 9).What this calculation does not include is a specific definition of the capital stock to be preserved. A detailed discussion of the possible interpretations can be found in subsection 1.5. One of the challenges of calculating the necessary stocks and possible utilities of future generations are difficulties when estimating future values. For example, Cost-benefit-analyses are a common instrument to evaluate policy measures. To analyze long-term effects, discounting (and thus making results comparable) is often the measure of choice, given a monetary estimation of the effect. This implies that all eventualities would have to be predicted and included in the calculation (BAYER 2004). The advantages of discounting are for one that individuals tend to prefer current consumption over future consumption, as is proved for example by the large number of credits to finance current consumption instead of saving and consuming in the future. Also, economic growth means that future generations will be better off, therefore discounting is justified; and lastly, there is uncertainty regarding future developments and preferences of future generations, which some take to justify a concentration on current generations' needs. These reasons are arguable, though. A preference for current consumption does not increase the right to deplete natural resources, thereby diminishing future generations' chances for consumption. Also, it is highly disputed if economic growth really leads to increased wellbeing (cf. subsection 5.7). And the third argument for discounting, the uncertainty and thus the right to bias accounting toward current generations, is difficult for moral reasons, as the simple existence of uncertainty does not justify passing on the risk to future generations (SRU 2002).

Another disadvantage of discounting is that long-term effects and yields are discounted and therefore systematically smaller than contemporary effects, and thus biased towards those political measures in favor of current and at the expense of future generations. This leads to measures with high current costs but high(er) future benefits not being realized, but favors measures with current benefits but high future costs (BAYER 2004).

Another aspect that has to be taken into account is the existence of discontinuities. As they cannot be anticipated in most cases and disrupt natural as well as socioeconomic and political systems, they contest the system of discounting and the predictions or extrapolations this is based on (MYERS, KENT 2008). The unpredictability of future generations needs does complicate the adoption of measures appropriate for intergenerational justice. This should not be used as an excuse to dispense with the concept as a whole or to abstain from taking measures, though. The current calculation methods, if inadequate and in need of improvement, do offer a basis to start from.

2.4 Institutions to Further Sustainable Development

To implement the guiding principle of sustainable development in all levels of society, law-making and everyday life in general, it is necessary to institutionalize it. The UN stresses the need to integrate sustainable development on all levels while recognizing interlinkages (UNITED NATIONS 2012). Sustainability is a guiding principle. Therefore, it has to be kept in mind that the superordinate institutions of sustainable development are norms and values. This includes the explicit implementation of sustainability in all fields of politics and society, but also more implicit applications such as adapted lifestyles or company principles. Some scientists even suggest the inclusion of a fourth dimension, institutions, into the concept of sustainable development with its currently more or less undisputed three dimensions (ecology, economy and social). This column would comprise participation and justice as well as fields like public health or social security and welfare. KLEINE (2009) considers this dimension rather as a cross-sectional task affecting the three traditional columns, because "institutions" concentrate on structural or procedural aspects rather than substantial aims. As the classical concept of sustainability assumes politics to be able to manage society, therefore showing a major potential to solve problems occurring when trying to reconcile the individual aspects of sustainability (WETZEL 2005), an efficient institutionalized approach is necessary.

The sustainability problem is a global one with local impact; institutions therefore have to be formed on a local, regional, national and global level. Apart from typical institutions on a government- or NGO-level, it is also essential to institutionalize sustainability as a guiding principle in education. This helps to establish sustainable development in all levels of society, thus raising acceptance and normalcy of the concept. Also, the topic has to be part of any technical and vocational training especially in, but not limited to, sectors where the lack of a skilled labor force can impede a country's sustainable development (JANN ET AL. 2006). When discussing institutions it has to be kept in mind that while the economic approach to choosing the appropriate instruments to implement a policy or a program is to promote overall economic efficiency and social welfare, the political approach would be to not only consider those aspects, but to also include political and administrative aspects (HOWLETT 1991). The difficulty with political and governmental institutions is that they are fragmented and allocated to specific fields – in social policy, for example, there are health, education, labor, etc. – but there are usually no entities that connect all those different fields, let alone with superior rights to force the fragmented institutions to follow one guiding principle. An operationalization of sustainability is therefore rather difficult and remains organized in very small sections instead of concentrating on the big picture. The problem of the fragmented institutions can be solved by building institutional frameworks to meet the challenges of sustainable development. These frameworks must concentrate on four principles:

(1) Improve governance

(2) Improve measurement, monitoring and evaluation systems

(3) Assess the roles of public and private actors

(4) Increase the resilience of human and natural systems (UN DESA 2012b).

The following Table 1 gives an overview over the institutions on the different levels. This overview is incomplete and must remain so, as the number of institutions changes constantly and it is, especially on the NGO-level at the national and local stage, hard, if not impossible, to identify all groups involved. The examples given are from a German point of view, thus choosing the European level as a reference between the global and national level, and german institutions on the national and local level.

INSTITUTIONS FOR SUSTAINABLE DEVELOPMENT				
Level	Global	European	National	Local
Political	- Rio- and Rio +10/20+ related: UNCSD, UNFCCC, Agenda 21, Johannesburg Plan of Action, SDG - UN DESA - UNEP - UNSDSN - ILO	- EU SDS - ESDN - Guidelines and decrees - EMAS-decree	- RNE - SRU - WGBU - Enquete Commission of the Parliament - National Sustainability Strategy - Environmental laws	- Local Agenda 21 processes
NGO/ company	- ESD - Dow Jones Sustainability Index - FTSE4GOOD - MSCI World ESG Index - Domini 400 Social Index - Green Cross International	-Green 10 (=10 biggest green NGOs in Brussels; eg. CAN Europe, FoEE, EEB) - EPE	- German Corporate Governance Index - Responsible Care - Germanwatch - NABU - BAUM	- Local youth organizations, environment groups, etc.

Table 1: Institutions and organizations concerned with sustainable development
(own selection)

Apart from the well-known institutions of the UN, it is interesting to note the institutions on the company level. Sustainability has become important enough for customers to incite the creation of company sustainability rules. Indices like the FTSE4GOOD, an ethical stock market index, ask companies who want to become part of the FTSE4Good Index to fulfill a number of criteria from different areas such as environmental management, climate change, human and labor rights, supply chain labor standards and governance related criteria, namely concerning bribery (FTSE 2011). The Dow Jones Sustainability Index (DJSI) operates in a similar manner: a defined set of criteria and weightings is used to assess the opportunities and risks deriving from economic, environmental and social developments for the eligible companies (DJSI 2010). Institutions not included in the overview, but nonetheless indispensable for sustainable development, are some religious institutions, but more importantly education and research institutions.

It has been widely discussed that profound knowledge about sustainability and sustainable development are elementary for an eventual successful implementation of measures towards a more sustainable world, and the mainstreaming of the general principle that has been called for cannot take place without educated societies that understand the concept and its pre-eminent significa nce. The exemplary institutions listed above are only a selection out of a very large number of institutions on every level that are concerned with sustainability. The existence of such a large number of institutions is a first success, but it also does pose problems. It has been discussed in subsection 1.2, that the parties concerned often choose their own definitions of sustainability or sustainable development according to their aims and approaches. Based on their definitions, they decide on aims and measures to be taken. But as the number of institutions multiplies, the number of interpretations of the concepts does, too. A large number of institutions working independently of each other, sometimes competing for funding, supporters and acknowledgment, may actually slow down the process if they do not cooperate with each other. One example for such cooperation in Germany is the forum environment and development, a federation of 35 NGOs who developed their own set of aims and indicators towards a sustainable development (HENSELING ET AL. 1999). The collaboration of small NGOs leads to a multiplication of the individual influences and can thus further the propagation of the concept and increase the likelihood of success.

To further the general acceptance of sustainable development as guiding principle, the general public, but also decision makers on all levels have to trust institutions responsible for furthering the concept. A GLOBESCAN survey among more than 24.000 people in 23 countries from all continents found that interviewees attest scientists and NGOs the best performance, while national governments are rated poorly. When asked which institutions have the highest impact, NGOs were not considered very successful, though. Only scientists were rated to have both a high impact and a high performance (cf. Figure 2) (GLOBE SCAN/SUSTAINABILITY 2012b). These results should be worrying the responsible institutions as those with the highest impact have low performances (excepting scientists) in the judgment of their peoples.

The survey also asked which institutions of sustainable development the interviewees trusted. Scientists ranked highest in their estimation with a net trust of 52 percentage points[11], followed by NGOs with a net trust of 29 percentage points. National governments enjoy a net trust of only 2 percentage points, an alarmingly low amount.

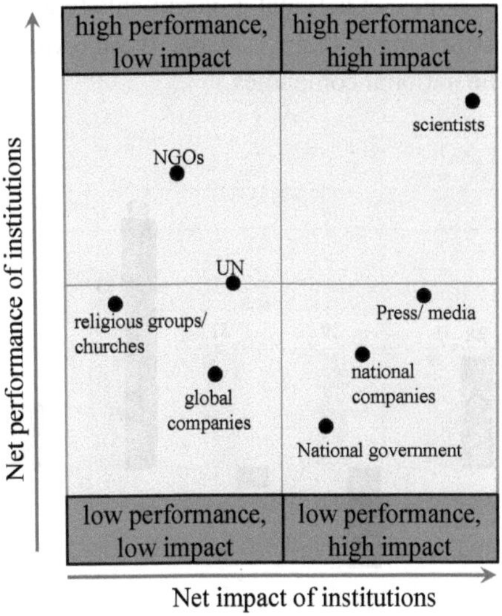

Figure 2: Potential impact and performance of institutions on sustainable development
(GLOBESCAN/SUSTAINABILITY 2012b, p. 12)

It has to be noted though, that there are large differences between industrialized an emerging economies. While in industrialized countries scientists are valued with a net trust of 63 percentage points, emerging economies award them a net trust of 43 percentage points. All in all, interviewees in industrialized economies were a lot more

11 The question asked was "And how much impact, if any, do you think each of these institutions can have in solving society's challenges? And how well would you say each of the following institutions are doing in helping make progress on these economic, social and environmental challenges?", with the answer categories "doing a very good job, "doing a good job", doing a poor job" and "doing a very poor job". Net impact is then calculated by answers "very good" and "good" minus "poor" and "very poor" in percentages (GLOBESCAN/SUSTAINABILITY 2012b).

critical towards (almost all) institutions than their counterparts in emerging economies. The biggest difference (apart from trust in religious groups and churches) can be seen in trust in companies. In emerging economies, global and national companies are rated as rather trustworthy, in industrialized countries the answers "just a little trust" and "not trust at all" prevailed (cf. Figure 3).

The most important and summarizing question, which institution the interviewed thought had the highest potential impact in solving society's challenges, varies widely among countries. While some put their hopes on national governments (e.g., in Russia, China and Brazil), others rather trust scientists (e.g., Canada, India, Australia, and USA) or, as is the case in Germany, the national companies.

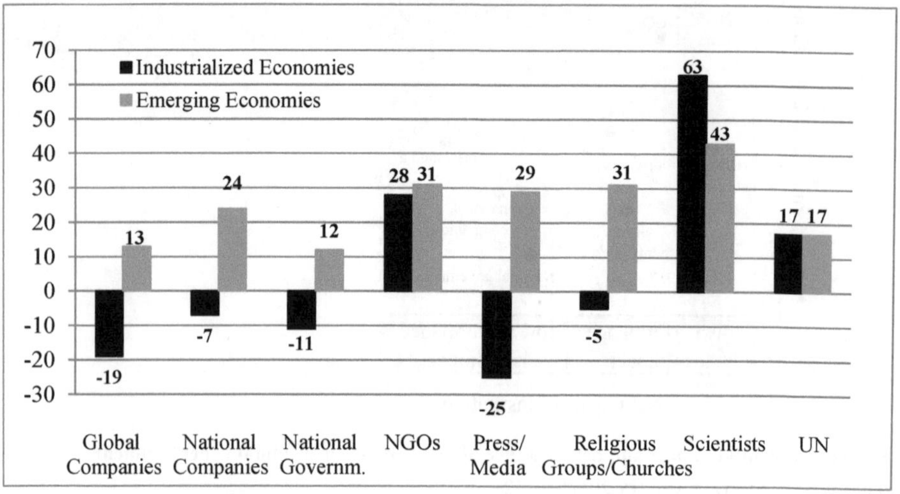

Figure 3: Net trust in institutions

Industrialized vs emerging economies, 2012 (GLOBESCAN/SUSTAINABILITY 2012b)

2.5 Characteristics of Sustainability

One of the areas where scientists', but also institutions' definitions and interpretations of sustainability greatly differ is the determination of the characteristics of sustainability. Assuming an agreement on one definition of sustainability or sustainability, for example on the definition of the Brundtland commission, the realization and implementation of the concept needs a closer inspection. The statement that "sustainable development, which implies meeting the needs of the present without compromising the ability of future generations to meet their own needs" (WCED 1987a) is necessary leaves a number of questions open. One of those is the interpretation of how the ability of future generations to meet their needs is to be sustained. The most basic interpretation is that the capital stock of natural resources has to be sustained to the extent that the welfare of future generations can be comparable to that of the current generation (PFISTER, RENN 1996). The question of welfare and its comparability shall be briefly discussed in subsection 4.7, the point to be considered here is the sustaining of capital stock. There are three different interpretations of this fact:

(1) Different kinds of capital[12] are interchangeable, but the total capital stock has to be constant. This means that it is acceptable to use all natural capital if it is replaced by another kind of capital stock. This concept is called weak sustainability.

(2) Substitution between different kinds of capital is not possible/ allowed. Therefore, natural capital cannot be used and then replaced with another kind of capital stock. This concept is called strong sustainability.

As a compromise between (1) weak and (2) strong sustainability, the concept of "reasonable" or "balanced" sustainability has been suggested. This concept assumes that natural capital can be substituted to a certain level. Factor mobility is, under certain premises, possible. This compromise takes possible future technological development into account, even though the assumptions necessary to do so are restrictive (BLAZEJCZAK, EDLER 2004).

The basic distinction between weak and strong sustainability is whether human-made capital and natural capital are pooled or considered separate capital stocks (DRESNER 2008). A typical model that stands for weak sustainability is SOLOW's neoclassic model. In this model, an intertemporal social welfare function aiming to ensure a non-declining level of benefit for current and future generations is employed. Limits to growth or the use of capital stock can be overcome by technological change, the substitution of manmade capital for natural capital and returns to scale. This allows for example for a degradation of the environmental situation if the decline of benefits caused therefrom can be compensated by an increased consummation of manmade goods. Other models, mainly argued for by ecologic economists, consider the protection of the environment as the only way to ensure sustainability (HOLSTEIN 2003; HAUFF, SCHIFFER 2013).

12 Suggested is for example a distinction between financial, natural, produced, human and social capital (GOODWIN 2003).

Both weak and strong sustainability have their advantages and disadvantages. One benefit of the concept of weak sustainability is that it simply assumes that the utility of future generations shall remain on the same level as that of current generations. This does not exclude the possibility of a future higher level of utility, of course, but also does not explicitly include it. This is due to the assumption that a higher utility in the future likely means that current utility could be increased without hurting the principle that future generations should be able to enjoy the same utility level. The idea of a certain utility level leaves open how that level is to be reached. As the same utility level can be achieved with different inputs or input combinations, it is not necessary that the current conditions are maintained. Thus, the concept is easier to implement than the concept of strong sustainability and the costs are likely smaller because there are more possibilities to find the most efficient way to realize the preservation of the welfare level.

A drawback of the model of weak sustainability is the non-predictability of technical progress. The concept allows for the substitution of natural capital with other forms of capital, so that the overuse of non-reproducible resources can be compensated by technical progress that allows to substitute the lost resources. As technological progress cannot be predicted, it is impossible to calculate the allowed actual use of natural resources to meet the conditions of sustainable development. In addition, most natural resources have different capacities; therefore a substitution of natural capital by technological progress has to fulfill all of those capacities, which will prove difficult in most cases (SRU 2002).

Strong sustainability, on the other hand, does not allow the substitution of natural capital. Thus, renewable resources may only be used to the extent of their regeneration. But non-renewable resources may not be used at all if adhering to the concept, that way neither current nor future generations would profit from the resources (SRU 2002). The concept asks for a comprehensive change of current production and consumption and will be hard, if not impossible, to implement.

The concept of "balanced" or "reasonable" sustainability has been introduced to combine the advantages of the two opposed concepts. It joins the ecocentric approach of strong sustainability and the anthropocentric view of the supporters of weak sustainability and develops an eco-anthropocentric concept that does not agree with the neoclassic efficiency triangle of technology, growth and market, but does not fully support the ecological approach of stopping economic growth altogether and concentrating only on ecology either. Table 2 offers an overview over the strategies discussed. All three options accept the constant capital rule as a foundation.

Types of Sustainability		
Constant Capital Rule		
Weak Sustainability	**Balanced Sustainability**	**Strong Sustainability**
• Purely anthropocentric • Harmony between growth and environment • Ecological capital fully substitutable • Pro-growth (with moderate environmental policy) • Strategy: efficiency through technology, growth and market • Conventional cost-benefit-analysis • Representatives: neoclassical economists (growth optimists)	• Eco-anthropocentric • Positive turnaround through environmental policy possible • Ecological capital partly substitutable • pro ecological/sustainable growth • Strategy: ecological consumption patterns and efficiency through technology, politics and market • Ecologically enhanced cost-benefit-analysis • Representatives: social scientists (growth optimizers)	• Ecocentric • Conflicts between growth and environment • Ecological capital not substitutable • Sustainable growth impossible • Strategy: stop growth, abdication and efficiency through individuals and politics • Against cost-benefit-analysis • Representatives: ecological economists (growth pessimists)

Table 2: Types of sustainability
(STEURER 2001)

2.6 Sustainability Models

An important aspect of mainstreaming the concept is to describe the theoretical models of sustainability in a clear and unambiguous way. Graphic representation is a factor that should not be neglected, as it helps understand the concept and eases the communication between different interest groups. Early sustainability concepts stress the ecological aspect and are therefore considered one-column-concepts, typically environment plans or –strategies (KLEINE 2009). Later models are more complex, the most important ones shall be described in the following subsections. The specific characteristics of each dimension will be discussed in detail in subsection 2.7.

2.6.1 The Pillar Models

The most basic model to depict sustainability is a three pillar or column model. The model is based on the assumption that all three pillars should be treated as equal. As the definitions of sustainability are often interpreted to refer to the three dimensions ecological, economic and social sustainability, especially after Rio 1992, the depiction is based upon those pillars. It is impossible to relate the three pillar model of sustainable development to a single author as it grew historically (KLEINE 2009). It is notable that each column stands for itself (cf. Figure 4). Sustainability is added as the uniting principle roofing the pillars.

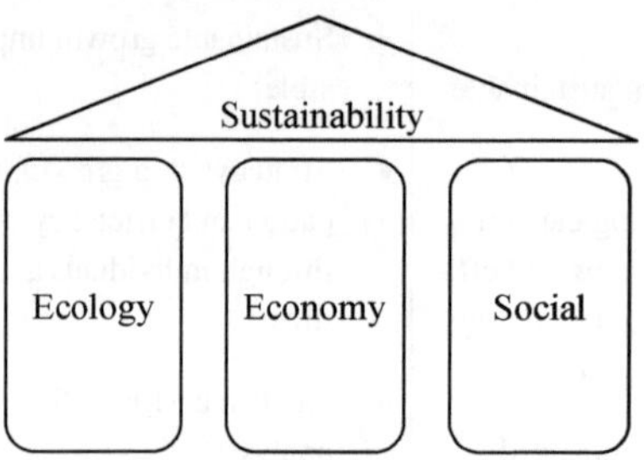

Figure 4: Three-pillar model of sustainability
(own depiction, model is used widely in scientific and popular publications in similar form)

The model has been politically influential in Germany and did further an increased appreciation of the ecological aspects, as it postulates the equality of economic, ecologic und social development. It is criticized, though, that the concept has been used as a kind of wish list, where individual preferences of stakeholders are written into one of the pillars, thus furthering arbitrary classifications and weightings (SRU 2002). Also, sustainability is increasingly seen as an integrated, holistic concept and the borders between the dimensions cannot be defined clearly (BUNDESREGIERUNG 2008). It is not always possible to distinguish, which action or right belongs to which column, and actions towards sustainability in one pillar may decrease sustainability in another sector (EKARDT 2005). If all pillars are treated as of equal importance, strong sustainability (cf. subsection 2.5) is impossible to reach. Without ecological boundaries, measures to realize economic and social sustainability would be allowed to deplete natural resources and could still be evaluated as successful.

Another version of the three-pillar-concept has been suggested by a joint committee of German and French experts on sustainability who, requested by the Franco-German

Ministerial Council, wrote a report on *monitoring economic performance, quality of life and sustainability*. Those experts suggest the following pillars to support political decisions:

(1) Economic performance and material well-being,

(2) Non-material well-being and quality of life,

(3) Sustainability (can the current level of well-being be sustained for future generations?)

(CONSEIL D'ANALYSE ÉCONOMIQUE, SACHVERSTÄNDIGENRAT ZUR BEGUTACHTUNG DER GESAMTWIRTSCHAFTLICHEN ENTWICKLUNG 2011). This approach tackles one of the problems of the three pillar model with equal dimensions: that the three pillars belong to very different scientific fields. Therefore, the scientific development in every pillar, the identification of qualitative and quantitative targets, the design of indicator systems and all related research, have developed independent of the other pillars. That was probably unavoidable due to the growing complexity of the topic, but hampers the realization of sustainable development policies (KLEINE 2009). With the suggestion of the CONSEIL D'ANALYSE ÉCONOMIQUE and the SACHVERSTÄNDIGENRAT, the interdependence of the three dimensions is taken into account.

When discussing a model of three pillars, it is also necessary to keep in mind that the model may be appropriate for developed countries, where economic and social sustainability may not be realized yet, but where those two dimensions have already been brought to a high level, thus easing the concentration on the environmental pillar. This may look different in a developing country, where survival and economic growth, or an improved quality of life, take precedence.

The most important objection towards this depiction of sustainable development is the lacking consideration of links between the three dimensions. The basic fields of politics are usually easily linked to one of the three dimensions, but every factor is influenced by and influences other factors, thus creating a complex, interlinked model. An example of those links is shown in Figure 5. As the world we are living in is not one-dimensional, but rather complex, it is necessary to find a visualization of sustainability that at least begins to capture this complexity. The three pillar model is therefore not or only for limited purposes the optimum depiction.

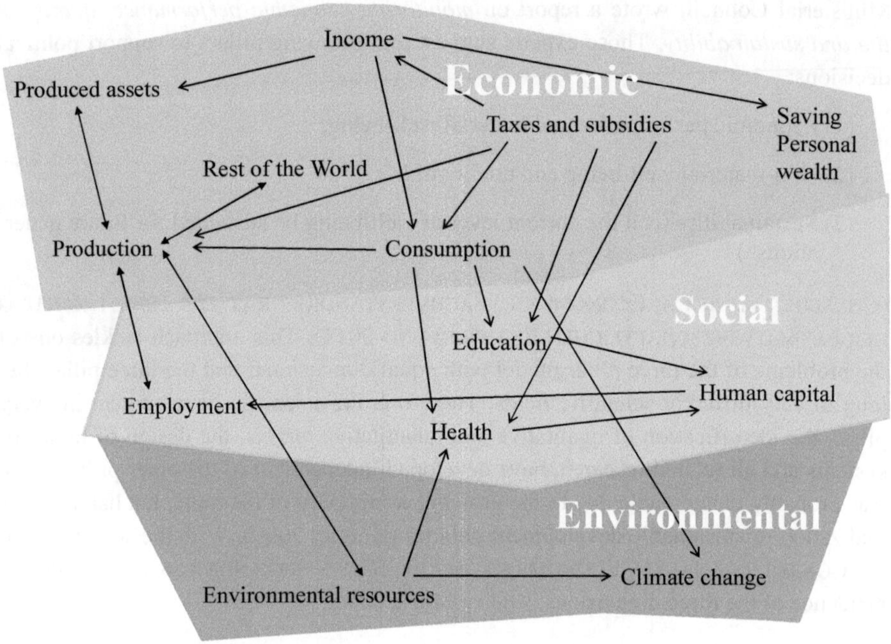

Figure 5: Links between the three spheres of sustainable development

(HARRISON 2000)

Several researchers advocate the inclusion of a fourth pillar into the three-pillar model (cf. subsection 2.6). This is a simple extension of the three pillar model comprising the ecological, economic and social columns and adding the institutional aspect (cf., for example, SPANGENBERG 2005). The intention of this fourth pillar is to ensure a comprehensive implementation of sustainability as guiding principle, and using the fourth pillar (or the roof for the other three pillars in some cases) as a cross-sectional task affecting the three traditional columns, because institutions concentrate on structural or procedural aspects rather than substantial aims (KLEINE 2009). This model faces the same criticism as the three pillar model as it does not observe the links between the pillars (aside from the institutional aspects) and does not depict a possible precedence of one column over the others. The three and four pillar model are in some cases complemented by an additional pillar depicting cultural aspects, but this dimension is rarely discussed extensively, as most argue that cultural aspects can be included in the social dimension.

2.6.2 Sustainability Triangle

Following the criticism of the pillar models, a triangle model has been developed to illustrate the dimensions of sustainable development with their links. The basic form of the triangle is shown in Figure 6. Measures and their effects can be allocated to either a point on the lines of the triangle, thus affecting only two dimensions, or any point within the triangle if all three dimensions are affected.

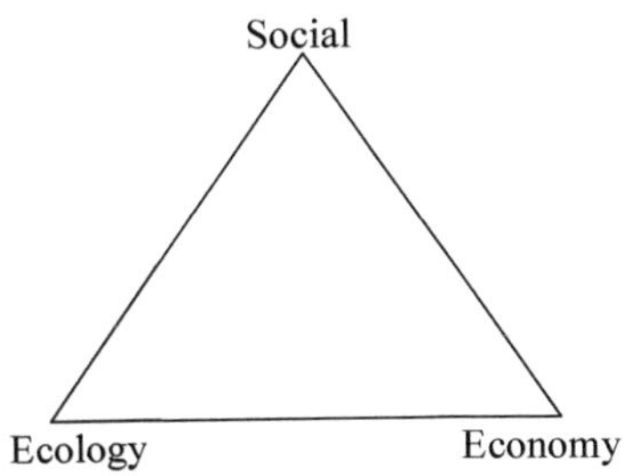

Figure 6: Basic sustainability triangle
(own depiction, model is used widely in scientific and popular publications in similar form)

The triangle is also endorsed by the german network for sustainable economics on the premise that the triangle is embedded within the boundary of the ecological limits (NETZWERK NACHHALTIGE ÖKONOMIE 2012a). The german government recently also turned away from the three pillar model and towards a triangle model that includes the absolute limit that the network for sustainable economics asks for.

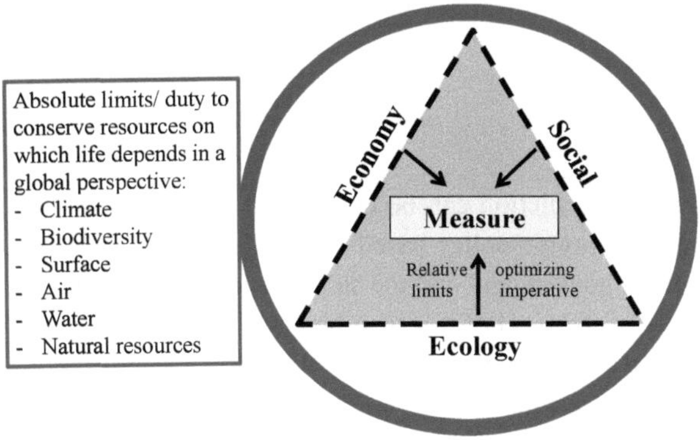

Figure 7: Sustainability triangle with absolute ecological limits
(SRU 2011, p. 5)

The sustainability triangle suggested by the GERMAN COUNCIL OF ENVIRONMENTAL ADVISORS (cf. Figure 7) is similar to the triangle used by the german government. It does stress the absolute ecological limit more clearly though and shows that sustainable development can only be realized within those absolute limits.

Another version of a Sustainability Triangle has been developed by VON HAUFF and KLEINE who favor a "magical" integrative triangle of sustainable development in an attempt to see the dimensions of sustainable development not as juxtaposing, but as an integrative concept that aims to harmonize the key aspects of sustainable development (cf. Figure 8) (KLEINE 2009).

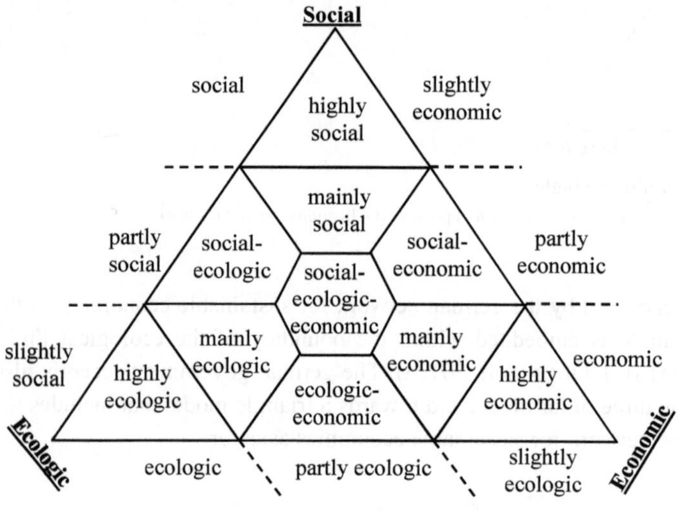

Figure 8: Integrative sustainability triangle
(HAUFF, KLEINE 2009)

The magical in the title of KLEINE's depiction can be considered analogous to the so called *magical square* of German economic policy based on the German Stability Law that postulates in §1 that the federal government and the states have to choose their political measures to ensure stability of the level of prices, high employment, a balance in foreign trade and steady and adequate economic growth (STABG). These four requirements are often depicted as corners of a square and then called the *magical square* because the legally mandatory concurrence all four dimensions is impossible to reach due to incongruity of the aims. While in some circumstances there is congruity[13], there is incongruity in other situations[14].

2.6.3 Sustainability Circles

Another option to depict sustainability and the connections between the dimensions is to use circles that overlap in the middle, symbolizing the connections between the dimensions. This version has the disadvantage that it is not possible to show the extent of the influence on one or the other dimension other than the attribution to one, two or three dimensions. In this case, the integrated sustainability triangle offers more exact options. Still, the basic circle model offers the advantages of showing the links between the dimensions and of allowing for the precedence of one of the dimensions. SCHRÖTER (2008) fills the dimensions with the corresponding properties, yielding an illustration as shown in Figure 9. For SCHRÖTER, the social component of the general principle comprises community development in all its forms – participation, meeting basic human needs, ensuring equity and justice, etc. The economic and ecologic dimensions are as expected. The distinctive feature of SCHRÖTER's model is that she only considers those measures, projects and situations as sustainable that are located in the intersection of all three dimensions.

HABER (2011) prefers a version with separate dimensions linked by certain actions depicting the influence from one dimension on the others (cf. Figure 10).

The dimensions are defined by the actions allocated to them: the economic sector is expected to secure material livelihood, the social dimension must concentrate on securing immaterial livelihood, while the environmental sector secures ecological stability. Both the economic and social sector must cater to the environmental dimension: the economy must reduce or avoid environmental impact and society must follow sustainability rules set by the environment. This leads to a certain precedence of the environmental dimension in the model.

---

13 cf., e.g., OKUN's law that states that economic growth leads to a high level of employment or more exactly, a 2% increase of GDP will lead to a 1% decrease of the unemployment rate. OKUN's law has been disputed and has been called a rule of thumb rather than a law as it is an empirical observation and not based on a theory.

14 cf., e.g., the Phillips curve that states that a decrease of the unemployment rate is correlated with an increased rate of inflation. This observation has been proved empirically for short term relations between the factors, but has been disputed for long-run predictions as both factors are influenced by many other parameters.

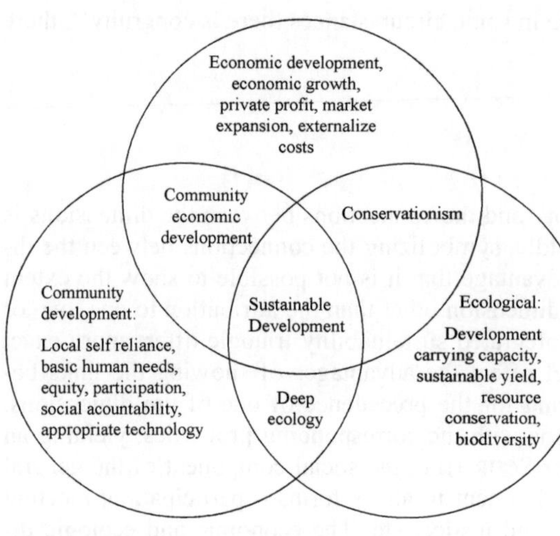

Figure 9: Properties of sustainable development
(SCHRÖTER 2008, P. 219)

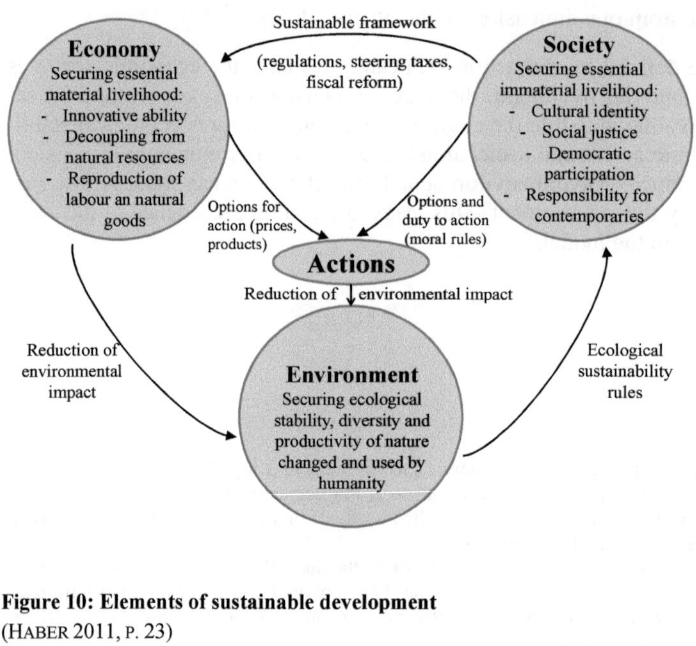

Figure 10: Elements of sustainable development
(HABER 2011, P. 23)

2.6.4 The HGF Sustainability Model

There are other concepts that should not be overlooked. The Helmholtz-Gemeinschaft (HGF), a community of German Research Centers of the Helmholtz Association, for example, suggest an approach to sustainable development that differs considerably from the common concepts based on the trinity of ecology, economy and social aspects, even though the HGF model acknowledges the three dimensions and adds institutions/politics as a fourth dimension. The basic elements of the HGF concept are inter- and intragenerational justice, globalism and anthropocentrism. The superior goals based on those elements are "assuring human existence, conservation of societal production potential and the preservation of the possibilities for development and action" (HARTMUTH 2004). The depiction of the concept is derived from the circle models of sustainability, but is complemented by a timeline and a geographical axis (cf. Figure 11).

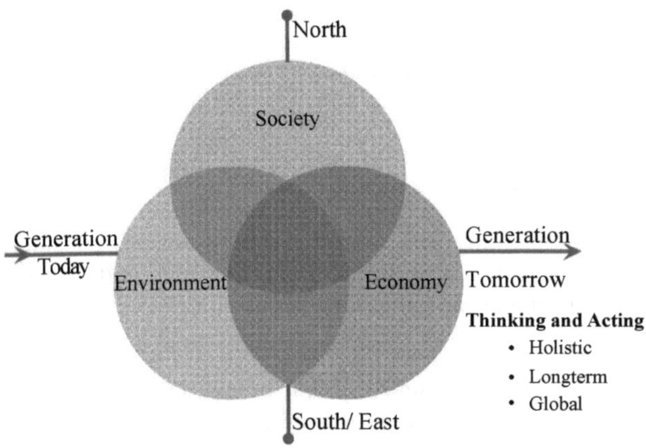

Figure 11: Integrative sustainability concept of the HGF
(KOPFMÜLLER 2011, P. 8)

As can be seen in, the basis for the HGF concept is the circle model of sustainability, supplemented by a North-South/East axis and another axis illustrating the different generations. This integrative concept leads to the development of an indicator set for sustainable development. Based on the determination of central sustainability problems and a thorough definition of the concept "sustainable development", its general objectives, minimum requirements and rules, indicators to evaluate sustainable development are compiled (cf. Figure 12). The authors participating in the project aim to find an integrated concept that analyses strategies and measures not as isolated facts for each dimension, but rather interdisciplinary (DIEFENBACHER ET AL. 2009).

Constitutive elements of the concept sustainable development

↓

General objectives of sustainable development

↓

Rules of sustainability: minimum requirements for sustainable development

↓

Indicators for sustainable development

↓

Central sustainability problems

Figure 12: HGF concept for sustainable development indicators
(HARTMUTH 2004, P. 7)

2.7 The Dimensions of Sustainability

Depending on the concept of sustainability followed, the dimensions are considered equal or the ecological dimension is given precedence. For a thorough understanding of sustainability, it is necessary to understand the dimensions and the corresponding policy areas.

There are many fields of politics. On every level (global policy, continental policy such as EU-policy, national policy, regional policy or local policy), the fields differ a little from those on other levels, for example in the responsibilities of the ministries or because the competence for certain fields is on a different level[15]. But all in all, the main fields of politics are similar for most levels and regions, even though the importance placed on a specific field will sometimes differ significantly according to the individual situation of the country or region. Figure 13 shows an example of possible political fields and the dimension of sustainability they belong to.

15 Foreign and security policy, for example, are usually only conducted on a national (or, in some cases an international) level, while cultural policy, school policy or transportation policy can also be found on lower levels.

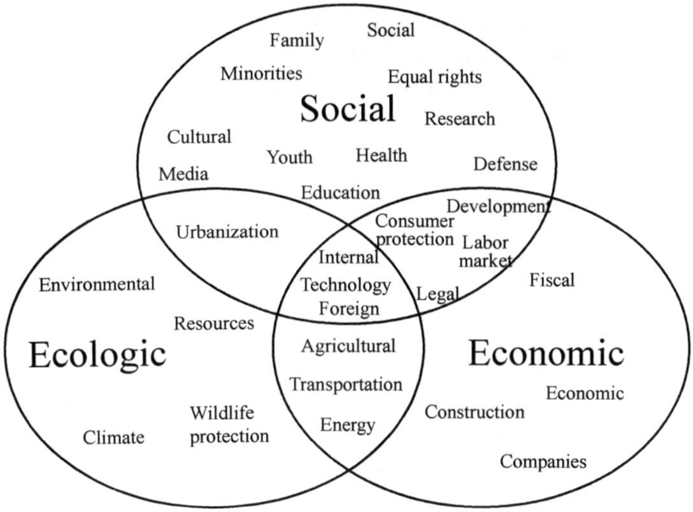

Figure 13: Policy fields
(author's own)

It is likely that the list is incomplete, and the fields mentioned are of different importance. It must also be taken into account that most areas are somehow related to all dimensions of sustainability. To provide an overview and to contribute to a better understanding and classification of policy fields and the sustainability dimensions, policy fields are assigned to the dimension they mainly affect. The dimensions shall be discussed in detail in the following subsections.[16]

2.7.1 The Ecological Dimension

The ecological dimension is what usually comes to mind first when sustainability is mentioned. This is partly due to the fact that the original sustainability models were based mostly on the ecological aspect, but also because public understanding of sustainability is very closely linked to this dimension. A 2012 survey by FORSA, a german

16 It is not the aim of this chapter to provide a comprehensive overview over the current state of sustainable development within each dimension. This would stray too far from the focus of this work, but is likely also impossible, as success and failure within the dimensions are hard to measure, but also too diverse within countries and regions. The discussion for the ecological dimension in Germany has been extensive as can be seen in various publications of the SRU (2002, 2012) or the WGBU (2011).

institute for social research, among citizens showed that they estimate the importance of actions to further sustainable development with a clear bias towards environment-related topics (FORSA 2012). This domination of the ecological dimension over the others is welcomed by many politicians and researchers who claim that such precedence of this dimension is imperative due to the irreparable damage that already occurred (HAUFF, JÖRG 2013). Environmental problems have considerable influence on economic and societal development; therefore a priority for decelerating climate change during a transformation towards a sustainable society seems the only logical solution (WGBU 2011). The economic costs for respecting the ecological limits may be very high, though, rendering the reparation of the environmental damage rather unlikely if the costs are considered inacceptable (COSTANZA ET AL. 2012). When talking about the ecological dimension of sustainability it is necessary to distinguish between political measures to further ecological sustainability and traditional concepts of environmental protection. While the latter's approach is to consider the protection of the environment as an objective to be pursued, the sustainability approach considers ecological sustainability one of many aims within the general principle of sustainability. Environmental protection is therefore rather a necessity to reach the overarching aim than the aim in itself. It is argued that ecological sustainability is a function for the furthering of social and economic development, thereby indicating that the limits of growth are not set by the environment but rather by the state of scientific and technical knowledge and the social organization thereof (BRAND, JOCHUM 2000). Often cited ecological aims are:

(1) Protection of earth's atmosphere

(2) Protection of the ecosystem

(3) Protection of resources

(4) Protection of human health

(5) Mobility within in the limits of the environmental space (ROGALL 2007).

To realize those aims is the explicit assignment of environmental institutions and laws; and rules and regulations have to be shaped accordingly. Their extent, but more importantly their enforcement, varies greatly among the nations.

When putting the ecological dimension in context with the sustainability concept, the distinction between strong and weak sustainability (cf. subsection 2.5) needs to be considered. Strong sustainability would imply a precedence of the ecological dimension, as it would prohibit the use of exhaustible resources, thus restricting the social and economic dimensions. Weak or balanced/reasonable sustainability would allow equality between the dimensions. The requirements of a sustainable policy for both cases would differ in the permission to use exhaustible resources, but would be equal in permitting emissions (which must be below the level of maximum assimilation of the medium they are put into) and the use of renewable resources, if the extraction rate is lower than the potential regeneration (cf. Figure 14). The latter provides another difference between the weak and the strong concept. Weak sustainability would allow the use of renewable resources even above the possible regeneration rate, as long as substitution is guaranteed.

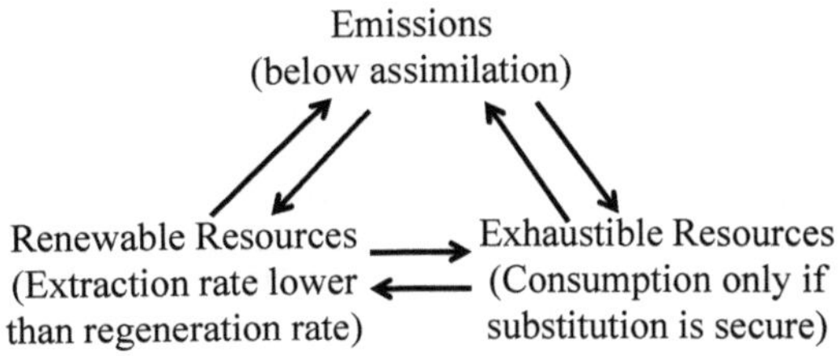

Figure 14: Connections between emissions and resources
(HAUFF, SCHIFFER 2013)

It has been discussed above (cf. subsection 2.5) that strong sustainability is unlikely to be realized, as it could not be enforced. Therefore, policy makers who choose either weak or balanced sustainability as their general principle also need to make assumptions about technological development and the existence of possible substitutes and choose their policy measures accordingly. Their assumptions, the resulting types of ecological policy and the results if the assumptions are right or wrong can be illustrated in a payoff matrix (cf. Figure 15). If a policy maker is optimistic about the development of substitutes for natural resources and chooses an optimistic type of policy that supports research and development (R&D) for substitutes for natural resources and at the same time allows the use of exhaustible resources as well as the overuse of renewable resources[17], then the outcome of this policy depends on the accuracy of the assumptions. If the assumptions were correct, the rewards for the measures will be high, i.e., the policy measures taken were an important step towards sustainability. But if the policy maker is wrong and the optimistic policy of overusing resources is not met with the necessary technological development to provide substitutes, than the result is disastrous for the goal of a sustainable world. At the same time, if a policy maker assumes a more pessimistic view towards the development and chooses the policy measures accordingly, not allowing the use of exhaustible and the overuse of renewable resources, and the assumptions are correct, then the outcome will be tolerable. There will be no regress in sustainable development. In case the policy maker's assumptions were wrong and technological development was more successful than expected in finding substitutes for natural resources, than the payoff will not be as high

17 *Overuse* refers to using more of the resource within a certain period of time than can be regenerated, thus depleting the stock of the resource.

as in the optimistic assumptions and policy/optimistic outcome scenario, but still positive.

		Actual state of the world	
		Optimists about technological development and possible substitutes for natural resources are right	Pessimists about technological development and possible substitutes for natural resources are right
Type of policy	Optimistic	High	Disaster
	Pessimistic	Moderate	Tolerable

Figure 15: Approaches to environmental uncertainty
(PEARCE ET AL. 1989)

Assumptions must also be made about the characteristics of the ecological systems that are relevant for a specific decision on policy measures. There are five possible characteristics: persistency (system is sustainable over time), constancy (system stays in status quo independent of external influences), resistency (system remains in equilibrium and withstands external disruptions), elasticity (system returns to status quo after strong external disruptions) and resiliency (degree of external disruptions a system can withstand and speed with which it returns to status quo afterwards) (DIEFENBACHER ET AL. 2009). If the policy makers assume a system to be sustainable over time, very elastic, constant, resistant and resilient, they will tend to make their decisions rather independent of possible environmental impact.

One of the problems of such assumptions and the decisions based on them is that the outcome will only be visible long after the decision is made. Therefore, a repetition of the decision process and the following choice of policy measures may be possible, but not within a short span of time. This would imply the need for a thoroughly informed decision, but, as will be discussed in subsection 3.3, as policy makers will most likely not face the results of their decisions and therefore not be punished for possible wrong decisions, they do not necessarily make prudent choices, but rather decide on those types of policy that will yield the highest agreement in society in the short run, and therefore the most votes[18].

18 As will be discussed in subsection 3.3, there are of course those decision makers that are not interested in their reelection, but rather in realizing the ideal of a sustainable development. But as those idealists can also only achieve their goals if they get enough time and power to do so, they still depend on votes and possibly on reelection.

There are different approaches to measure the status quo and the development of the ecological situation. There are single indicators provided by the statistical offices of various countries and institutions, but also aggregated indicators such as the Happy Planet Index as a complete sustainability index or the ecological footprint as an index for the ecological dimension of sustainability. The advantages and disadvantages of single and aggregated indicators will be discussed in detail in chapter 3, at this point of the work it suffices to present some data.

The ecological footprint is a measure to calculate environmental impact. It is a metric measure of the amount of land required to sustain a country's consumption, including the area to (re)produce the renewable resources that are used by a country's citizens, the area that is used for the country's infrastructure, and the area that is required to absorb the country's CO_2 emissions. It is measured in global hectares (gha). A combination of biocapacity data with the current global population yields the upper limit of gha that could be consumed if the consumption is to be sustainable. This limit has been calculated at 1.8 gha per capita for the current generation. The countries with the worst ecological footprint p.c. are Qatar (11.7 gha p.c.), Luxembourg (10.7 gha p.c.) and Kuwait (9.7 gha p.c.); the countries with the lowest ecological footprint per capita are Bangladesh, Haiti and Afghanistan, all three with an ecological footprint of less than 1 gha p.c. Germany has an ecological footprint of 4.6 gha p.c. (NEW ECONOMICS FOUNDATION 2012).

There is a strong correlation between p.c. GDP and ecological footprint; the explanations for this correlation being obvious (cf. Figure 16).

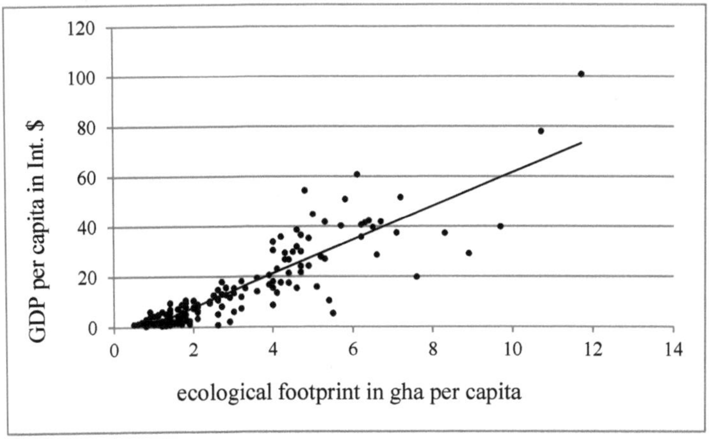

Figure 16: Ecological footprint and GDP

(author's own, data from NEW ECONOMICS FOUNDATION (2012), INTERNATIONAL MONETARY FUND (2012), trend line OLS-estimation, $R^2 = 0{,}778$)

The implications for sustainability are quite discouraging: if the correlation between the ecological footprint and GDP per capita is – and remains – positive, realizing intragenerational justice will lead to an increased GDP for poorer regions, but also to a growing ecological footprint. The alternative would be to either reduce GDP for the developed countries and to hope to thereby reduce their ecological footprint – a measure that will most likely not find any political majority – or to develop technologies and adapt lifestyles to break up or lessen the correlation between GDP and ecological footprint. The GLOBAL FOOTPRINT NETWORK (2015) estimates that current resources use would need 1.5 planet earths. When forecasting future resource use based on moderate UN scenarios on consumption, demographic development and estimated growth of crop yield, the current resource use would require two planets by 2030.

The German Network for Sustainable Economics set a number of ecological management rules that must be followed if sustainability is to be realized (cf. Figure 17). The first rule, climate protection, refers to the requirements shown in Figure 14. Emissions must not be higher than maximum possible absorption, thereby protecting the climate. The second point stresses the fact that human interference into environment must allow for enough time for nature to self-stabilize. The third rule refers to another aspect discussed in Figure 14, the requirement that renewable resources must not be used above their rate of regeneration (this requirement is objected to by advocates of weak or balanced sustainability, cf. subsection 2.5). The same holds for rule four, also disputed between advocates of the different specifications of sustainability. The last rule aims at the humans' quality of life, but also the environment, asking to restrict pollution, radiation and noise. This rule also demands the consideration of the impact of political and economic decisions on human health, the environment and the quality of life (NETZWERK NACHHALTIGE ÖKONOMIE 2012b).

(1) Climate protection

(2) Environmental compatibility, protection of species, protection of landscape diversity

(3) Sustainable use of renewable resources

(4) Sustainable use of non-renewable resources

(5) Healthy living conditions

Figure 17: Ecological management rules
(NETZWERK NACHHALTIGE ÖKONOMIE 2012b)

2.7.2 The Economic Dimension

The economic dimension of sustainability is complex and there are quite a few disagreements between the parties involved in the discussion. To define rules of economic sustainability, authors use different approaches. DALY (2007b)[19], for example, assumes that "the economy is a subsystem of the larger ecosystem, and the latter is finite, non-growing, and materially closed", thus claiming that the economic dimension is subordinate to the ecologic dimension. He is supported by von HAUFF and SCHIFFER (2013) who state that the economic and social system cannot be sustainable in themselves. They need a certain quality and stability of the ecological system to work, therefore, stakeholders' adaption to the resilience of nature is necessary. The alternative to this approach is offered by the representatives of the sustainability models claiming equality for the dimensions.

A specific of the economic column is the creation of value, which is not necessarily limited by the laws of nature, as natural input is combined with knowledge. Therefore, the criteria for economic sustainability have to include not only physical capital and natural resources, but also human capital and technical and organizational knowledge (sometimes summed up as social capital). But apart from some general rules like the preservation of assets, criteria suggested differ widely, mostly based on different assumptions regarding factor mobility (BLAZEJCZAK, EDLER 2004). The German Network for Sustainable Economics developed a set of economic management rules to comply with the requirements of a sustainable development (cf. Figure 18).

(1)	Consideration of economic consequences
(2)	Guarantee of fulfilling basic needs with sustainable products
(3)	Prices have to be appropriate and fulfill a controlling function
(4)	Balance in foreign trade with high self-sufficiency
(5)	A functioning budget with an adequate endowment with merit goods

Figure 18: Economic management rules
(NETZWERK NACHHALTIGE ÖKONOMIE 2012b)

The first rule sounds simple but has not always been followed to date: that one has to consider the economic consequences of economic actions. The second rule, the guar-

19 Herman Daly is one of the Founders of the International Society for Ecological Economics and can be counted among the advocates for the precedence of ecology.

antee of fulfilling basic needs with sustainable products, means that individual and societal needs must be fulfilled efficiently, but within ecological limits. Therefore, economic policy must encourage all innovations and changes towards sustainable production. The appropriateness of prices means that they have to include externalities. The balance in foreign trade is a common requirement, but the sustainable addition is that goods are only exchanged if they cannot be produced efficiently (i.e., if internalizing all externalities the foreign goods are still cheaper or better) within the country. This would also reduce economic dependency on other countries. The last rule, a functioning budget, is also extended with the demand for an adequate endowment with merit goods. That means that the functioning budget has to go hand in hand with sufficient collective and merit goods to improve education and human capital, among others (NETZWERK NACHHALTIGE ÖKONOMIE 2012b). To fulfill those requirements, three main actors within this dimension have to be taken into account: the government/politics, companies and consumers.

2.7.2.1 Politics

In Germany, the political basis for the economic dimension is the so called *magical square*. The German Stability Law demands in its §1, that all economic and fiscal decisions must be made so that they simultaneously contribute to the stability of the price level, high employment, balance in foreign trade and steady and adequate economic growth (STABG). The fiscal and expense topics have been given a de facto antecedence by the inclusion of the brake on debt into the German Constitution and the European fiscal pacts. To comply with those rules, it may be necessary to neglect or even disregard the other dimensions of sustainable development, thus giving the economic sector precedence (DULLIEN, VAN TREECK 2012).

As much of the German economic and monetary policy is interdependent with the European market and politics, it has to be kept in mind that the BUNDESBANK, for example, has not much influence on the stability of the price level anymore, because the potent instrument of monetary policy has been given up in favor of the European Central Bank (ECB). It has often been suggested to extend the *magical square* to a pentagon or hexagon with the additional corners social justice, livable environment or just distribution of income and wealth, as the traditional magical square does not meet the requirements of the current environmental, economic and social situation. Some authors go one step further and suggest the adjustment of the objectives. DULLIEN and VAN TREECK (2012), for example, suggest the following goals for economic policy: material well-being, provided by a moderate economic growth; ecological sustainability to ensure that natural resources are not endangered in the long run; social sustainability to avoid/reduce social inequality and sustainable public policy and public finances to secure the public capital stock for future generations. The latter three points are largely derived from the established definitions of sustainable development, but the suggestion also recommends „moderate economic growth“ as a measure towards sustainability, a characteristic that is increasingly disputed. In this context it is used to provide material well-being, but as the welfare of citizens is increasingly uncoupled from economic growth (HAUFF, SCHIFFER 2013), at least in societies where a certain level of economic well-being has been reached, it is arguable whether economic growth should be an important political aim for industrial nations at all. For developing countries, the exclusion of growth and wealth in the measurement or evaluation of sustainable measures is hypothetical. If intragenerational justice and the meeting of basic needs are declared aims of sustainable development, then countries where economic growth is essential to fulfill those basic needs will necessarily concentrate on economic growth. In any case, the association of growth with economic topics is a very common one. For many, economic growth and material well-being are almost synonymous with overall well-being. As sustainability is often defined as necessity to ensure current and future generations' well-being, a short discussion of well-being will follow in subsection 5.7.

2.7.2.2 Consumers

The consumers are an important factor in the course of sustainable development. For one, consumers are also voters. If they do not agree with the politics suggested by the ruling parties, they may well punish them in the next election. As politicians need to be elected to realize their ideals and goals, they are likely to adjust their suggested measures to the extent that is just acceptable to the voters. The beliefs and convictions of voters are often investigated. A 2012 poll found, for example, that of about 1.000 people interviewed, a vast majority (84%) believed that stronger economic growth is possible while protecting the environment and ensuring sustainability (cf. Figure 19).

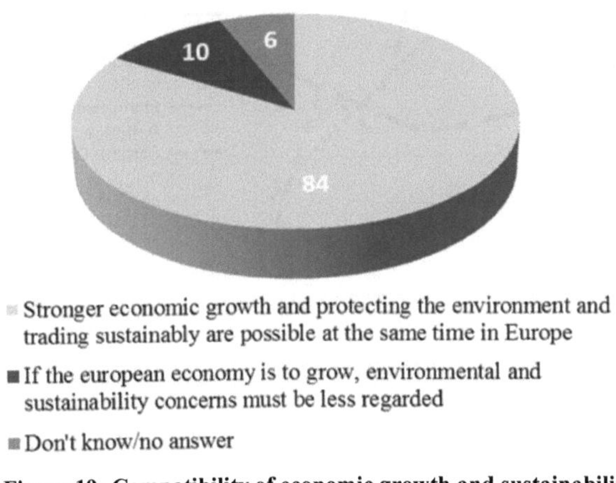

Figure 19: Compatibility of economic growth and sustainability
(TNS EMNID, BERTELSMANN STIFTUNG 2012)

Only 10% of the interviewees believe that for the economy to grow, it is inevitable that environmental protection and striving for sustainability must be neglected. As most scientists lean toward the latter assumption, this is another proof of the necessity of sustainability education among the general public in order to further the understanding of the meaning and also the implications of sustainability and sustainable development.

To realize sustainable development it is also imperative that consumers change their consumption patterns towards the sustainability paradigm. The consumption of products harmful to the environment must be reduced and consumers must be more alert and informed about the goods they consume and their environmental impact (GEYER-ALLÉLY, EPPEL 1998). PAECH and PFRIEM (2007) see this as a crucial aspect, but stress that especially in developed nations, consumption is not necessarily used as a means to satisfy needs, but that companies aim to create (imaginary) needs that can be satisfied by their products. Consumers need to be aware of the influence of companies' marketing on their wishes and presumed needs and make conscious decisions to avoid overconsumption. In addition, as consumers are usually also voters, they need to inform themselves (and be informed) about pressing issues that should be tackled on a way towards a sustainable society. Current studies show that economic problems for example are considered by far more important than environmental topics (cf. Figure 20).

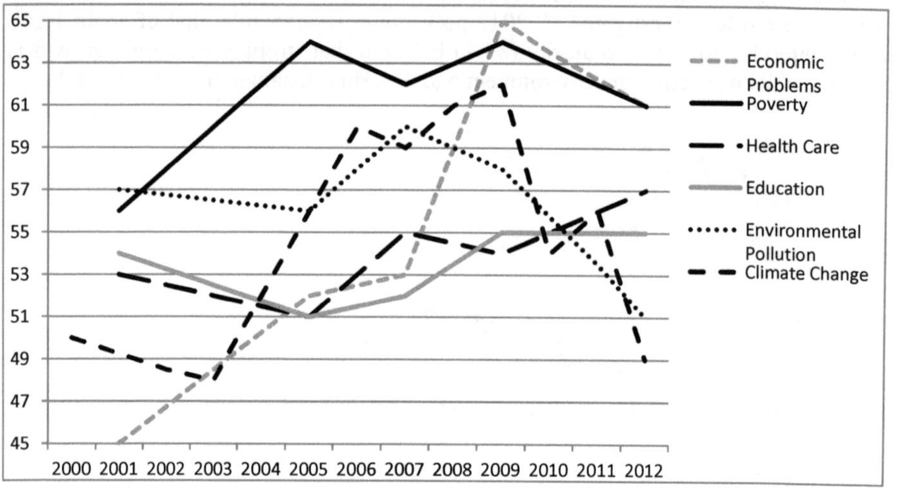

Figure 20: Importance of future challenges

Survey 2000 – 2012, answers "very serious challenge", average of 14 countries (Brazil, Canada, China, France, Germany, India, Indonesia, Kenya, Mexico, Nigeria, Spain, Turkey, UK, and USA) (GLOBESCAN/SUSTAINABILITY 2012c, p. 7)

It is also interesting to note that the estimation of the seriousness of economic problems has grown considerably over the last decade, while environmental pollution and climate change are becoming less important. This may, at least in part, well be a consequence of the selection of interviewed persons because, as mentioned before, the importance assigned to different topics varies greatly between emerging and industrialized countries. As the data set includes developing as well as developed countries, though, the results cannot simply be dismissed on grounds of an insufficient choice of countries in the sample, but provide a relevant insight.

These results give important hints for policy makers trying to establish sustainable development as the leading paradigm all over the world. No matter whether one leans towards sustainability definitions with equal importance for all dimensions or towards a precedence of the environmental pillar, it is necessary to convince people of the damage that may be done if short-term economic growth is given pre-eminence before environmental concerns. A possible strategy to include the consumers in the process of realizing sustainable development is described by OTT and DÖRING (2007), who suggest to adapt the guiding principle and the according measures to the different social milieus such as those suggested for Germany in the renowned study of the SINUS-Milieus (2013), where ideals and moral concepts of citizens are evaluated and classified.

2.7.2.3 Companies

First and foremost, companies will adapt their production, if a) government rules and regulations force them to and b) if customers demand it. In the last years it has become more common to declare Corporate Social Responsibility (CSR) or Corporate Sustainability (CS) their guidelines. Both are voluntary guidelines that exceed legal obligations with which companies aim at a more responsible production. CARROLL (1991), for example, describes a company's situation as a triangle (cf. Figure 21).

The basic necessities for a company are to be profitable (= economic principle) and to act lawfully (= legal principle). If those necessities are fulfilled, a company can add ethical and eventually philanthropic issues to its strategies. Those two latter aspects are not required to run a company, but as customer awareness of ethical and social issues is growing, it may well be advantageous the company's sales to include those topics into their strategies. The ethical dimension includes the obligation to avoid harm, the philanthropic dimension adds the responsibility to improve the quality of life and contribute resources to the community (KAS 2012). In current discussions about CSR, the economic, legal and ethical dimensions are rather understood as integrated than as separate dimensions that must somehow be mentioned in the company's strategies. Instead, CARROLL and SCHWARTZ developed a circle-model for the core dimensions of a CSR that is integrative and offers the options to place the company's strategy on any combination of the three dimensions (cf. Figure 22). In this model, the philanthropic responsibilities are not included anymore.

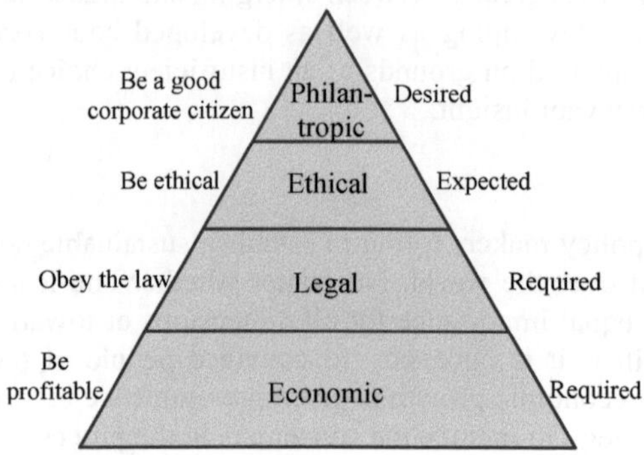

Figure 21: Pyramid of CSR
(CARROLL 1991)

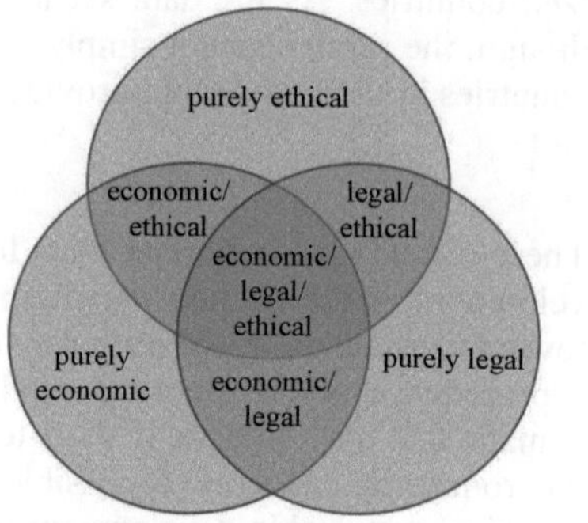

Figure 22: Core dimensions of CSR
(SCHWARTZ, CARROLL 2003)

Companies have reacted to customer's growing interest in sustainable products and services. They are increasingly informed about social and environmental standards and expect companies to adhere to those standards[20]. Starting with standards for organic food and various ecolabels, a large number of certificates and standards exist now. Some of these standards have been developed by individual companies, but many have been launched by NGOs or social movements supported by NGOs. Many of the standards and certificates are specifically for the food industry. In addition to purely product related labels ("bio"/"organic" food), there are also labels that evaluate the production process (e.g., the working conditions, transport, etc.). Those labels can be considered labels that evaluate sustainable development, as they include the different dimensions.

Apart from the food-industry labels, a number of other standards and certificates have developed. Institutions such as EUROSIF, the European Sustainable Investment Forum, or its members such as the FNG, the German, Austrian and Swiss Sustainable Investment Forum, aim to further sustainable development through the financial markets. The DJSI (Dow Jones Sustainability Indices) for example are considered a global sus-

20 A number of studies have been conducted to prove that customers "punish" companies that are not perceived as responsible and sustainable. One of those studies is the Global RepTrak 100 Study that measures how the 100 most highly regarded companies across 15 countries are perceived and how customers react to that perception in terms of purchases (REPUTATION INSTITUTE 2013).

tainability benchmark, but apart from the global comparison, they also offer regional analyses[21]. In Germany, for example, the German Association for Financial Analyses and Asset Management (DVFA) develops key criteria to assess companies, including ecological, social and governance indicators. Most of the sustainability indices include more than 100 single indicators for every company, thus enforcing a weighting and the setting of priorities.

To achieve good results in those sustainable company rankings, companies need to set up sustainability strategies as mentioned above. These strategies should include cooperations with other stakeholders in sustainability. But while sustainability experts believe that in respect to sustainable development policy, the most effective approach for companies is to work with multi-actor collaborations, including government (58%), only 30% of the experts think that this is the approach that companies are most likely to take according to a 2012 survey among development experts and practitioners from all sectors involved[22] (GLOBESCAN/SUSTAINABILITY 2012a). It is also advocated that companies should be included in mapping out ways to sustainable development as their collaboration is crucial; most of them doubt the approach taken by the companies so far (GLOBESCAN/SUSTAINABILITY 2012a). The experts were asked whether individual direct action or collaboration with multiple actors were most effective for multinational companies aiming to achieve positive results with regards to sustainability. They believed that most actions should involve collaboration with multiple actors, even elementary company internal options like engaging the employees on sustainability issues or the development of sustainable products or services (GLOBESCAN/SUSTAINABILITY 2012a).

Another important part of economic sustainability is the labor market. This field is not only relevant for the economic, but also the social dimension (cf. subsection 2.7.3). In the 1990s, companies considered the environment as an important factor for location decisions. Environmental laws and regulations were considered an obstacle for the decision. At the same time, the quality of the environment was regarded a soft factor, especially important to attract employees (GRABOW ET AL. 1995). If the protection of the environment is seen as killing jobs that means there is a trade-off between the ecologic and economic and social dimension (PETSCHOW ET AL. 1998). Following this train of thought, companies would be located in those places where the balance between high costs for compliance with environmental regulations and an environment that attracts qualified labor was even. Current theories of economic geography lean more toward

21 The DJSI, a group of indices that evaluate the sustainability performance of companies listed on the Dow Jones Index, are offered by RobecoSAM Indices and S&P Dow Jones Indices and partly use the data of the conventional Dow Jones with added environmental and social criteria.

22 The sectors involved are "corporate, government (including multi-lateral institutions), NGOs, Institutional (e.g., academics) (and) Service (e.g., consultants, media)" (GLOBESCAN/SUSTAINABILITY 2012a).

behavioral theory[23] and Krugman's new economic geography[24], and do not place the same importance for location decision on environmental costs for the companies anymore.

Another economic factor are jobs in green sectors. They have become more numerous as the importance of environmental friendly production has grown. It has been found that employees have reported increased job satisfaction working for companies that embrace or promote sustainability principles (JANN ET AL. 2006).

2.7.3 The Social Dimension

It has been mentioned before that the economic and social system cannot be sustainable in them, but instead need a certain quality and stability of the ecological system to work. Some scientists claim that the social dimension is usually not only dominated by the ecologic dimension, but by the economic one as well, thus leaving the social aspects a subordinate position (EBRINGHOFF 2005). This position is also supported by HOLSTEIN (2003) who states that social sustainability cannot be realized unless the economic and ecologic requirements are met.

The social dimension is also often considered a special challenge as social capital is not as clearly defined as ecological and economic capital. It is sometimes described as the structures underlying production such as public institutions; newer definitions include the possibility to satisfy needs, to realize social integration and to advance a society (HAUFF, KLEINE 2009). It must be kept in mind, though, that social sustainability is always defined in the context of the situation it is used in and that in praxis, the realization of social sustainability is usually rather based on ad hoc decisions than on a sound concept. MUTLAK and SCHWARZE (2007) therefore state a deficit in the development of theories on the social dimension. The aims that are usually attributed to the social dimension of sustainability are

(1) social security

(2) democracy and rule of law

(3) inner and outer safety (peace)

(4) social integration and equal life chances (including gender equality)

---

23 The inclusion of behavioral theory in location theories supports the assumption that entrepreneurs have not only economic, but also other goals and will therefore often accept locations or strategies that are not optimal in the strict economic sense.

24 KRUGMAN was the first who, in the 1990s, developed a new approach to economic geography. In his theory, he includes factors such as economies of scale, external effects and others. Thus, he supports the theory that location decisions are not solely based on a strict calculation of location costs.

(5) quality of life and health (ROGALL 2007).

Similarly, LAMPERT AND ALTHAMMER (2001) offer an assignment of political areas to social policy that shows, which areas of life are touched by the social dimension (cf. Figure 23). International and supranational social policy can be roughly divided into the same areas, although many of the social policy decisions are still made on a national level, so the supranational social policy has been neglected in the depiction.

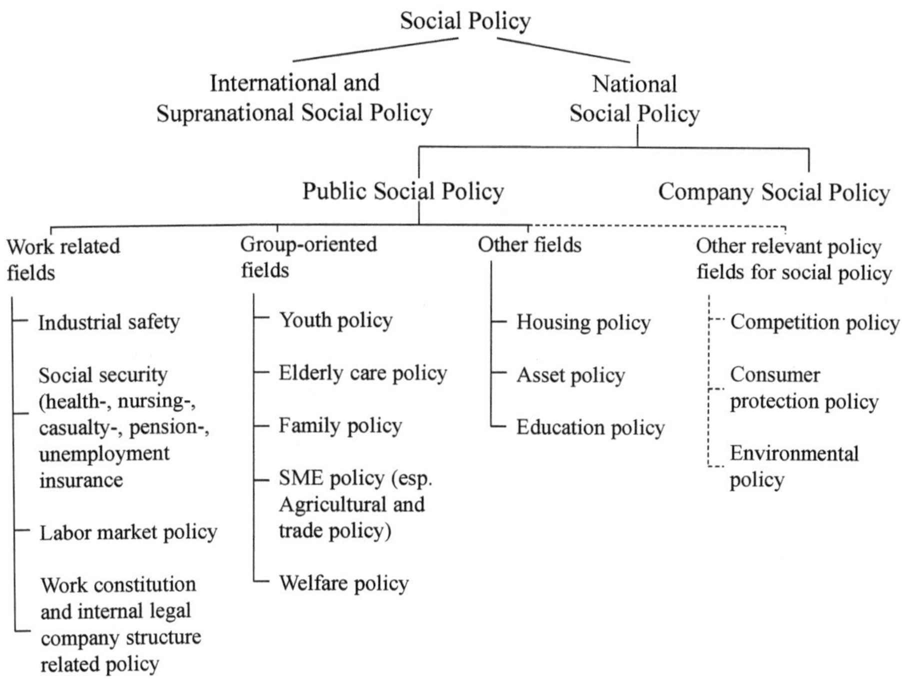

Figure 23: Areas of social policy
(LAMPERT, ALTHAMMER 2001, p. 159)

Education in all its forms – schooling, training for a job, but also lifelong learning – and access to culture (often defined in a broader sense, including art and literature, but also forms of life, basic rights, value systems, traditions, etc.) are especially important for reaching social sustainability (HAUFF, SCHIFFER 2013). In many countries education is seen as a very serious challenge to society. A GLOBESCAN/SUSTAINABILITY survey from 2012 shows that in many countries, education is seen as one of the most important challenges to society.

Interestingly, when those survey results are plotted against the GDP purchasing power parity (PPP) per capita there is no clear correlation between the estimated importance of the educational challenge and p. c. GDP[25] (cf. Figure 24). There are several ways for education to have impact on sustainable development. Education increases human capital, thus influencing the economic dimension of sustainability by furthering economic growth and (sustainable) innovations. The social dimension is influenced as well, as a better education leads to a sensitization for sustainability problems (GRUNWALD, KOPFMÜLLER 2006).

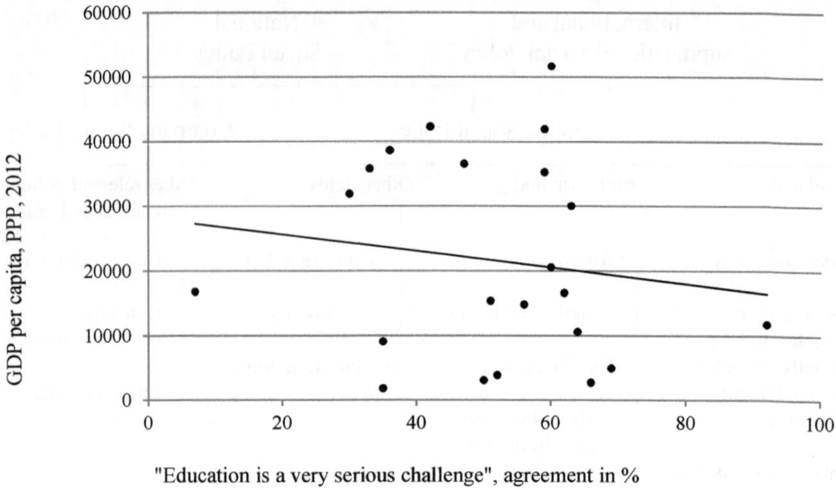

Figure 24: Challenges to society: education and GDP
(GLOBESCAN/SUSTAINABILITY 2012c; IMF 2013), trend line OLS estimate

The labor market, an important part of the social dimension, influences the social dimension of sustainability in various ways. For one, employees (and employers) pay taxes, thus financing the public system. Having a job also is important for welfare as will be further discussed in subsection 4.1 and for overall social cohesion. Jobs and labor are concerned in many fields of social policy (cf. Figure 23); among them all directly work-related areas, but also in youth and family policy, or policies for small and medium enterprises (SME). Education policy is linked with the labor market, as are

25 The OLS estimate yields an insignificant negative correlation with an R2 of 0,021. This correlation can therefore be neglected.

competition and environmental policy. Many political decisions to be made influence the labor market directly or indirectly, either immediately or with an impact in the long run. The labor market is only indirectly regarded by the generational balance, though. The sustainability gap used as an indicator of the sustainability of the social sector and the expenses of the government[26] indicates that economic booms in the last decade did not result in an improved sustainability gap (RAFFELHÜSCHEN ET AL. 2007). It shall be discussed in subsection 4.4, whether inter- and intragenerational justice is aspired to in labor market policy decisions. A 2012 survey among sustainability experts showed that RAFFELHÜSCHENs opinion is supported by many of his colleagues. When asked about the worlds' progress on economic, environmental and social causes, the experts assert that there has been progress in the first two areas, but regress in rising to the social challenges (GLOBESCAN/SUSTAINABILITY 2012b).

As for the economic dimension of sustainability, the network for sustainable economics developed a set of management rules to follow if social sustainability is to be realized (cf. Figure 25).

(1) Good Governance

(2) Social security, no poverty

(3) Equality of opportunities, social integration and distributive justice

(4) Conflict avoidance

(5) Techniques without risk

Figure 25: Social-cultural management rules
(NETZWERK NACHHALTIGE ÖKONOMIE 2012b)

The good government targets corruption, the abuse of power, short-term management and other destructive and undesirable policy influences. It is imperative that democratic and constitutional rules are observed; and market failure has to be corrected by the state. Point two of the social-cultural management rules asks that every member of society receives benefits from the social systems according to his or her contributions or corresponding to their need. The authors stress, that to be sustainable, those benefit may only grow with the extent of economic productivity and all members of society must contribute according to their abilities. Equality of opportunities, social integration and distributive justice have to be ensured by policy makers, who also need to make

26 The sustainability gap is an extended version of the debt-to-GDP ratio. It does not only include the explicit national debt, but also the implicit debt that will be incurred in future years (MOOG, RAFFELHÜSCHEN 2013).

sure that those requirements can be fulfilled for current and future generations while respecting the limits of natural capacity. The fourth rule, conflict avoidance, refers to an avoidance of any policy that could destabilize international security; the fifth rule forbids the use of technologies that involve unjustifiable risks.

2.8 Summary

In this chapter, a short overview over the evolution over the general principle of sustainable was given. Based on the insights gained at each milestone of the development, definitions of sustainable development were reviewed. As the definitions are only a vision, and realization of the idea needs concrete requirements, the transfer from the general idea towards a concept was described and the minimum requirements for the realization of the concept discussed. The most common definition of sustainable development includes an underlying stipulation of intra- and intergenerational justice. These two concepts were analyzed, especially with regards to the meaning of justice and fairness. The quantification and various methods to calculate intra- and intergenerational justice were surveyed. Taking into account the necessity of assertive institutions to ensure the implementation of sustainability strategies on all levels of society, institutions to further sustainable development are then discussed.

Those introductory topics were followed by a discussion of the possible characteristics and a specification of the ecological, economic and social dimension of sustainable development, including an analysis of the stakeholders, especially in the economic dimension. The concluding subsection summarizes the chapter by attributing possible sustainability models and depictions to the changing understanding of sustainability in the last decades and thereby showing the complexity of the general principle.

3. Realizing Sustainable Development

As has been shown in subsection 2.2, sustainability is widely acknowledged as overarching goal; and sustainable development is a generally accepted principle und guideline for political action. The degree of familiarity with the concept has increased considerably in the last decade; and sustainable development has been institutionalized and mainstreamed into many areas of politics and everyday life. But the simple fact that the concept is known and has been introduced into rules for decision-making on many levels and in many countries does not necessarily mean that the world is closer to realizing sustainability than before. It is common knowledge that knowing is not the same as doing; and added to this, the many facets of sustainability and sustainable development may not be as well understood as surveys asking about the familiarity with the concept imply. In Germany, for example, sustainability is translated as "Nachhaltigkeit", but the word "nachhaltig", sustainable, is often used to simply describe something as long-term. Someone may answer the survey positively and indicate his or her familiarity with the concept; but may only connect sustainability with a long-term consideration of a problem or situation. It is therefore helpful to take a closer look at past achievements and successes or failures of the implementation of the concept. It is even more important to then discuss the reasons of the successes and failures as those reasons will be helpful later on when discussing indicators to measure sustainable development, as a number of institutional indicators may have to be included in the indicator set.

As is the case with strategy building in general, the transition from a general principle towards the formulation of a strategy must include the formulation of targets. This step is essential when trying to find the correct instruments to realize the aims (GÜNTHER, SCHUH 2000). Sustainable development strategies must follow the same rules as any other strategies concerning political measures and must include the potential of reaching the targets as well as political feasibility. As depicted in Figure 26, the basis for the development of a strategy for sustainability is a thorough understanding of the general guiding principle and its underlying values. Those values must be the foundation for the development of guidelines or operating principles that are then specified as aims or conditions and the criteria to substantiate them must be collected. Only then does the choice of appropriate instruments, followed by the implementation of the measures, take place. Therefore, strategy building for sustainability measures and programs will also be discussed in this chapter.

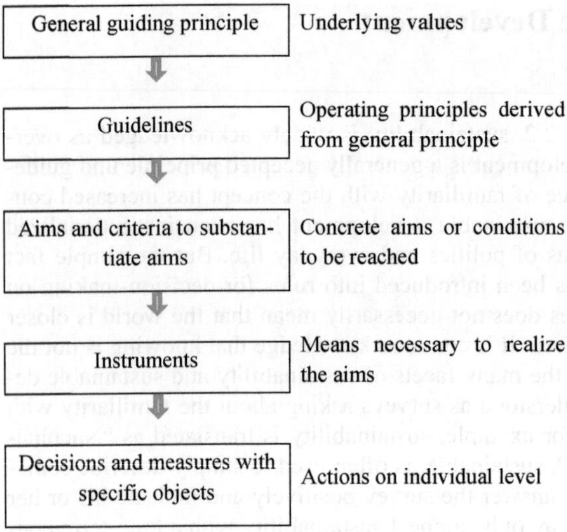

Figure 26: From general principle to realization
(GÜNTHER, SCHUH 2000, p. 13)

3.1 Past Achievements

Sustainable development has been on political agendas for at least two decades, and many states instigated sustainability strategies. In 2012, the UNITED NATIONS stated that 77% of the European countries had implemented sustainability strategies, followed by 64% in Oceania, 57% in Asia, 46% in the Americas, and 40% of the African countries (UN DESA 2012). That is a first, and not a small, step towards realizing sustainability, but the question remains whether the implementation of a strategy is enough. A strategy has to be ambitious enough to reach the goals set, but also be politically enforceable and practical enough to be realized. The progress of implementation and the steps towards reaching the goal must also be closely monitored to render adaption possible if the measures chosen do not work as anticipated. The requirements for realizing sustainability will be further discussed in subsection 3.2.

3.1.1 Citizens

Public opinion on the progress made in improving economic, social and environmental aspects is very diverse and varies greatly among regions. A 2012 GLOBESCAN survey among citizens in 22 countries found that on average, environmental protection is estimated to have improved over the last 20 years (46% of the interviewees said that it "got a lot/somewhat better", opposed to 29% saying it "got somewhat/ a lot worse"), while progress in economic wellbeing (39% better/ 36% worse) and the creation of healthier and more equitable societies (39% better/ 29% worse) is judged a little less favorably (GLOBESCAN/SUSTAINABILITY 2012b). The data varies greatly among the countries, though (cf. Figure 27).

	Australia	Brazil	Canada	China	France	Germany	Ghana	Greece	India	Indonesia	Nigeria	Pakistan	Peru	Russia	South Korea	Spain	Turkey	UK	USA
Economic wellbeing	-6	47	-28	79	-52	13	32	-61	47	27	-13	7	16	25	1	-32	2	-24	-42
Creating healthier and more equi-table socie-ties	7	41	7	71	-14	10	42	-57	34	22	-5	13	10	5	-2	7	0	9	0
Protecting the envi-ronment	31	38	16	62	36	41	25	-37	20	41	0	5	-10	-1	-3	17	-1	37	23

Figure 27: Global public opinion report on the state of sustainable development
(GLOBESCAN/SUSTAINABILITY 2012b)

The scores for every country were calculated as balance between the percentage of interviewees saying that the item asked about "got a lot better" or "got somewhat better" minus percentage of interviewees stating that it "got somewhat worse/ a lot worse". Over all countries participating, the balance for environmental protection is in favor of improvement with 17 percentage points. Progress in economic wellbeing is judged less favorably with a balance of only 3 percentage points in favor of improvement; the creation of healthier and more equitable societies comes in at a balance of 10 percentage points in favor of improvement (GLOBESCAN/SUSTAINABILITY 2012b).

As mentioned above, the answers vary significantly between regions. While interviewees in developing economies, especially in Asia, consider economic wellbeing to have improved significantly over the past twenty years (China: 82% "got better", India: 63%, Brazil: 59%), Westerners tend to think that their economic wellbeing worsened (Greece: 77% "got worse", France: 69%, USA: 64%). Germany ranks somewhere in the middle with 37% saying it got better, 33% it stayed about the same and 25% it got worse (GLOBESCAN/SUSTAINABILITY 2012b). How the assessment of the citizens compares with statistical data will be discussed in this subsection.

One of the most important factors that link citizens with sustainable development is the awareness of the concept and the willingness to act accordingly. For the ecological dimension, PREISENDÖRFER (1999) analyzed ecological awareness and actual environmental relevant behavior from data of the German 1998 census and found four clusters or types of environmental behavior (cf. Figure 28):

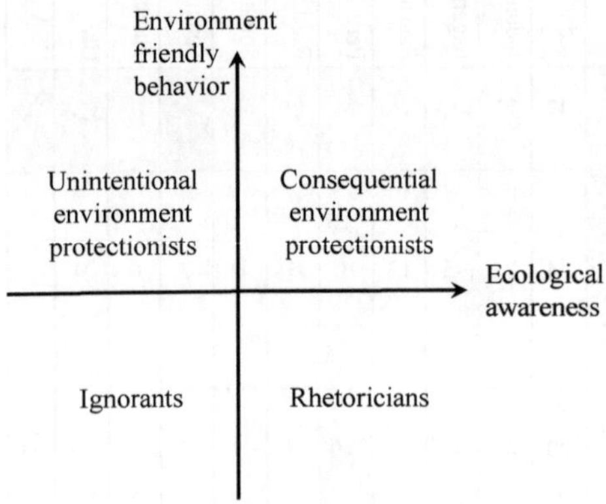

Figure 28: Types of citizens in terms of the environment
(author's own, based on PREISENDÖRFER 1999)

- *Ignorants* with both low ecological awareness and low environment friendly behavior, estimated at about 10% of the German citizens
- *Rhetoricians*, who have a high ecological awareness but low environmental friendly behavior, estimated at about 30% of the German citizens
- *Environment protectionists* without the environmental values, who have a low ecological awareness, but an environmental friendly behavior, also estimated at about 30% of Germans
- *Consequential environment protectionists* who have an above-average ecological awareness as well as above-average environmental friendly behavior. This group includes about 30% of Germans.

The percentage of citizens belonging to each group varies over the years, but about 60% of the german population being – either intentional or unintentional – environment protectionists is not a bad start for raising awareness and improving environment-friendly behavior. It has to be kept in mind, though, that the simple term "environment-friendly behavior" does not indicate whether it is friendly enough to be sustainable, and the description "above-average environmental friendly behavior" shows that the data is not matched to actual requirements for environmental friendly behavior. An example for a certain ambiguity in the public when sustainable actions are concerned is a study about the preferences of college and university graduates when choosing a future employer. In a 2015 survey, 46% of the surveyed graduates in business, economics and engineering stress that working for environmentally responsible companies is very important for them. In addition, 55% expect their future employers to be socially responsible. On the other hand, 34 % of those asked in the representative study say that they would work for a company with a negative reputation if the compensation is adequate. Interestingly, the graduates' favorite future employers are five globally playing automobile companies - an industry that is not exactly known for its sustainable production (WERLE 2015).

Consumption as a whole is a very important topic for sustainable development. If the typical economic assumption that consumption is the aim of production is true, then all negative ecological and social impact caused by production are at least indirectly caused by consumption and consumers (SCHRADER, HANSEN 2001). SCHRADER and HANSEN also offer a definition of sustainable consumption that is closely derived from the BRUNDTLAND COMMISSIONs definition of sustainable development (cf. subsection 2.2): "Consumption is sustainable, if it contributes to the satisfaction of current generations needs without compromising the needs of future generations" (SCHRADER, HANSEN 2001). Private consumption takes up 57.5% of GDP expenditure in Germany, government consumption adds a share of 19.5%. Consumption is therefore an important starting point for any sustainability strategy.

One relevant question is whether consumers are interested in sustainable products. The data from PREISENDÖRFER (cf. Figure 28) suggests that this is the case, but does empirical data for food consumption, for example, match his findings? In Germany in 2011, for example, the share of organic products in total food sales was only 3.3% (SCHAACK ET AL. 2013). This means that even the 60% of interviewees that were classified as environment protectors do spend only a minority of their food budget on organic food and drinks. Also, the use of primary energy has only decreased by 5.8% in the last 25 years, despite an increase of energy efficiency of more than 35%. Specifically, the energy consumption of private households increased by 8.4% between 1990 and 2010, although the increase mainly happened between 1990 and 2000, and private energy consumption nearly stagnates since then (STATISTISCHES BUNDESAMT 2012). The data for Europe is not much more positive. EUROSTAT (2012) analyses comparing data for the EU 28 from 1990 to 2012 show that final energy consumption increased by 2.2% within those 23 years. Residential energy consumption increased by 5.6% within the same period. Critics argue that it is difficult to decrease energy consumption or increase energy efficiency to a degree that will positively influence sustainable development. So far, this explanation has often been used as an excuse to not do anything. The same holds true for food and drink consumption: organic food markets and brands seem to be everywhere and surely anyone claiming to lead an environment-friendly life will buy a large share of his or her food supply organic, but as the data cited above indicates, the translation of good intentions into action is still deficient.

3.1.2 Companies

The companies' role in sustainable development has been described in subsection 2.7.2.3. Companies will either aim for sustainable products and production out of their own initiative, because of the beliefs and convictions of the owners, for example, or, and those cases are most likely much more common, driven by their (potential) customers wishes or government laws, rules and regulations. In the 1990s an often heard argument was that strict rules for environmental protection would hurt the competitiveness of german companies. The environment was considered a two-sided location factor, though: environmental laws and regulations were considered an obstacle for production; at the same time, the quality of the environment was regarded a soft factor, especially important to attract employees (GRABOW ET AL. 1995).

By now, several studies prove that the environmental protection sector is, at least in Germany, a growth area and a positive effect on total employment was proven by some scientists. It has to be kept in mind, though, that there are empirical difficulties with the analysis of the sector and that some studies did not find any such effects, so the argument of increased employment due to strict environmental regulations is not strong (HAUFF 2007), but on the other, no increase of unemployment due to environmental protection has been proven either. Data based on the IAB-company panel[27] estimates that in 1999 a minimum of 2.7% of all employees included in the panel work in the environment protection sector. The companies expected the number of employees in this sector to grow by 24.4% in the following five years (KOMAR 2001). „Green jobs" will be discussed in more detail in subsection 4.4.

A survey among sustainability professionals showed that while most of the experts believe that companies should be included in mapping out ways to sustainable development as their collaboration is crucial, most of them doubt the approach taken by the companies so far (GLOBESCAN/SUSTAINABILITY 2012a). In a 2011 survey of the sustainability communication of Germanys 150 biggest companies (GEBAUER, GLAHE 2011), companies answered questions on the different expectations of sustainability reporting. Overall, employees and NGOs require the most information about sustainability, with 65% of the companies stating that the employees are always, very often or often taking interest in the reports, 63% stating the same for NGOs. Customers are also rather interested in the reports (60%), as well as the capital market (60%). The simple fact of their interest does not imply that they will draw their conclusions from the information they receive. But other studies show that a company's reputation as a responsible company leads to significantly higher willingness to recommend the company's products (REPUTATION INSTITUTE 2013).

---

27 The IAB-Betriebspanel is a company panel of the German Institute for Employment Research

3.1.3 Politicians and Scientific Assessment

Despite the successes to implement sustainable development, statistical analyses show that the implementation of sustainable development, and, as a first step towards this implementation, the increase of awareness of the concept and its implications, has been insufficient so far. Even though *sustainable development* and *sustainability* have become commonly used or even obligatory catchphrases in political speeches and programs, the concept of sustainable development has not yet been incorporated into all aspects of politics. Mainstream economic policy, for example, does not pay particular attention to sustainability. A routine integration of environmental and social issues into economic decisions would be vital to success, but has not been realized yet (JANN ET AL. 2006). In environmental and social politics, sustainability is more implemented, but the integrated approach to combine all dimensions of sustainability is not yet mainstreamed into all areas of political decisions.

In 2003, national sustainable development strategies (NSDS) had been implemented in 12% of the countries worldwide. Implementation varied widely among the continents, though, Europe leading with 33% of its 46 countries having implemented a NSDS. 33% can hardly be called a sweeping success, but the worldwide average of 12% (Africa: 6% of 53 countries; Asia and the Pacific: 9% of 45 countries; Western Asia: none of 12 countries; the Americas and the Caribbean: 6% of 35 countries) shows an even more critical picture (UN DESA 2004).

In their 2012 study *The future we want*, the UNITED NATIONS acknowledged "the need to further mainstream sustainable development at all levels, integrating economic, social and environmental aspects and recognizing their interlinkages, so as to achieve sustainable development in all its dimensions" (UNITED NATIONS 2012, § 3). The report stated that since Rio 1992, insufficient progress and setbacks in several areas prevented the fulfillment of the hopes of the Rio conference. It was also stressed that most problems on the road to sustainability cannot be solved independently from others by one single party, thus creating the need for common action. Reasons for not reaching the goals stated in Rio 1992 are for example changing geopolitical realities such as new emerging powers (UN DESA 2012a). The Johannesburg Plan of Implementation[28] listed hundreds of commitments, many of them with numeric specification and dates by which these goals were to be reached. There is no regular monitoring of the complete list, but it can be said that many of the commitments have not been achieved (UN DESA 2012a).

28 The World Summit on Sustainable Development in 2002 took place in Johannesburg. One of the results of the conference was the Johannesburg Plan of Implementation that included quantifiable goals for the realization of sustainable development, for example the reduction of poverty, the reduction of negative impacts of chemicals on health and environment and a better protection of biodiversity.

A survey among sustainability experts showed that when asked about the world's progress on economic, environmental and social causes, the experts assert that there has been progress in the first two areas, but regress in rising to the social challenges (GLOBESCAN/SUSTAINABILITY 2012c). In Germany, the progress in sustainable development is controlled by the quantifiable data collected according to the government rules of the Agenda for Sustainable Politics (BACHMANN 2002). The rules state that the Strategy for Sustainable Development is to be strictly monitored. The indicators are updated every other year; a progress report is issued once every four years, including an evaluation of the implementation of the strategy (BUNDESREGIERUNG 2011b). An overview over the status of the indicator set is given in Table 3. Only the indicators that are marked as ++ are on track towards the indicated targets, whereas + and - indicate that there is still a long way to go to reach the targets, even if the development is in the right direction towards an improvement. The -- stand for indicators where the current development is contrary and the gap between target and reality is widening. As the targets are already a compromise between scientists' predictions of necessary changes to ensure sustainable development and political feasibility, the abundance of +, - and -- markers is critical. In addition, some of the indicators are only of a limited informational value. While it is, for example, commendable to increase the share of renewable energy sources in electricity consumption, this indicator – one of the few indicated as ++, i.e., right on track towards meeting the target – does not say anything about the development of electricity consumption in total. If, e.g., total electricity consumption has increased[29], then even with an increased share of renewable energy sources the consumption of energy from non-renewable sources may have increased in absolute numbers. Therefore, the indicators have to be interpreted with caution.

In summary, while the awareness for a necessity for sustainable development has increased, much remains to be done if sustainability is to be realized. The data below has been collected for Germany. To judge on a global level – which would be necessary to make an informed judgment, as most effects do not stop at national borders – it is necessary to compare global data on those indicators. Sadly, this is not a realistic plan of action as global data collection is rather patchy. But the data for a developed country like Germany gives a useful first insight in the sincerity and success with which sustainable development is pursued.

29 This is not true in the case of Germany, according to the working group for energy balances (AGEB) (ARBEITSGEMEINSCHAFT ENERGIEBILANZEN 2013), but the argument holds for example in the case of developing countries.

Indicator	Target	Status	
		2008	2012
Resource Conservation			
Energy productivity	To be doubled between 1990 and 2020	+	-
Primary energy consumption	To be reduced by 20% by 2020, 50% by 2050, compared to 2008	n/a	-
Raw material productivity	To be doubled between 1994 and 2020	-	+
Climate protection			
Greenhouse gas emissions	To be reduced by 21% by 2008/2012, 40% by 2020, 80 to 95% by 2050	++	++
Renewable energy sources			
% of renewable energy sources in final energy consumption	To be increased to 18% by 2020 and 60% by 2050	++	++
% of renewable energy sources in electricity consumption	To be increased to 12,5% by 2010, to at least 35% by 2020 and to at least 80% by 2050	++	++
Land use			
Built-up area and transport infrastructure expansion	Increase to be reduced to 30 hectares a day by 2020	-	-
Species diversity			
Species diversity, landscape quality	Increase to index value of 100 by 2015	--	--
Government debt			
General government deficit	Ratio of government deficit to GDP less than 3%	++	--
Structural deficit	Structurally balanced public spending, national structural deficit of no more than 0,5% of GDP	n/a	--
Government debt	Ratio of government debt to GDP no more than 60%	n/a	--
Future economic stability			
Gross fixed capital formation in relation to GDP	Increase in gross fixed capital formation share in GDP	++	++
Innovation			
Private and public spending on R&D	To be increased to 3% of GDP by 2020	++	++
Education and training			
18-to-24-year-olds without school leaving certificate	To be reduced to less than 10% by 2020	--	++
30-to-34-year olds with tertiary or post-secondary education	To be increased to 42% by 2020	n/a	++
Share of students starting a degree course	To be increased to 40% by 2010, followed by further increase and stabilization on high level	--	++
Economic output			
GDP per capita	Economic growth	++	++
Mobility			
Intensity of goods transport	To e reduced to 98% by 2010 and to 95% by 2020, compared to 1999 levels	--	--
Intensity of passenger transport	To be reduced to 90% by 2010 and to 80% by 2020, compared to 1999 levels	-	-
Share of rail transport in goods transport performance	To be increased to 25% by 2015	-	-
% of inland freight water transp. in goods transportation performance	To be increased to 14% by 2015	--	--

Farming			
Nitrogen surplus	To be reduced to 80kg/ha of agricultural area by 2010, further reduction by 2020	-	-
Organic farming	Share of organic farming land used for agriculture to be increased to 20% in coming years	-	
Air quality			
Air pollution	To be reduced to 30% by 2010, compared to 1990	+	+
Health and nutrition			
Premature mortality (cases per 100.000 under 65: men)	To be reduced to 190 cases per 100.000 residents by 2015	++	+
Premature mortality (cases per 100.000 under 65: woman)	To be reduced to 115 cases per 100.000 residents by 2015	+	+
Smoking rate amongst young people (12-to-17-year olds)	To be reduced to under 12% by 2015	++	++
Smoking rate amongst adults (15 years and older)	To be reduced to under 22% by 2015	-	-
Proportion of adults suffering obesity (18 years and older)	To be reduced by 2020	--	--
Crime			
Criminal offences	To be reduced in number or recorded cases per 100.000 residents to under 7.000 by 2020	++	++
Employment			
Employment rate (total, 15-to-64-year-olds)	To be increased to 73% by 2010 and 75% by 2020	+	-
Employment rate of older people (55-to-64-year-olds)	To be increased to 55% by 2010 and 60% by 2020	++	++
Prospects for families			
All-day care provision for 0-to-2-year olds	To be increased to 30% by 2010	-	-
All-day care provision for 3-to-5-year olds	To be increased to 30% by 2010 and 60% by 2020	++	++
Equal opportunity			
Gender pay gap	To be reduced to 15% by 2010 and to 10% by 2020	--	--
Integration			
Foreign school leavers with a school leaving certificate	To be increased to rate of german school leavers with at least lower secondary schooling by 2020	-	+
Development cooperation			
Percentage of expenditure for official development assistance in GNI	To be increased to 0,51% by 2010 and 0,7% by 2015	-	-
Opening markets			
German imports from developing countries	Further increase	++	++
++ target achieved or will be achieved (deviation < 5%) until time indicated, if trend continues			
+ development in correct direction, gap of 5-20% to target remains if trend continues			
- development in correct direction, gap of > 20% to target remains if trend continues			
-- development in wrong direction, distance to target increasing if trend continues			

Table 3: Sustainable development indicator status, Germany 2008-2012
(STATISTISCHES BUNDESAMT 2008, 2012)

3.2 Strategies for Sustainable Development

The Brundtland Commission states that "in its broadest sense, the strategy for sustainable development aims to promote harmony among human beings and between humanity and nature" (WCED 1987b, p. 57). This definition of a strategy is too vague, but the quotation shows the complexity of the concept. To develop a strategy that includes all aspects of sustainable development and is politically feasible is a considerable challenge. The prerequisites and necessary rules shall be discussed in the following subsections.

3.2.1 Overview

The Brundtland commission, one of the acknowledged authorities on the topic, has compiled a list of requirements for the pursuit of sustainable development which contains the following elements that are deemed essential for a successful strategy:

- A political system that secures effective citizen participation in decision making
- An economic system that is able to generate surpluses and technical knowledge on a self-reliant and sustained basis
- A social system that provides solutions for the tensions arising from disharmonious development
- A production system that respects the obligation to preserve the ecological base for development
- A technological system that can search continuously for new solutions
- An international system that fosters sustainable patterns of trade and finance
- An administrative system that is flexible and has the capacity for self-correction (WCED 1987b).

It is stressed that the requirements must be the underlying guidelines for all actions to ensure that the development is sustainable. But the Commission also clearly emphasizes that this development can only be realized if the goals are sincerely pursued and if developments in the wrong direction are corrected quickly and efficiently (WCED 1987b).

The rules listed above are the groundwork for successful sustainable development strategies. But what exactly is a strategy for sustainable development? It is undeniably difficult to find an all-encompassing definition. Due to complexities and uncertainties, it is rather impossible to define exact parameters. If approximations and assumptions are applied and parameters developed as a basis for strategies, said parameters may be subject to unexpected changes in the future; and, in the case of ambivalent parameters the development in one direction may be good for one dimension, but critical for the others. A typical example for this phenomenon is the fertility rate, where the decline may be favorable to ecological issues, but problematic for economic and social issues (BAECHLER 2012). Apart from those parameter-based problems, anyone defining and developing a strategy for sustainable development will also face political challenges, such as a usually unfavorable cost-benefit outcomes in the short term, uncertainties in the calculation and prediction of long-term outcomes, differing definitions and priorities for sustainable development and appropriate measures, and a lack of political feasibility and public acceptance for many of the more radical measures. Those obstacles will be discussed in more detail in subsection 3.3.

3.2.2 Strategies

When discussing strategies for sustainable development, it is necessary to have an understanding of the requirements and characteristics of strategies. The basic requirement is strategic competency, i.e., a fundamentally existent power for target-oriented, consistent and homogeneous action. This competency is the basis for the development of a strategy, which is normally done by carrying out the following steps: the formulation of precise targets, followed by an analysis of the current state, strategic calculations and an analysis of different options, and, based upon the former evaluation, a decision which option to take. The decision and the subsequent implementation then have to be supervised to ensure possibly necessary adaptions of the strategy to reach the targets set for the process. In addition, especially in politics a strategy has to be accompanied by a strategic communication, because it is hard to reach a wide acceptance of the approach chosen without the support of the voters (TILS 2005). The strategy must be supported by a number of guidelines and specified principles that permit the operationalization of the concept. Those guidelines and principles must be supported by indicators to control the successes in achieving clear and quantifiable or qualifiable goals (TILS 2005). The requirements for, and possible difficulties with, indicators will be discussed in detail in subsection 5.2.

The usual steps during the development of effective sustainability strategies are defined by RENN ET AL. (2007) as the following: First comes the *orientation* phase. In this phase the normative basis is decided on and the time period for realization is fixed. This is the setting of the strategic targets that are described above. This step is followed by the stage of *explanation and connections*: the analysis of the status quo and the target situation and the investigation of (dynamic) connections between variables influencing the way from status quo to the target situation. This step corresponds with the strategic analyses and calculations mentioned above. Once those requirements are fulfilled, the third step, *transformation and action*, takes place: The options about measures appropriate to realize the target must be discussed and weighed based on the analyses of step two. The implementation and supervision are the necessary fourth step.

However, for the discussion of sustainability it has to be kept in mind, that political strategies do not always follow the same rules as company strategies. For one, political decisions are often made in a more complex and diverse environment. The impact of strategies (and measures to realize them) on other fields must be considered, because the consequences of decisions usually have a far greater impact than decisions on the company level (cf., for example, subsection 3.2.5 about the mandatory regulatory impact analysis in Germany). In addition, political strategies do not only have to pass impact analyses and the evaluation of their effectiveness, but have to take into account all stakeholders opinions and preferences. Decision-making on a political level is also complicated by the large number of interested parties who have their own ideas and interpretations of adequate strategies, goals, and measures. The difficulties to find reliable indicators to determine not only immediate, but also long-term impact add to the complicated process. The distinctive characteristics of political decision-making will be discussed in more detail in subsection 3.3.

3.2.3 Sustainable Development Strategies

As a basis for the development and implementation of sustainability strategies, RITT (2007, pp. 74-75) suggests two possible strategies: the efficiency- and the sufficiency strategy. The former strategy aims at reducing negative impact on the environment per output unit, the latter provides absolute limits for the use of natural resources. A combination of both rules is most efficient, because simply following the efficiency strategy might reduce the negative impact on environment per output unit, thereby possibly decreasing the price, thus increasing consumption, which would negate the positive effects. The reason for the design of a sustainability strategy from the political point of view is to clearly signal the importance of the topic and the interest to specify aims and measures and to reach the targets set. It is also a way to help citizens or stake holding institutions to get information and orientation. It raises awareness of the topic and generates votes if sustainability is a crucial priority in voters' minds. Therefore, it is important to show activities to realize sustainable development. The overview over sustainability strategies in politics of the German Council of Environmental Advisors (SRU) (cf. Table 4) is based on ecologic sustainability and considers the other dimensions as of merely secondary importance, due to the SRUs interpretation of sustainability.

Their approach is to develop strategies and measures directly connected to the environment and, in a second step, to develop measures for all fields related to the environment. This approach can be transferred to the other sustainability dimensions as well, so that an enhanced model would not only include environmental strategies, but also economic and social issues. The second pillar of Table would then be rather small as most topics are somehow related to one of the dimensions. In the case of an extended interpretation, the second pillar would rather have to deal with the connections between the dimensions.

Strategies for Sustainability	
- Show social consensus about sustainable development - Signal political intentions to reach sustainability targets - Offer orientation to stakeholders	
Environmental Strategies	Sectoral Strategies with Relevance for Environment
- Broach ecological issues - Bring relevant knowledge into politics - Express ecological requirements	- Develop strategies consistent with environmental targets for political fields concerned

Table 4: Sustainability strategies in politics
(SRU 2012)

The German Advisory Council on Global Change (WGBU) supports the SRUs argument for the priority of the ecological dimension and considers the remodeling of economy and society as means towards a climate compatible society, therefore seeing the two columns as support for the ecological column. The process necessary to realize this remodeling is called the "great transformation", in tradition of former great transformations, the neolithical revolution (i.e., the development of society towards an agricultural and livestock-breeding society) and the industrial revolution (i.e., the transformation from the agricultural society towards an industrial society) (WGBU 2011).

ROGALL (2007) suggests a less environment-centered approach and advocates the implementation of three concurrent strategies: an efficiency strategy that aims at increasing resource efficiency; a substitution- and consistency strategy to further the development of sustainable goods and sustainable production; and a sufficiency strategy that targets the design and implementation of new lifestyles, including new consumption patterns. To make those strategies successful he suggests a mix of instruments to realize a change of society towards sustainability, as he rightly claims that a single instrument cannot efficiently solve all pending problems. He also criticizes that many instruments are not used with full force but rather are the results of compromises that were reached after political negotiations, thus making it even more necessary to apply a larger number of measures (ROGALL 2007). The latter criticism and its entitlement can be observed in everyday political discussions and decision-making. The implementation of sustainability with the help of a large number of measures creates a number of problems, among them the incompatibility of measures or rivalry between measures so that one measure might further the realization of one aim and at the same time lessen the impact of another measure intended to reach another aim. In addition, the decision for the prevalence of one of the dimensions is based on the classical assumption that politics are able to manage society and therefore show a major potential to solve problems occurring when trying to reconcile the individual aspects of sustainability (WETZEL 2005). These political difficulties and challenges shall be further discussed in subsection 3.3.

3.2.4 Sustainable Development Rules

If a sustainability strategy has been developed (cf. subsection 3.2.3), the next step is to specify rules that must be followed to reach the goals set for sustainable development. ENDRES and RADKE (1998, p. 30) suggest setting two priorities for sustainability: to ensure "that critical stock of all societal components of assets that are considered relevant is never reached or are below the target", and to "adequately assess that changes of all societal components of assets that are considered relevant accumulate to zero". RADKE refines these priorities into three basic rules for sustainability:

1. *Harvesting Rule*: Renewable natural resources have to be used in a way that ensures that the harvest does not excess their capability to regenerate.
2. *Extraction Rule*: Exhaustible natural resources must only be extracted to the extent where functionally equivalent substitutes can be provided.
3. *Emission Rule*: Pollution of environmental elements is only allowed at or under the level of their capacity to assimilate. (RADKE 1999)

The rules set are all based on the concepts of sustainable policy discussed in subsection 2.2. If those basic rules are followed, and if a concept is decided upon, it is necessary to deal with the concrete rules. In the case of Germany, the government has developed a set of rules that must be adhered to if sustainability is to be realized (cf. Table 5).

(1) Every generation has to solve its own problems and must not burden future generations with them. Furthermore every generation has to provide for foreseeable future liabilities.

(2) Renewable natural assets (such as wood or fish stock) may in the long run only be used within the scope of their capability of regeneration. Non-renewable natural assets (e.g., mineral resources or fossil energy sources) may in the long run only be used to the amount to which they can be substituted by other materials or energy sources.

(3) The release of substances may, in the long run, not be bigger than the adaptability of the natural systems such as climate, woods, and oceans.

(4) Dangers and unwarranted risks for human health have to be avoided.

(5) Structural change that has been triggered by technical developments and international competition has to be economically successful, but also ecologically and socially compatible. To do so, political fields have to be integrated, making sure that economic growth, high employment, social cohesion and protection of the environment can be realized.
(6) Energy and resource use as well as traffic capacity have to be decoupled from economic growth. Simultaneously, an increased demand for energy and resources created by growth must be compensated by increased efficiency. To a good portion, that has to be done by creating knowledge through research and development and knowledge transfers through specific trainings.
(7) Public budgets are bound to generational justice. Thus, budgets have to be balanced on all levels (federal, state, community). In a second step, public debt has to be reduced continually.
(8) Sustainable agriculture must not only be efficient and competitive, but also environmentally compatible and meet the requirements of species-appropriate livestock management and have to ensure preventive and health-related consumer protection.
(9) To further social cohesion, poverty and social exclusion have to be prevented; all social strata shall be enabled to participate in the economic development; adaption of politics, economy and society to demographic change shall be timely; everyone shall be enabled to participate in social and political life.
(10) The international general framework has to be designed so that all people in all countries can live a humane life after their own beliefs and in tune with their regional environment and can partake of the economic development. Environment and development form a unit. Sustainable global action is based on the United Nation Millennium Development Goals. With the help of an integrated approach, the combat against poverty and hunger shall be linked to respecting human rights; economic development; protection of the environment and good governance.

Table 5: Sustainability rules of the German Federal Government
(BUNDESREGIERUNG 2011b, p. 28)

If the first rule is observed, intragenerational justice is realized, as the rule does not allow living at the expense of future generations. The following rules address specific scopes of application. Rule (2), for example, implies weak sustainability (cf. subsection 2.5), allowing the substitution of non-renewable resources with other resources and thereby implicitly accepting possible depletion of resources. Rule (5) focuses not only on the ecologic, but on all dimensions. This rule is hard to follow, though, as the integration of the political fields poses – as has been mentioned before – a number of problems, among them the contrarious impact of measures on different dimensions and the reality of non-integrated ministries and responsible institutions that follow their own agenda. Therefore, to implement this rule it is necessary to create an overarching authority that is able to influence the agendas of all other decision makers. Rule (8) is rather concrete and could lead to clear policy measures and, eventually, to results, even if "species-appropriate" is a term that will most likely be interpreted differently by different stakeholders and will therefore be debated. Nevertheless, it should be possible to find a compromise. Rule (9) is more complicated, though. Enabling all citizens to participate in economic development would mean to decrease unemployment, increase labor market participation and increase contributions to those who are not able to earn their own income. This will become harder in those countries with an aging population[30], as demographic change continues due to the "existing structure of the population, persistently low fertility and continuously increasing number of survivors to higher ages" (GIANNAKOURIS 2008). The next challenge is posed by the requirement of a timely adaption of institutions to changes. It is well known that the response time of the political institutions is less than desirable, and the postulation that politics, economy and society should react simultaneously and adequately to such a big challenge is – while correct and necessary – likely too ambitious. Rule (10), the international guideline, is copied from the goals of the UNITED NATIONS. National action will not or only marginally contribute to the successful implementation, and international action depends on the cooperation of at least most of the developed, but also the emerging nations. If it is hard to come to an agreement on precise measures on a national level, it is even more so on the international level.

The german strategy for sustainable development also states about 30 mostly quantified targets that can also be used as indicators, and includes, apart from the ecological dimension and adequate indicators, aims such as generational justice, quality of life, social cohesion and international responsibility. The SRU, for example, criticizes the abundance of aspects and the inclusion of a number of topics that are not closely related to sustainable development and therefore lead to a diminished clarity of the concept by trying to include too many topics. The SRU also regrets the lack of public interest in the development of a strategy for sustainable development. The heterogeneity of the concept that includes targets from all fields of politics is believed to be one of the reasons for that lack of interest, as it leads to a loss of contours (SRU 2002).

There are sets of rules that are closer to the original definition of sustainability and sustainable development. Those usually set clearer limits to the use of natural capital and put their focus on the ecological dimension, based on many scientists' conclusion that due to the current state of the environment and the damage and (over)depletion of resources that has already taken place a prevalence of the ecologic dimension is inevitable.

A suggestion for a general system of sustainability rules is depicted in Table 6, where the rules are subdivided into substantial and instrumental rules. The latter are necessary to ensure the openness of the process as well as the adaptability of the strategy

30 The projected median age of the EU27 population, for example, is projected to rise by 7.5 years in the next 50 years. During that time span, the share of people aged 65 years or older is predicted to increase from 17.1% to 30%. In total, the relation "working age people to persons aged 65 years or older" is projected to change from 4:1 in 2008 to 2:1 by 2060 (GIANNAKOURIS 2008).

during the implementation process if the need arises and the in-process evaluation shows that the targets set cannot be reached if the rules and strategies are not tuned and adapted.

System of Sustainability Rules		
Substantial Rules and their Classification		
Securing human existence	**Securing societal productive potential**	**Conservation of options for future development and action**
Protection of human health	Sustainable use of renewable resources	Equal opportunities in education, career and information
Ensuring basic provision (nutrition, education,…)	Sustainable use of non-renewable resources	Participation in public decision processes
Ensuring possibility for an independent provision for individual existence	Sustainable use of environment as depression	Conservation of cultural heritage and cultural diversification
Fair distribution of the right to benefit from the environment	Avoidance of unjustifiable technical risks	Conservation of cultural cpacity of nature
Equalization of extreme differences in income and property	Sustainable development of real, human and knowledge capital	Conservation of social resources
Instrumental Rules		
• Internalisation of external ecological and social costs • Appropriate discounting • Limiting public debt • Fair global economic framework conditions • International cooperation • Openness to feedback of public institutions • Reflexivity of public institutions • Ability for self-organization • Balance of power		

Table 6: General system of sustainability rules
(GRUNWALD, KOPFMÜLLER 2006, p. 57)

3.2.5 Sustainability Management in Germany

In Germany, sustainable development is translated into constitutional law. When the constitution was adopted, sustainable development was not yet a commonly used word and much less a guideline for political action. Still, § 20a of the German constitution states that *"the state protects the responsibility for future generations nature and animals within the framework of the constitution (...)"* (GG 1949). The sustainability rules of the German government have been discussed in detail above. But apart from those rules that are, in a way, rather guidelines than specific operating instructions and can be interpreted in different ways, there are other measures to implement sustainable development in all law making processes and thereby into all levels of society.

To allow for the complexity and the cross-sectional character of sustainability, the competence for sustainability in Germany lies with the German Chancellery (cf. Figure 29). The chancellery is supported by the federal statistical office that provides, for example, data for the sustainable development indicators cf. Table 3), the Commission on Sustainable Development and a parliamentary advisory board as well as several commissions and boards from the federal states and the communal organizations. The administration office for sustainable development is responsible for decisions that must be realized by the departments that, in turn, report their results to the administration Office.

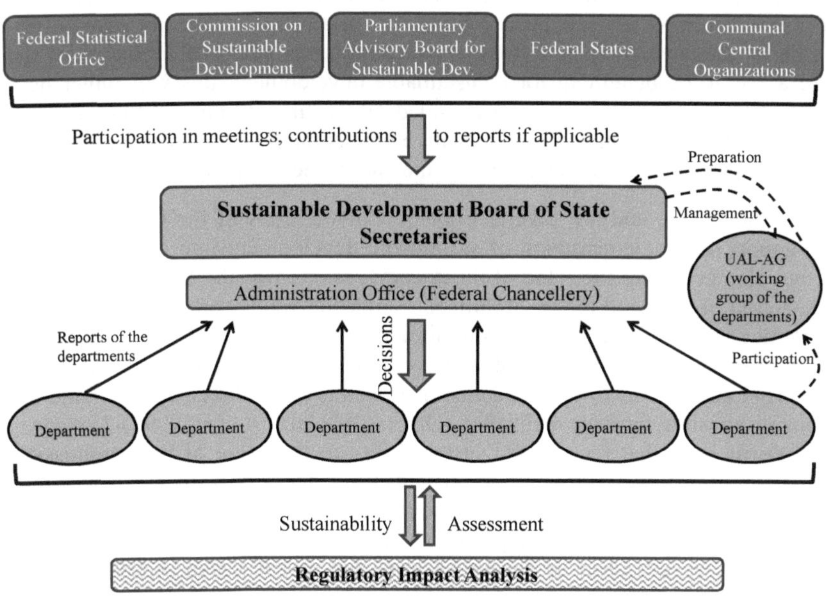

Figure 29: Sustainability management in Germany
(BUNDESREGIERUNG 2008, p. 34)

The system of responsible and executive units is supported by the institution of a mandatory regulatory impact analysis. The German Parliamentary Rules of Procedure (GGO) regulate the organization of federal ministries and their cooperation, but also the rules of law-making (Bundesregierung 2011a). In §43 s. (1) no. 5 GGO, e. g., legislators are obligated to conduct a regulatory impact analysis before ratifying new laws. Impact analyses take into account intended effects, but also unintended side effects of new laws and regulations. The analysis must include long-term impact and a prediction of a new law's concurrence with the guidelines for sustainable development (Bundesregierung 2011a). As all areas of politics are concerned and must follow the rules of the GGO and have to conduct sustainability assessments for all laws and regulations, it makes sense to include a first impact analysis in the planning phase for a new law. If the goals of a specific government initiative are inconsistent with the sustainability rules, a positive evaluation of the drafted law is unlikely; therefore the law or rule must not be passed (TIESSEN ET AL. 2011).

This is, in theory, very logical. But this mandatory regulatory impact analysis does not have the intended effects yet. It was hoped that it would be applied during the process of law-making. Instead it is only conducted after drafting the law; and possible negative effects and the suggestion of alternative regulations are mostly set aside (SRU 2011). This is, in a way, understandable because of the complexity of the topic. It is almost impossible to precisely predict a measure's impact on all dimensions of sustainable development. In addition, if the impact analysis is only conducted after the draft of a potential new law has been completed, sustainability does not play an important role for the lawmakers; and if the impact analysis or later evaluations show the impact of a law to be beneficial for a sustainable development, this will rather be a side effect of lawmaking instead of an intended effect. In addition, existing laws are not affected by the GGOs rules, so that negative impact on the goals of sustainable development must be rectified in other ways, if they are detected at all.

In addition, there were and are several Enquete Commissions of the German parliament to support the implementation of sustainable development into every aspect of politics, but also everyday life. One of those commissions was the Enquete Commission "Protection of man and the environment – aims and framework requirements for sustainable development". Aim of the commission appointed in 1995 was to not theoretically discuss sustainability, but instead develop practical and realizable advice for everyone. That advice was to include aims, instruments and actions; and to name the institutions responsible for their realization (DEUTSCHER BUNDESTAG 1998). However, it has been criticized, that (economic) sustainability in the sense of the commission does not encompass a basic principle of sustainability: the global approach. It rather concentrates on preserving the economic, social and human capital that has been accumulated, whereas a more global approach should discuss whether it is necessary in some regions to surrender part of the wealth to ensure global sustainability (EKARDT 2005).

A review of Germany's sustainable policies is provided by the German Council for Sustainable Development (RNE). It covers issues such as administrational implementation, vertical integration in federal states, management frames in the private sector, governance issues arising with the ongoing input of scientific evidence, civil societies input, leadership and governance, the issues of global transition and technologies, economy, development and sustainability, and the governance of advisory schemes (RAT FÜR NACHHALTIGE ENTWICKLUNG 2009). The institutions and rules aiming to mainstream sustainable development and to implement measures to further sustainability are manifold in Germany. But the successes have, according to the SRU and the RAT FÜR NACHHALTIGE ENTWICKLUNG, not been sufficient so far, and the rules and concepts are still lacking. Even the underlying model of sustainability is challenged by some, because while the sustainability model of the federal government of Germany with its concept of equality between social, economic and ecologic elements explicitly respects an absolute limit when it comes to the conservation of nature, this limit is not defined. Also, the government does not specify how respecting this limit is to be ensured (SRU 2011).

SWOT ANALYSIS FOR SUSTAINABLE DEVELOPMENT IN GERMANY			
Strengths	Weaknesses	Opportunities	Threats
Deep roots	Weak horizontal and vertical coordination	Building on what has been achieved	Increasing global pressure
National Sustainability Strategy in place	Weak cooperation between public and private sector	Speeding up change	Demographic change
Institutional competencies	Confusing information to consumers and business	Building the Grand Design	
Research and development	Lack of vision		

Table 7: SWOT analysis for sustainable development in Germany
(RAT FÜR NACHHALTIGE ENTWICKLUNG 2013, p. 19)

There is still a long way to go if Germany wants to realize its self-professed place as a role model for sustainable development. The German Council for Sustainable Development has conducted a SWOT Analysis (i.e., an analysis of Strengths, Weaknesses, Opportunities and Threats) and found, apart from a number of (mainly institutional) strengths, also weaknesses and threats critical to a realization of sustainable development in Germany (cf. Table 7). Those weaknesses have to be tackled and, apart from the existing measures, a number of hard decisions have to be made and priorities have to be set. Before those decisions can be implemented, they must be politically accepted, and laws and regulations must be passed. This poses a number of difficulties which will be discussed in the following chapter.

3.3 Challenges in Implementing Sustainable Development

It has been discussed in chapters 1 and 2.1 that the concept of sustainability is popular and widely accepted by citizens as well as politicians. There is also extensive research done on the topic. So why is there so little progress and where does the knowledge-action-gap come from? Some possible reasons have been detailed in former chapters. One is the concept itself: sustainability is a "contestable concept: one that affords a variety of competing interpretations or conceptions. Many political objectives are of this kind: liberty, social justice and democracy, for example. These concepts have basic meanings and almost everyone is in favour of them, but deep conflicts remain about how they should be understood and what they imply for policy" (JACOBS 1991, p. 60). This elusive concept is open to manifold interpretations, owing to the lack of operationability of many of its components (BÖHRINGER, LÖSCHEL 2004). Thus, the concept has become a vessel for all kinds of interpretations and adaptations. A person or group developing a definition of sustainability may have different objectives – benevolent or not. A political party might plan to maximize votes, companies are more interested in minimizing costs or gaining customer interest and approval, a group for nature and environment protection will focus on the environment (TREMMEL 2003). They will tailor the definition and interpretation of sustainability to fit their intentions and will set priorities accordingly.

In addition to those conceptual difficulties, the very nature of sustainability poses an obstacle. Sustainability has to be realized by international, national, regional and communal institutions as well as the civil society. The concept cannot simply be commanded by the government but has to be put into action by all parties concerned (BUNDESREGIERUNG 2008). This is due to the fact that sustainability is a normative agreement and not enforceable (HAUFF, JÖRG 2013), even if specific aspects of a sustainable development can be enforced by law. A specific challenge to the implementation of any reform, even if they are not as complex as sustainability-related reforms, is the stickiness of existing social structures. Reforms often do not change much; in some cases they even destroy the harmony between people and institutions. To change existing situations and institutions, it is necessary to understand reality as a complex of interdependent layers. Those layers have developed in a process of necessity and coincidence, and to instigate changes (e.g., in the form of reforms) it is crucial to understand that new systems always develop between two existing layers (PATZELT 2014). To implement a reform that needs extensive changes in behavior or values, the most promising approach is to stimulate changes between two existing layers (cf. Figure 30). Other challenges to the realization of sustainable development will be discussed in the following subsections.

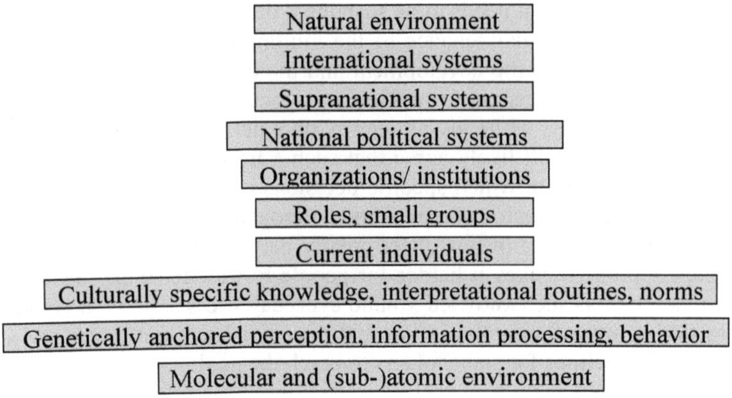

Figure 30: Layers of social reality
(PATZELT 2014)

3.3.1 Communicational Challenges

As can be seen in the section above, one of the challenges and a crucial point for success when mainstreaming and implementing sustainable development is communication. The difficulties with a distinct definition that have been discussed above and in subsection 2.2 complicate communication of the concept. People, whether in their role as voters, politicians, scientists or simply consumers, need an understandable idea of the concept that, in the case of agreement with the idea, can be translated into actions to further it.

A very basic problem arises in german speaking countries, for example. The german translation of *sustainable* has two meanings: one that is used in common language and means intensive or durable and another one that depicts a whole concept, the one that is used in this work. So if a politician speaks about sustainable policy measures it is not clear whether he only refers to a long-term approach, or to the considerably more complex concept of sustainability that includes several dimensions and generations. The double meaning (or rather, its ambiguity, as the simpler version is at least part of the complex concept) may be capitalized on, for example to do some greenwashing (GROBER 2010).

The UNITED NATIONS state that sustainability is not a clear vision, presenting a future world with clear images of its design in all areas. Rather, it is a concept, a way of thinking that allows to imagine – and to create – a large number of different future worlds. This implies that a successful concept of sustainable development must include minimum requirements (what needs to be sustained, developed) as well as showing possible paths to realize the maintenance of the minimum requirements, leaving policy makers and all involved in the development and the execution of measures towards sustainable development freedom to set their own focus points. This guarantees a common denominator globally, while giving leeway on a national and regional level (UN DESA 2012a). Scientists will likely agree that such a framework definition with guidelines and band widths within which specific decisions can be made are the only open course of action in case of such a complex and heterogeneous world, where conditions, requirements and available means differ greatly between nations and regions. But such a complex approach makes it harder for people to transfer their theoretical knowledge (given that there is such knowledge) into everyday life's actions. It is therefore necessary to find a way of communication that does not leave out too many aspects but gives clearer guidelines for stakeholders to reach the goal.

In addition, media communication on the topic is rather sparse in mainstream media or, in the case of Germany, sustainability is mainly referred to in the simpler sense described above, i.e., as a synonym for long-term. It is also observed by some scientists that the media of the developed countries has put "sustainability" together with "environment" and "development" – topics considered to be of immediate importance to developing countries, but not to the developed nations (GROBER 2002). As the media's influence on knowledge and engagement of citizens is undeniably large, a clearer communication of the urgency of changes towards a sustainable development is desirable.

3.3.2 Challenges in Society

While the responsible institutions' communication related to sustainability needs improvement, and a lack of appropriate action can be asserted, institutions cannot be made out to be solely responsible for the insufficient success of implementing sustainable development so far. This would take away all responsibility from citizens and would ignore that an information transfer and the following actions can only work if all stakeholders want to be involved. It only takes a few moments to find information about sustainability and sustainable development; and if the information is too complex, there is a large number of basic, introductory leaflets and books for non-experts to start on the topic. Therefore, the typical excuse that the topic is too complex is not viable as far as basic information is concerned. The gap between perception and action has already been discussed in the 1972 publication *The Limits to Growth*, where the fact that the problem is perceived, but the causes, significance and the interdependencies of its many components are not understood, thereby prohibiting appropriate action, is attributed to the complexity of the topic and the lacking understanding for dynamic processes (MEADOWS ET AL. 1972).

EKARDT (2005), on the other hand, believes that lacking knowledge and information are not the cause for the inactivity of individuals where a sustainable lifestyle is concerned. Instead, he sees a motivation problem, possibly "influenced by unintended or unconscious incidental consequences of our actions" as the cause for non-action. BOSSEL describes the motivation of humans in time and space, based on MEADOWS ET AL. (1972), as follows (cf. Figure 31): individuals place the highest importance on the spaces closest to them: their family and, to a lesser degree, their community. The nation and the whole world are considerably less important in their decisions, and they act accordingly. Studying the importance of time spans yields similar results: the closer the time difference is to the current time, the more importance is placed on it. Consequently, the connection between time and space can be classified into three different "horizons": the horizon of responsibility, the horizon of attention and the horizon of influence, marked by the dotted lines in Figure 31. The idea behind the horizons is that people feel responsible for the people (and, to a lesser degree, the environment) closest to them in space and time (= horizon of responsibility). They are aware of situations, problems and challenges for people in their own lifetime and within their own nation or closer environment, but do not feel responsibility for them and therefore do not plan their actions according to their requirements (= horizon of attention). The time after their own lifetime, and space outside their nation is neither an important part of their responsibility nor their attention, but their intended or non-intended influence on both dimensions is undeniable (= horizon of influence).

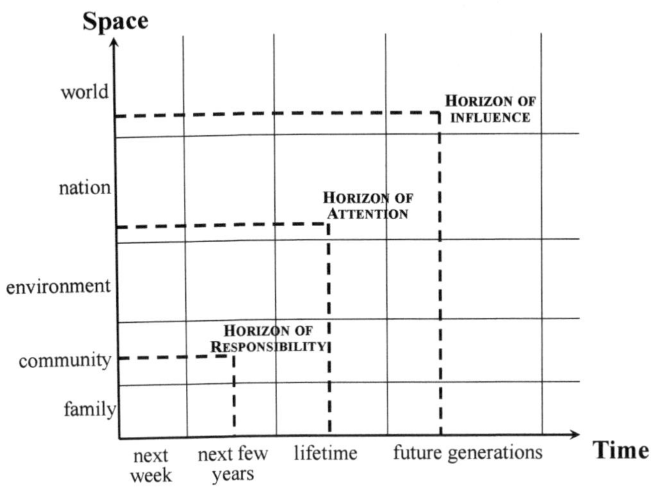

Figure 31: The horizons of influence, attention and responsibility in space and time
(BOSSEL 1999, p. 50)

Sustainable development with its stipulation for intra- and intergenerational justice requires an equal treatment of current and future times, as well as an equal consideration of spaces and spheres close to one's own and those that are more distant. Therefore, the horizon of responsibility and the horizon of influence should be one and the same. In practice, the difference between them is considerable, and to change this, a fundamental value shift would be necessary to increase the willingness to change lifestyles toward more sustainable ways of living and to bear the short-term cost of doing so. If this value shift takes place, a sustainable lifestyle would not only be accepted, but rather required by society (SCHÄPKE, RAUSCHMAYER 2012).

If a value shift is desirable, it is necessary to examine the variables influencing sustainable behavior of individuals. Those influences include the personal environmental norms, social norms, the awareness of problems and the awareness of consequences, individual cost/ benefit expectations, the awareness of consequences of behavior and the ascription of responsibility, the perceived personal agency and behavioral control, and the individual habits (SCHÄPKE, RAUSCHMAYER 2012). Therefore, to change individuals' behavior towards a more sustainable one, there are two main starting points: changing social norms or changing individual norms, attitudes, habits and behavior. Both points are correlated with each other, so that changing one could lead to a change in the other.

Generally, changing a system over time is realized by changing parameters of the system, the structure or the functions of the system or its identity (BOSSEL 2007). But those changes take time and are thwarted by a number of problems, such as those OLSON (2002, p. 2) describes in what he calls his zero contribution thesis: "[U]nless the number of individuals in a group is quite small, or unless there is coercion or some other special device to make individuals act in their common interest, rational, self-interested individuals will not act to achieve their common or group interests"[31]. SCHMID describes changes of social norms as a movement between legitimacy and legality (cf. Figure 32).

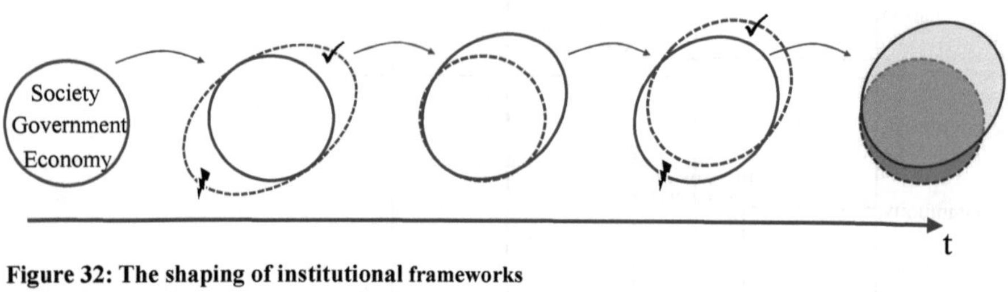

Figure 32: The shaping of institutional frameworks
(SCHMID 2014)

31 This is a typical case of the nonconformance of individual and collective rationality, as it is for example described by the prisoners' dilemma in game theory.

He describes a system where breaking existing legal rules could be seen as an innovation, create acceptance in a society and eventually lead to a change of the existing rules or norms. The same holds true the other way round: if legal rules exist that override the social norms and rules of a society, it is possible that in a long-term process, societies' norms will change towards an acceptance or even requirement of the legal rules. For sustainability this could mean that law makers should first set rules that go further than social norms in terms of sustainable behavior, and that social norms will adapt in time.

Another reason for the difficulties of implementing sustainable development is the difference between short-term costs and long-term benefits. This can be illustrated by two individuals facing the following pay-off matrix (cf. Figure 33):

Short-term pay-off

Individual 1 \ Individual 2	effort	no effort
effort	-5 / -5	-7 / 0
no effort	0 / -7	0 / 0

Long-term pay-off

Individual 1 \ Individual 2	effort	no effort
effort	10 / 10	0 / 7
no effort	7 / 0	-10 / -10

Figure 33: Short- and long-term incentives for cooperation
(author's own)

To make an effort towards a more sustainable lifestyle is costly (-7). If both individuals make the effort, the costs are reduced to (-5), as for example organic food becomes cheaper with increased demand and costs for innovations towards more sustainable products are distributed between the individuals. If the individuals do not make an effort, there are no costs. In the short-term there are no benefits either, so that the pay-off for the individual is either negative (i.e., it equals its costs, whose amount depends on the involvement of the other individual) or zero, if no effort was made and therefore no costs arose. In this scenario, a rational individual (1) would, independent of individual (2)s behavior, always choose to make no effort, as the payoff is better with this (therefore dominant) strategy. The same holds true for individual (2) who will always rationally choose the "no effort" option. Thus, the Nash-equilibrium[32] in this pay-off matrix is a symmetrical one, where both individuals choose to make no effort. But the short-term consideration does not suffice in the case of sustainability. The pay-off of any effort made will most likely only occur in the long run – improved or non-deteriorated resources, decreased or not increased pollution, the realization of intergenerational justice, for example. Therefore, the pay-off matrix from the short-term consideration must be extended by long-term gains. If both individuals put an effort into a more sustainable lifestyle in the short run, the long-term gain is valued at 15, so the long-term pay-off after subtraction of the short-term cost is 10 for each individual. In the case of only one individual's short-term effort, the long-term gains per player are smaller (+7); therefore the individual making the effort has a long-term gain of 0, while the one making no effort has a gain of 7. If both do not make an effort, in the short-run they face no costs, but the long-term consequences are substantial, in this example they are at -10 for each individual.

The difference between the long-term pay-off matrix and the short-term version is that in the former the dominating strategy for both individuals is to make an effort, as this would yield higher gains independent of the other player's strategy. In this case, the Nash-equilibrium is symmetrical as well, but this time, with the long-term benefits included, it exists in the case of both individuals making an effort. The example serves to illustrate the general idea that individuals tend to concentrate on solving immediate problems before taking on problems within larger space and a larger timeframe (MEADOWS ET AL. 1972). This is intensified by the difficulty of calculating future costs in comparison to short-term costs and benefits. Apart from the challenge to exactly estimate the necessary extent of effort to achieve sustainability, this is due to the fact that predicting long-term outcomes is complicated by uncertainties regarding future developments and external effects. In addition, scientists do not agree on the correct scientific method of calculation. As the calculation of long-term costs and benefits depends to no small amount on the method of discounting chosen, this is a relevant are of open research (RABL 1996). Another barrier towards the implementation of a sustainable lifestyle is the complexity of the topic and the little influence that people have on the long-term outcome given the impact of all other individuals together.

The arguments above imply that people are able to correctly estimate their effort and their performance, but studies show that individuals on average overestimate their performance. This positively biased perception of one's own performance holds even if the individuals concerned are aware that their peers evaluate them not as positive as they do themselves. It has, however, no significant effect on their actual performance

32 The Nash-equilibrium, a possible solution in game theory in case of non-cooperative games, where each player knows the possible strategies and pay-offs of the other player(s), is defined as a set of chosen strategies, where no player benefits from changing his strategy given the other players' strategy.

(ROBINS, BEER 2001). If individuals mistakenly think they act sustainably or if they at least overestimate the sustainability of their lifestyle, they may not make a big enough effort to achieve the level of sustainable living necessary to make a positive and sufficient impact. This is important because the impact of every consumer is relevant, as – if the typical economic assumption that consumption is the aim of production is true – all negative ecological and social impact caused by production are at least indirectly caused by consumption and consumers' choices (HANSEN, SCHRADER 2001).

The discussion about public action for a sustainable development is complicated by the fact that paradigms in sustainability are a question of belief, not of proof, so a final public decision on one of the paradigms is not in sight (STEURER 2001). As with so many issues where values and attitudes are important, the different values within generations as well as between generations make an agreement on measures and possible impact even more difficult than the mere complexity of the topic does. If, as HAYEK says, "(...) it requires for society as a whole the same kind of complete quantitative scale of values as that which manifests itself in the decision of every individual, but on which, in an individualist society, agreement between the individuals is neither necessary nor present" (HAYEK, CALDWELL 1997, p. 201), then this does not bode well for the realization of sustainable development. Even if people are not as individualist as the often discussed and oftentimes dismissed concept of man, the *homo oeconomicus,* implies[33], it is nearly impossible to first find a set of values for a single society and then find one that applies to more than one society, especially as sustainable development explicitly includes almost all areas of everyday life. If, in HAYEK's distinction, the three sources of human values are (1) genetic (i.e., inherited), (2) rational and (3) cultural (i.e., abstract) (HAYEK 1973), then it will take a long time to change the inherited values, a lot of information to change rational values and both of those things to change the cultural values towards a more sustainably inclined way of living.

The essential information to help consumers understand the necessity but also their options towards a sustainable lifestyle, ideally including clear guidelines, is not so easily available, though. For a number of reasons that shall be detailed in the following chapter, the scientific community is not in agreement on sustainable development as a concept, the required measures as well as the methods of implementation, therefore making information for citizens without a specific scientific education that helps them to understand the implications of sustainable development very, or in some cases even too, difficult.

33 For an overview over experimental tests on whether individuals behave as the assumptions of the *homo oeconomicus* imply, see for example FALK (2001). He shows that most experiments prove that many individuals behave reciprocal, i.e., they sanction perceived "unfair" behavior and reward perceived "fair" behavior, which contradicts the classical *homo oeconomicus'* behavior.

3.3.3 Scientific Challenges

Comprehensive research on sustainable development, but also on possible adaptions of current production cycles and all kinds of input, is essential for a successful implementation of sustainable development. There are a number of challenges in this area, many of them in very specific fields of research. The focus in this work will be on the general challenges of sustainability research.

3.3.3.1 The Concept of Sustainability

The biggest scientific challenge, and the one that is fundamental for all other challenges, is the concept itself or the way it is understood and defined by different stakeholders. The scientific literature abounds with definitions that differ more or less from each other. Two years after the publication of the Brundtland report in 1987 there were more than 20 scientific and/or political definitions of sustainability. Four years after the publication scientists counted at least 40 definitions and by the mid-1990s there were more than 60 (STEURER 2001), in 1997 over 70 definitions were counted (JÜDES 1997). It can be assumed that the following years brought even more definitions with the growing popularity and wider application of the concept. But with the growing acceptance of the concept of sustainable development, it loses its outlines and precision due to the additions to the concept that stakeholders make according to their priorities (DYBE, WEITH 2004).

It is of course very important to have a lively debate over such an important concept, as its implementation has an extensive impact on many aspects of government action, everyday-life and company strategies. But this debate must come to some agreement or at least compromise if the concept is to become more than a mere theoretical idea. To be ready for implementation, a concept must be precise[34] and unambiguous[35] (TREMMEL 2003, pp. 33-36). Those two requirements can only be met if there is a definition of sustainability that all or at least a majority of the stakeholders can agree on. The most basic definition that most likely the most stakeholders can agree on is the definition from the Brundtland report:

> "Sustainable development is development that meets the needs of the present without compromising the ability of future generations to meet their own needs"

34 "A concept is precise if a person who knows the meaning of the concept can decide for every fully described issue whether the concept applies or not." (TREMMEL 2003, pp. 33-36)

35 "A concept is unambiguous if all persons who know the meaning of the concept come to the same decision regarding the application of a fully described issue to the concept." (TREMMEL 2003, pp. 33-36)

(WCED 1987b, p. 41/1-3). This definition is too ambiguous, though, and is not sufficient for the formulation of specific and concrete goals. The specifications that have been made to remedy this ambiguousness are discussed in detail in subsection 2.2. While scientists still argue which model is the most useful to capture all aspects of sustainability, most agree on the three basic dimensions ecology, economy and social aspects.[36] But one of the greatest challenges to science (and politics, although to a lesser degree, because it is hoped that politicians base at least a part of their decisions on the findings of scientists and experts) is the weighting of those dimensions. A typical approach to integrative sustainability is to consider the aims of the three columns of sustainability as equal, which often complicates the implementation, and later the assessment of measures and results, by a conflict of objectives (BLAZEJCZAK, EDLER 2004). This conflict of the dimensions can only be solved if priorities are set, conflicts are minimized and possible synergies are investigated. An equal treatment of the dimensions makes it possible to avoid the setting of priorities and therefore makes it easier to reach common acceptance of the general principle and its definition, but it dilutes the concept and opens it to manifold interpretations (BÖHRINGER, LÖSCHEL 2004).

The setting of priorities is a considerable challenge but is inevitable, if clear and successful strategies shall be developed. The partial interconnectivity of the dimensions must be analyzed and especially in the case of contrarious impacts of measures on interconnected aspects prioritizing is imperative. In addition, limited means to implement measures further enforce a prioritization. This setting of priorities is complicated by conflicts of values (cf., e.g., subsection 3.3.2). Those slow the implementation of projects and measures as they complicate the setting of priorities and the weighting of different goals. Such conflicts of value are object of social-ecologic transformation research and will remain an important part of current sustainability research (GRIEßHAMMER ET AL. 2012).

3.3.3.2 Connecting Fields of Research

In general, due to the existence of the different dimensions, it is necessary to make much of the current sustainability research more transdisciplinary[37]. To raise scientists' awareness of the actualities and important factors of the other dimensions, it is also helpful to enforce multi- or interdisciplinary research that aims for a problem-driven application of knowledge and methods. They concentrate on scientific topics in

36 The institutional dimension that is added by some does not alter the basic argumentation and is therefore left out in this discussion.

37 Transdisciplinary research is based on disciplinary research but supplements it with knowledge about interdisciplinary integration and societal relevance (GRIEßHAMMER ET AL. 2012).

the areas of contact of the research fields concerned.[38] All in all, the complexity of the topic calls for frontier research, i.e., research between the traditional distinction of basic and applied studies. It is very helpful to combine fundamentally new knowledge, possibly from different areas, with knowledge about the implementation of the conclusions drawn from this knowledge and the problems encountered when doing so (JAHN 2009). This is the only way to ensure that research comprises applied considerations such as possible measures to realize sustainable development as well as knowledge about their implementation and political feasibility.

This trans-, multidisciplinary or frontier research faces problems that traditional monodisciplinary research does not, or not to such an extent, know: that the inclusion of ignorance, uncertainty or heterogeneity in the problems and the work within a complex system leads to a limited precision of the predicted outcomes or even the impossibility of a prediction (JAHN 2009). This lessens the communicability of the results as it is clearly easier to communicate a single and unambiguous indicator than an ambiguous "the outcome depends on a large number of eventualities and ranges between two extremes that are very far from each other" or a similar statement; and it is of course also easier to develop measures based on clear facts than on imprecise numbers or even only unquantifiable data.

3.3.3.3 Defining and Measuring (Future) Needs

Much of the planning of measures to implement sustainable development depends on the definition of future and current needs that are part of most of the common definitions of sustainable development. Future needs pose an important challenge as their prediction is necessary to decide on the amount of resources that may be consumed by current generations. But even if basic needs are known or can be predicted with more or less precision, information about their norms, consumption structures, production functions or political structures, among others, is lacking (GRUNWALD, KOPFMÜLLER 2006). In addition, long-term predictions are complicated by discontinuities. They are "(1) profoundly disruptive of systems whether natural or socioeconomic/ political, and (2) catch us unawares by overwhelming our anticipatory and preventive capacities" (MYERS, KENT 2008, p. 46), thus making it almost impossible to correctly predict the information above for future generations, much less two or more generations ahead.

In addition, many predictions that are made today are based on current data but leave out possible effects of current actions with delayed results. This leads to an often observed optimistic underestimation of effect delays (HABER 2011). But even if predictions are made, the time ranges considered in forecasting and trying to determine fu-

38 Differentiating between transdisciplinary and multidisciplinary research, JAHN (2009) stresses that the former comprises multi- and interdisciplinary research and enhances them with the incorporation of the societal context, aiming to make the research results fit for application.

ture developments range between a few months to four or five years (a policy cycle) up to 20 or 30 years in very few cases, for example for the demographic development (MYERS, KENT 2008). Considering the discontinuities and the difficulties in predictions described above, any prediction that claims to be correct beyond a conservative time range[39] may at least be doubted. In addition to the imponderables, there is also the issue of measurability. While economic issues are often expressed in monetary units, ecological data is often gathered in physical units and social situations can be best described using temporal or qualitative data. So far there is no possibility to adequately compare the three (HAUFF, KLEINE 2009). This dilemma is aggravated by the difficulties of data collection that will be discussed in more detail in chapter 4.

All in all, the way to a sustainable development is characterized by searching, learning and collecting experiences. Researchers have to deal with incomplete and sometimes fragmentary knowledge and information; and results and conclusions are often provisional. Those reasons are often used as justification for inaction, because the lack of sound information is supposedly making it impossible to find adequate measures. The provisional character of research results should stop neither citizens nor institutions from acting more sustainably, though, even if on the lowest common denominator.

3.3.4 Structural Political Challenges

DALY, a seasoned advocate for sustainable development, admonishes politicians to not subordinate sustainable development to economic growth, which he sees as the current political goal dominating all others. He warns, that

> *"Currently it seems that we are witnessing the conflict between a physical impossibility (continual growth) and a political impossibility (limiting growth). But in the long run the physically impossible is more impossible than the merely politically impossible."*

(DALY 2007b, pp. 10-11) and thereby addresses two important topics for the political feasibility of the sustainability concept: (perceived) political impossibilities and long-term considerations. The third factor, the concept of growth, shall not be discussed here, it shall suffice to mention that there are many concepts that address wellbeing or happiness rather than growth as the aims to be reached (cf. subsection 5.7). DALY's "political impossibilities" refer to an often used excuse not to take a certain measure or set a specific priority, even though it must be admitted that at the time of the decision-making, impossibility seems very real to the actors. According to (HOWLETT 1991, p. 8), there are four basic attributes of instruments for policies:

---

39 What is to be considered a "conservative" time range depends on the individual indicator. The prediction of demographic developments, for example may be less susceptible to discontinuities than other indicators, thus making predictions over longer time ranges more reasonable than in other cases.

(1) resource intensiveness
(2) targeting (precision, selectivity)
(3) political risk (support, opposition, public visibility, chances and consequences of failure), and
(4) constraints on state activity

The first two attribute have been discussed before in this work, with focus on the difficulties of a prediction of costs and necessary resources for the realization of a policy. The attributes (3) and (4) shall be discussed in more detail in the following subsections, especially the following six political obstacles for the realization of sustainable development: the necessary collaboration of different institutions, the enforceability of the concept, temporal considerations, costs, the self-interest of individual stakeholders, and communication.

3.3.4.1 Institutional Collaboration

It has been stated in the chapters above that sustainability is a complex and almost all-encompassing concept. Therefore, its implementation and realization naturally does imply that different institutions must work together. For the international level, this will be discussed in subsection 3.3.5; for the national level, the example used shall be german political institutions. In theory, the division of powers in Germany would mean that it is sufficient to discuss only the legislative power. In reality, there is a close link between legislative and executive powers, so that both shall be considered. As the german government puts it, sustainability has to be realized by national, regional and communal institutions as well as the civil society. The concept cannot simply be commanded by the government but has to be put into action by all parties concerned (BUNDESREGIERUNG 2008). But present policy making concentrates on fragmented aims belonging to different departments, where cooperation and collaboration are rather the exception than the rule (cf. subsection 3.3.4.3 for a discussion of selfishness/self-interest as one possible reason for this lack of cooperation). For sustainable politics that – in theory – concentrate on the connection between economic, ecologic and social aims, this is a less than optimal situation and leads to conflicts of aims, especially in the short run (BACHMANN 2002).

In addition, the fragmented organization of sustainability law-making and management lessens the chance to use possible synergies between actions of different responsible institutions and raises the likelihood of redundancies, overlapping or even opposing actions in those cases, where there is a conflict of aims. Linkages between sectors are often overlooked – due to an inability to detect them, but also often due to strictly separated areas of responsibility (MYERS, KENT 2008). This leads to situations where, for example, one ministry will specialize in increasing economic growth, while another ministry will deal with the corresponding pollution, even though it would be more effective to couple competencies and power. This is an often unsolvable problem in the current system of institutions that were "established on the basis of narrow preoccupations and compartmentalized concerns" (WCED 1987b, p. 17/32). But to enable integrated, trans-sectoral decision-making, it is necessary to choose a concrete number of goals followed by a prioritization among all problems and issues that are gathered under the superordinate concept of sustainability (HABER 2011). This is complicated by the complexity of the concept and the actual situation of the environment, leading to inevitable ignorance and provisional assessments that cause conflicts of values and judgment, disputes over priorities and the necessity to weigh goals and options (GRUNWALD, KOPFMÜLLER 2006).

3.3.4.2 Enforceability of the Sustainability Concept

Sustainability is a general principle, more a vision than a concrete goal, due to the rather vague definition that leaves the concept open to manifold interpretations. It is a normative agreement (HAUFF, JÖRG 2013), not an enforceable and clear concept. JACKSON states that "Impossibility theorems confront us at every turn. Economies can only survive if they grow. People won't relinquish materialism. The state is powerless to intervene." (JACKSON 2011, p. 171) But this "impossibility" brings us back to DALY's statement that in the long run, political impossibilities are less impossible than physical impossibilities (cf. subsection 3.3.4.). If the concept is not directly enforceable by law, but there is common agreement on the necessity to realize sustainable development, the alternative is to enforce it indirectly. This can, for example, be realized by a compulsory sustainability assessment before passing laws and regulations as well as during the ex ante evaluation of possible measures in all political fields and on all political levels. Another option is an improved information strategy and the implementation of sustainability as a subject (or better even, a topic in various subjects) at schools, universities and all other educational institutions. This is necessary if the political impossibility mentioned above shall be overcome. All those possible measures are hampered by a serious problem of politics and politicians: the self-interest of political protagonists and their priorities. Those interests will be discussed in more detail in the following chapters.

3.3.4.3 Self-Interest of Stakeholders

If the implementation of sustainable development as a guiding principle toward sustainability for all aspects of life were only dependent on the implementation of reasonable and constructive laws that are "only" complicated by the complexity of the concept and competing priorities of the dimensions of sustainability as well as a lack of information and a free rider problem on the side of the consumers, researchers could concentrate on solving the complex problems and finding a weighting of priorities that is, if not optimal, at least a second best solution; and politicians could develop methods and explanations to further societies' understanding of sustainability and the realities that lead to the absolute necessity to implement sustainable development to ensure intra- and intergenerational justice.

But there is another considerable barrier towards the implementation of sustainable development: the motivation of the legislative and executive protagonists. If the optimal legislative actor is a benevolent dictator[40], who realizes a Pareto- or Kaldor-Hicks-Optimum (cf. subsection 2.3.1), then the optimal executive protagonist implements the benevolent dictator's decisions without transaction costs. In reality, there is no perfect information, there are transaction costs and the legislative and executive actors are mostly not benevolent (or in some cases, if the results of their actions coincide with the public optimum, coincidentally benevolent, not intentionally), but instead have their own interests at heart. There are also frictional losses through the division of powers between law-making and law-enforcement. Those frictional losses can be described with the economic concepts of information asymmetries and incomplete contracts as well as transaction costs.

The basis for those concepts are a principal-agent relationship, first described in those terms by JENSEN and MECKLING (e.g., 1976) in the 1970s, their work being based on the theoretical works of COASE (1937), among others, about property rights, incomplete contracts and transaction cost theory. The idea of principals and agents has been broached before, for example by BATT in 1929. He discusses the relationship between masters and agents vs. masters and servants, noting that "That which distinguishes an agent from a servant is not the absence or presence of a fixed wage or the payment only of commission on business done, but rather the freedom with which an agent may carry out his employment" (BATT 1929, p. 7). Therefore, "an agency relationship has arisen between two (or more) parties when one, designated as the agent, acts for, on behalf of, or as representative for the other, designated the principal, in a particular domain of decision problems" (ROSS 1973, p. 134). This principal-agent relationship can easily be transferred to the relationship between policy-makers and their voters or the public in general. The principal, i.e., in this case the people, choose the agent, i.e., the politician, to act for them in the domain of political decision making. The causes for those frictional losses in principal-agent-relationships are information asymmetries, more specifically the following three cases of an information asymmetry between principal and agent:

(1) **Hidden Characteristics.** This category has been prominently discussed by AKERLOF who used the *market for lemons*, i.e., the market for used cars of a bad quality, to describe the connection between quality and uncertainty. He argues that in the case of used cars, before the conclusion of a contract the owner has a clearer idea of the specific good he wants to sell than the potential buyer

40 The benevolent dictator can be described as an imaginary individual who acts purely rational and has perfect information, which he uses to maximize the utility of all economic subjects. Therefore, the benevolent dictator is independent of all political influences and does not succumb to self-interest or particular interests of other actors.

who only knows the average quality of the good. Independent of the real quality of the good, the risk neutral[41] buyer's willingness to pay will be based on the average quality of the good, because he has no knowledge of the real state of quality. Therefore, a seller of a good quality will receive a payment that is lower than the real worth of his good, whereas the seller of a bad quality, i.e., a lemon, receives a higher payment than he would in the case of information symmetry. The problem of hidden characteristics can at least partly be solved by signaling by the seller or screening by the buyer (AKERLOF 1970).

(2) **Hidden Information**. In this case the information asymmetry only occurs ex post, i.e., after the conclusion of the contract. If the principal can observe the agent's actions but cannot judge their quality, then the agent is said to have hidden information (ARROW 1984). A typical example for this case of information asymmetry is a medical consultation.

(3) **Hidden Action.** This information asymmetry occurs ex post as well. In the case of hidden action the result is known, but the principal cannot directly observe the agent's actions, and indirect observation by inference from result to action to reach said result is also impossible (ARROW 1984). This is the case, e.g., if a manager's actions cannot be completely observed, but the company performance is known. In this case, it is impossible to attribute the outcome directly to the manager's actions.

The transfer from theory to application can be made as follows: if the principal is the people, and their chosen agent a politician, for example, then the information asymmetries can be interpreted as follows:

(1) **Hidden Characteristics**. Voters likely have an opinion about politicians in general and politicians belonging to a certain party in particular. But they usually do not have the necessary information to judge whether a single person available for election is more likely to represent their specific agenda than the average politician (or the average politician of a certain party) or less. The politician has more information about himself (even if some actions after an election cannot be determined in advance and may depend on party guidelines or other external factors), but if his character is above average and the voter does not know that and instead assumes that it is average, then his chances for election in proportion to his characteristics decrease. If the politician is below average, then his chances to be elected are the same as those of an above-average politician. There is a certain risk of above-average politicians dropping out of the election if their efforts are not adequately rewarded by votes; it is also possible that a politician reduces his or her efforts to average if that means less effort, but the same result. Both options lead to a decrease of the average performance.

41 A risk neutral person being defined as someone who only judges a situation by the expected payoff, independent of the risk connected with the payoff.

(2) **Hidden Information**. As described above, this asymmetry occurs ex post, i.e., after the election. Even if voters can observe a politicians actions (e.g., by monitoring their votes in parliament or following their public communication), it is hard to judge the quality of their action. For example, political work includes bargaining for parliamentary votes, i.e., a politician may vote in favor of a topic that he is indifferent about or that has no high priority for him in exchange for a favorable vote from someone else for a topic that is important on his agenda. The observer only sees the votes, but has no information about the – possibly implicit – bargaining.

(3) **Hidden Action**. If a voter knows the outcome of a certain situation – an important law passed, changed regulations, increased subsidies, for example – he cannot deduce the politician's actions from this outcome. Whether the result came about in spite or because of the politician's actions or whether the effort the politician put into the topic was high or low is not known to the voter.

In addition to the information asymmetries and the self-interest of the politicians, i.e., the legislative branch of a government, there are barriers towards the implementation of sustainability (or, in fact, most integrated concepts) in the executive branch as well. In a world of budget restrictions, institutions in themselves have the tendency to concentrate on their own survival, therefore they can be barriers to changes and adaptations to an ever changing environment (MYERS, KENT 2008).

NISKANEN (1968, pp. 293-294) summarizes the priorities of an executor of political will as follows: "Among the several variables that may enter the bureaucrat's utility function are the following: salary, perquisites of the office, public reputation, power, patronage, ease of managing the bureau, and ease of making changes". He then observes that with current compensation schemes that are independent of their success in applying either the principle of maximum output with a given input or realizing a given output with minimum input, bureaucrats try to maximize their budget (NISKANEN 1968). This budget maximization thwarts one of the basic requirements for the implementation of an integrated concept: the cooperation and collaboration of different institutions and bureaus. If the interest in budget maximization and power, thus the right to make important decisions, take priority over the collaboration, then the conflicts of aims that exist with the realization of sustainable development will be aggravated. As a lack of cooperation leads to interferences in content and the right for decision-making, the allocation of resources (human as well as financial) in the executive branch is inefficient.

Another hindrance for the implementation of sustainable development as guiding principle for all actions are the decision-making processes of the legislative. Individual decision-making of every representative is based on a number of aspects, among them the decision-guidelines of their party, their own ideas and beliefs, their conscience, their knowledge about the topic to be decided upon, and their interest to be re-elected. Therefore, their ideas about the voters' information and interest (if the voter-interest in a topic is nil then the individual representative does not have to be too considerate of voters' wishes) as well as their estimated preferences, and the importance they place on a topic (and therefore the amount of energy they put into making an informed decision and into possibly convincing other representatives of their point of view) will vary, in some cases greatly. In many cases, representatives will be expected to go along with their party's suggestions, even if there is no openly expected obedience to party guidelines, such as the caucus-discipline sometimes expected in Germany or the whip-voting activities in Great Britain or the United States. Another necessity for policy makers is to decide on their individual attitude toward risks. An evaluation of public policy must include a weighting of uncertainty. It is therefore necessary to define an adequate attitude toward taking risks that a policy maker should assume (ARROW, FISHER 1974). Also, the existence of irreversibility is not necessarily a reason not to undertake the project leading to the irreversible situation. But the effect of the irreversibility must be calculated and then included in a balance of costs and benefits (ARROW, FISHER 1974). In those cases, when choosing between realizing a development that uses natural resources and preserving those resources, the following calculations have to be made: developments that are estimated to be currently profitable should not be undertaken if the development has to be reversed in the foreseeable future. In addition, if net benefits from realizing the development decrease over time relative to estimated net benefits from preservation, it is necessary to realize the development as soon as possible (FISHER ET AL. 1972).

If the direction of the decision-making has been decided upon, the representatives then have to choose the kind of policy they prefer: reactive, i.e., ex post, or anticipatory, i.e., ex ante policy. PEARCE ET AL. describe the factors affecting the choice between those policy options as follows (cf. Table 8):

FACTORS AFFECTING THE CHOICE OF POLICY STANCE		
	Policy Stance	
Factors	Reactive Policy	Anticipatory Policy
Time Preference (discounting)	+	-
Information by delay	+	-
Cost escalation	-	+
Uncertainty	-	+
Irreversibility	-	+
Sustainable development	-	+

Table 8: Factors affecting the choice of policy stance

(PEARCE ET AL. 1989)

If there is a time preference, i.e., if current worth is valued above future worth, then a reactive policy is chosen. The same holds true for the case of delayed information, where the choice of a reactive policy is obvious. In the case of expected cost escalation and uncertainty, an anticipatory policy is advisable, and, especially relevant for all environment-related topics, if irreversibility is apprehended, ex ante policy is mandatory. Summarizing, it can be said that for sustainability-related decision, an anticipatory policy stance is advisory. In the case of already occurred damages of natural resources and existing laws and rules as well as situations that oppose the basic rules of sustainability such as intra- and intergenerational justice, it must be attempted to remedy those by reactive policy.

3.3.4.4 Temporal Considerations

It has been mentioned above that time preferences and possible information delays influence the choice of the policy stance. Another aspect connected to temporal considerations are the time lags between action and result. Sustainability is explicitly defined as a long-term concept. That does not diminish the importance of short-term successes, but the long-term effects of political and personal actions must take priority over short-term results in most cases. But measurable results of actions, laws or guidelines towards a sustainable development, often demanding current voters' cooperation and sacrifices (financial, life-style, etc.), rarely occur within the same legislative period as the costs. Therefore, consequential public costs are often deferred to some point in the future – a practice that may lead to an increased possibility of reelection if voters calculate their cost-benefit-relations with a short-term view, but causes welfare losses in the long run (BERTELSMANN STIFTUNG 2009). Thus, the long-term character of sustainability does not fit into the four or five year political election cycle, at least as long as voters do not realize that while the realization of sustainable development might leave more losers than winners in the short term, in the long run that will change if the right actions are taken (MEIMETH 2012). The result of this lack of long-term thinking on the side of the voters as well as the executors typically leads to a treatment of symptoms that promises short-term results, thus suggesting appropriate and successful actions and decisions on the side of the political actors. But as sustainable development explicitly demands the institutionalization of the rights of future generations, sustainable development within a political situation that concentrates on short-term results is almost impossible.

A simplified rationalization is described in the pay-off matrix of a one-time game below (cf. Figure 34), where voters' and politicians' temporal preferences and orientations are described.

		Political stance	
		short-term oriented	long-term oriented
Voters' stance	short-term oriented	Politician: re-elected Sustainable development: treatment of symptoms	Politician: not re-elected Sustainable development: not realized
	long-term oriented	Politician: not re-elected Sustainable development: treatment of symptoms	Politician: re-elected Sustainable development: realized

Figure 34: Short- vs. long-term thinking in politicians' and voters' stances
(author's own)

The politician will most likely try to approximate his stance to the (assumed) voters' wishes. If voters look for short-term successes (e.g., because of a preference for short-term gains and an accordingly biased discounting of long-term benefits, e.g., if long-term successes cannot be monitored, or due to a lack of information about long-term risks), then the politician will choose a short-term orientation as well. This results in his (or her) reelection without the realization of strategies towards sustainability, but with a treatment of symptoms sufficient to convince voters that the politician acted successfully and should thus be re-elected. For the sake of simplicity in this example, it is assumed that for the treatment of symptoms as well as for the long-term measures to realize sustainable development, the correct measures are chosen and the results are positive. If the politician faces short-term oriented voters, but chooses a long-term oriented approach in his political decisions, there will be no or few positive short-term results, but high short-term costs; thus the politician will not be re-elected and sustainable development will not be realized as the politician will not be able to continue his long-term approach. There is, of course, a possibility that in a repeated game the politicians that will be elected in succession will maintain the measures and laws implemented by the first politician and therefore, sustainable development is realized as planned by the first politician to choose that stance. Nevertheless, this possibility is only likely if all succeeding politicians choose the long-term approach over their own interest to be re-elected.

If voters favor a long-term oriented policy, but the politician chooses a short-term oriented approach, then the result for sustainability will be that only symptoms are treated and sustainable development is not implemented. For the politician this means that he will not be re-elected (assuming that voters can monitor the politician's actions) and sustainable development is not realized, but there is a treatment of symptoms.

The matrix above shows a simple mind game whose outcome depends on a number of factors, among them: the voters' ability to monitor political actions, politicians' ability to predict their voters' preferences, the self-interest of politicians and their priorities, time preferences, and the success and its measurability. If those factors are interpreted or their specification is assumed according to current studies, the result would most likely be the field where voters prefer a short-term policy stance. This is due to time preferences, the impossibility to predict the outcome of long-term processes and measures and to monitor the influence of the politician on specific measures and outcomes; but likely also to a lack of information about the absolute necessity of a sustainable development.

The problem with the decisions about long- and short-term stances as described above is that politicians have the choice to either attempt the prevention of unsustainable production and consumption cycles (i.e., an ex ante approach that would be considered a long-term stance in Figure 34) or to choose an ex post approach and try to repair or reverse occurred damages. The former approach faces the problem of prediction of future developments and can therefore only be based on a number of assumptions, while with the latter tactic it might be too late to reverse irreversible damages. This, with the added aspect of the desire to be re-elected makes for a complicated decision process. Therefore, some suggest a precautionary approach that stipulates political intervention before the damage is done. This approach requires reliable prognoses as well, though (NETZWERK NACHHALTIGE ÖKONOMIE 2012).

3.3.4.5 Costs

The fifth political obstacle is the expense factor. It has been discussed in subsection 3.3 that a cost-benefit analysis for measures to realize sustainability faces a number of challenges. Especially important in the case of sustainable development is the fact that costs are usually entered in the present period, while benefits mostly occur in future periods. Therefore, it is necessary to find a way to compare future benefits with current costs. This poses a challenge as the calculation of long-term costs and benefits depends to no small amount on the method of discounting chosen (RABL 1996) so that it is difficult to determine an objective value.

With regard to the national budget, the annual cash flow of the current year is what counts most when making political decisions. Long-term strategic considerations usually only mean "considerations until the end of the legislative period", as voters will often judge the success of political action by the debts accumulated or the growth achieved (HAGIST ET AL. 2006). The formal evaluation of policy measures also includes the aspect of „relative costliness" (HOWLETT 1991)[42], forcing politicians to act within strict budget limits and to justify their spending with results. If those results do not occur within the same legislative period as the spending, the typical conclusion is that the spending was a waste, because there are no measurable successes. It must be said, though, that so far there have not been any comprehensive studies on the (short- and long-term) costs of sustainable politics compared to conventional politics.

In addition, there are measurement problems. Economic growth, the pre-eminent aim of political actions in many countries, is often measured in GDP growth. Ironically, non-sustainable actions such as the contamination of natural resources and the subsequent cleaning may in some cases (and in the short-term only) lead to a growth of GDP[43], and unsustainable production that reduces the companies' costs increases GDP as well, because environmental degradation is not included in the measure. Therefore, any politician whose performance is mainly judged by indicators such as the GDP is lacking a convincing incentive to change his priorities. Other measures for economic growth that include ecological or social aspects have been developed (cf. subsection 5.7) but are not widely accepted and established.

3.3.4.6 Communication

Communication is one of the most important aspects when trying to mainstream a guiding principle such as sustainability. It has been discussed before that consumption is one of the drivers of sustainable development. If consumers change their lifestyles towards sustainable consumption, they force suppliers to adapt their production, to use sustainable input, technologies and distribution methods. In addition, consumers usually are voters as well, so their election decisions directly influence the political priorities and policy measures, at least in the long run. It is therefore a condition *sine qua non* that consumers and voters are informed about sustainability, the necessity to implement sustainable development, possible measures, necessary relinquishments and

---

42 HOWLETT (1991) summarizes the criteria for evaluating policy measures in his „synthetic policy design approach" as follows: 1. Complexity of Operation (Low ... High), 2. Level of Public Visibility, 3. Adaptability across users, 4. Level of Intrusiveness, 5. Relative Costliness, 6. Reliance on Market, 7. Chances of Failure, 8. Precision of Targeting.

43 GDP determination with the expenditure approach as: GDP = private consumption + investments + government spending + exports – imports; the income approach measures GDP = wages + rents + interests + profits + statistical adjustments. In the case of the expenditure approach, the cleanup of an oil spill, for example, may raise government spending and thus, GDP. The income approach would be influenced by additional labor employed for a clean-up, whose wages would also increase GDP. It must be noted, though, that there are consequences of spills or pollution that directly decrease GDP, such as reduced income due to less output in the agricultural and fishing sector, for example. Whether environmental pollution leads to an increase or decrease of GDP depends on the balance of those factors. Either way, the negative impact of pollution is always softened by measures to clean up.

options for personal measures to support sustainable development. In a democracy, on the side of the voters there is an obligation to collect this information; but there also is an obligation to deliver it on the side of the politicians, as they – at least in many cases – have more information or easier access to information and there are a number of experts at their disposal to give informed and well-founded information and advice. These advantages must be shared with the public, if sustainable development is to be realized.

But there is an inherent problem with the concept. Its open formulation is intended and necessary for such an all-encompassing concept. But this openness invites arbitrary interpretations, and reality shows that the political dealing with the concept has become a kind of wish list where every actor adds whatever he considers important (SRU 2002). For a merely theoretical concept that would only mean a broad discussion and the necessity to find connections between the points on the wish list. As sustainability needs to be implemented, and rules to do so need to be enforced, the definition of absolute limits is necessary. But setting those limits and thereby creating a base for informed decision in favor of sustainability is complicated by the multidimensionality and complexity of the principle (SRU 2011). In addition, it is necessary to set priorities regarding the dimensions of sustainable development, as well as the method of discounting with regard to intergenerational justice. It is also necessary to deepen the commitment to sustainable development by entering precise engagements, substantiated by binding goals (BUNDESREGIERUNG 2008). So far, this has not – or too little – happened (DRESNER 2008).

3.3.5 International Challenges

In addition to national challenges to the political realization of sustainable development, there is another political dimension that is likely even more complicated: the international aspect. This is important in two ways: firstly, pollution does not stop at national borders. If there is to be a solution to major environmental problems, it must be an international one. Secondly, if intragenerational justice is to be realized not only within one country's borders, countries have to cooperate. The first steps of international cooperation were made in the environmental dimension (cf. subsections 2.1.3 and 2.4). But the idea of international action towards the protection of the environment was by far not embraced by all. Especially developing countries who did not have the problem of too many factories polluting the environment, but rather the opposite, apprehended the utilization of the environmental excuse towards new trade barriers and towards a slowing of those countries' development (JOHNSON 2012). In addition, lessening the huge differences between developed and developing countries will severely deteriorate the ecological pillar, as economic growth without further burdening the environment is not conceivable, as long as it is not coupled with a significant decrease of environmental burdens caused by developed countries, so that the total international environmental burden is below the absorption- and regeneration levels (and, in the case of weak or balanced sustainability (cf. subsection 2.5) being applied to the measurement, below possible substitution levels). As this significantly decreased contamination by developed countries is unlikely, economic growth of developing countries will put an even higher strain on the environment. The alternative, no economic growth of developed countries, will sever economic and social aspects, though, and prevent the realization of intragenerational justice (BAECHLER 2012).

It is therefore necessary to develop a framework of international cooperation to enable developing countries to increase or even converge their standard of living towards that of developed countries. If this is to be done without further burdening the environment, research and development for the substitution of resources, sustainable production technologies, etc., must be increased to keep consumption and production at the status quo in developed countries. At the same time, the ecological footprint[44] of that production must be reduced, so that the environmental burden decreases significantly. At the same time, developing countries must be encouraged and enabled to use sustainable technologies and possible input substitutes for non-renewable resources to further their economic growth. This will in many cases be more costly than conventional technologies and resources, so that financial support must be available.

It is hard to imagine that developed countries will agree to large investments to make their own economy more sustainable, to convince their citizens to radically change their lifestyles and at the same time to financially support developing countries. This is especially unlikely in the light of politicians' motivations and their wish to be re-elected (cf. subsection 3.3.4). Successful international cooperation is even less likely in the light of the lacking national sustainability strategies. As the UN states, if governments adopt sustainable development as an overarching goal without renouncing other objectives, that leads to dual policies in many areas. And in most countries, sustainable development has never reached a level of institutionalization that could influence relevant budgetary and policy choices (UN DESA 2012a). So why would countries that do not even deem sustainability important enough to implement it into their own politics support the concept on an international level? The UNITED NATIONS are one of the most important institutions with international influence. Their declared main purposes are:

- "to keep peace throughout the world;
- to develop friendly relations among nations;
- to help nations work together to improve the lives of poor people, to conquer hunger, disease and illiteracy, and to encourage respect for each other's rights and freedoms;

44 An ecological footprint can be roughly described as "the ecological footprint can be represented as the aggregate area of land and water in various ecological categories that is claimed by participants in that economy to produce all the resources they consume, and to absorb all their wastes they generate on a continuous basis, using prevailing technology" (WACKERNAGEL, REES 1997, p. 7).

- to be a center for harmonizing the actions of nations to achieve these goals",

and they proclaim that their goal is to "coordinate efforts for a safer world for this and future generations" (UNITED NATIONS 2014). They also named sustainable development as one of their most important issues by resolving "to take urgent action to achieve sustainable development" (UNITED NATIONS 2012, § 12). Therefore, they are one of the most important institutions for mainstreaming sustainable development internationally. But the institution's own organization is not directed at sustainable development (yet). Social policy as one field of activity, for example, has been fragmented into secondary silos, including health, education, labor, human rights and gender issues, all of them with at least one (and sometimes several) United Nations agency devoted to them. But there is no single entity connecting the dots. In addition, while there are clearly critical linkages between these areas – and between social and economic and environmental policy as well – those linkages are poorly recognized in the international system and, as a result, they have not been operationalized (JANN ET AL. 2006).

It is not surprising that so far there has not been much success in strengthening the international cooperation for sustainable development. Governments, civil society groups, academia and the public have very different opinions on the progress made so far and the approach to be taken in the future. In addition, opinions vary greatly on whether the path to be taken is clear, the means are there and the only thing lacking is the political will or whether the plan and the means are lacking as well. The only thing most groups concerned agree on is, that the path taken at the moment is unsustainable (UN DESA 2012a). The recognition of a currently unsustainable path is a beginning. It must be followed by the recognition that sustainability must be realized and that to do so it is necessary to establish and enforce international rules, guidelines and limits. This does not seem very likely to happen in the near future, but without such cooperation countries will concentrate on their own economic growth or welfare, and the free-rider problem[45] will not be solved.

3.4 Summary

In chapter 3, the realization of sustainable development was discussed. A description of past achievements with special attention to the role of citizens, companies, but also politicians, was followed by a discussion of sustainable development strategies and rules, with the example of Germany. The following subchapter then discussed challenges for the implementation of sustainable development into everyday life and into the political agenda. Apart from challenges in communication, in the society and on

45 A free rider problem occurs in the case of common goods and can be described with a prisoners' dilemma where it would be collectively rational to cooperate and implement sustainable development because then, in the long run, the benefits would exceed the costs; but where it is individually rational to defect, i.e., to not implement sustainable development and instead profit from other countries efforts without carrying the costs.

the international level, special attention was given to political challenges. Structural political challenges that are imminent in the political systems were discussed with the help of theories from institutional economics, and the main obstacles for a realization of sustainable development were identified.

4. Sustainability and Labor

The sustainability strategy of the German government demands the implementation of sustainability as guiding principle for all political actions. This includes the obligation to assess every new regulation and law regarding their impact on the indicators for sustainable development (BUNDESREGIERUNG 2008). As labor market policy (LMP) is a substantial dimension of political actions, it must follow the guiding principle and consider it in the decisions and measures. In addition, indicators for an evaluation of the implementation of sustainability in LMP must be identified or developed. So far, sustainable labor as a comprehensive construct has not been discussed. There is research about "green jobs" and also about other individual aspects of labor that are part of a sustainable development. But there is no definition of sustainable labor, and therefore realizing sustainable LMP is almost impossible. In the following chapter, a few general observations on LMP will be made, followed by an attempt to define and outline the most important aspects for sustainable labor.

4.1 The Importance of Labor

From a strictly capital-oriented point of view, the importance of labor for the economy is obvious. If the resources an economy, or institutions within an economy, can draw upon can be roughly divided into real capital, human capital and financial capital, as many conventional economic models do, then the maintenance of improvement of human capital must be in the interest of all. For the labor market, the relevant type of capital is mostly human capital. It is interesting to note that newer research differentiates human capital into human capital (i.e., competencies), organizational capital and social capital (i.e., relationship-resources) (LEANA, VAN BUREN 1999). This classification enables a more differentiated view at the aspects which make labor so important for an economy.

The interpretation of the importance of human capital is evident. The human capital necessary for the production of goods and services can be provided or increased by training and qualification measures. In this case, qualification can be understood as adaption of abilities and skills of the employee to the requirements of the industry (MIKL-HORKE 1991). The improvement of human capital also means an increase of productivity. Investments in the training or education of workers (i.e., altering the stock of human capital) can be realized by companies, individuals and by the creation of appropriate measures by policy makers. Policy measures include the encouragement of mobility of resources, improving the quality of job matches and policies that reduce social conflicts, thus improving the relation between employees and employers (OECD 2007). Generally, the importance of work in people's lives varies greatly among countries and cultures. In a worldwide survey by a global network of social scientists, the World Value Survey, participants were asked which importance they placed on work.[46] Figure 35 shows the percentage of participants answering that work is very important or important for them for the 58 countries for which data was available for the time period between 2010 and 2014[47].

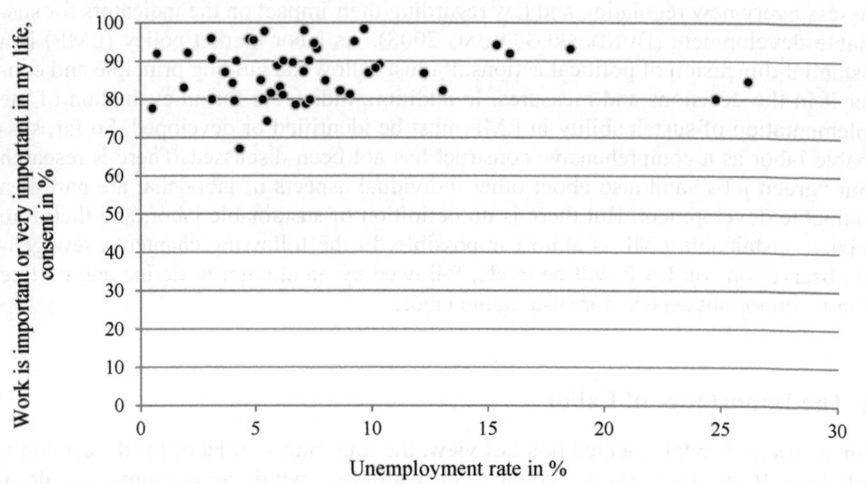

Figure 35: Unemployment rate and the importance of work
(Data for the 58 countries participating in the World Value Survey wave 2010-2014), (IMF 2014a; WVS 2014; own compilation)

The reasons for the variance in the answers are likely manifold. The seemingly obvious hypothesis that the unemployment rate or the GDP influence the importance that is placed on work cannot be proven. As an example, Figure 35 combines the reported unemployment rate for 2013 with the percentage of answers stating that work is "very important" or "important" in their lives. The answers vary between 67.1% (Bahrain) and 98.4% (Colombia), with the majority of countries ranging between 80 and 95%. Germany belongs to the lower ranking countries with 79.9% of those surveyed answering that work is (very) important for them.

46 The exact wording of the questions was: "For each of the following, indicate how important it is in your life. Would you say it is: very important; rather important; not very important; not at all important?"; the item considered here is "work" (WVS 2014).

47 The surveys are conducted in waves of four years; therefore the questions are not answered at the same time in every country.

In any case, the vast majority of those surveyed consider work to be an important part of their lives. This is due to a number of factors. On the one hand, employment provides income and thus the necessary provision for households. On the other hand, there is also the aspect of social inclusion. Unemployment reduces the social appreciation of the unemployed (ABRAHAM, HINZ 2008). JACKSON (2011) finds that one of the key factors towards happiness is meaningful employment. In the 1930s the renowned *Marienthal* study was conducted, a project of empirical social research in a region where the unemployment levels were very high after the shutdown of a big company. The study analyzed the psychological consequences of the unemployment and concluded that work is not only important for the provision of income, but also for social reasons such as a sense of a person's worth, a time structure, and a sense of belonging (JAHODA ET AL. 1960). Empirical studies of the 1970s and 80s supported that research and showed that social and psychological aspects of unemployment are an at least as important factor as the economic aspects. The extent of the social impact of unemployment depends on a number of factors (e.g., duration of unemployment, existing social nets, individual factors and the monetary framework) and on the specific situation of the affected persons. Those social aspects of unemployment are based on the importance of labor in a society and the implied feeling of a "duty to work", which may lead to a feeling of being stigmatized if one is out of work (MIKL-HORKE 1991). This is mainly due to many current societies' organization as working societies, i.e., as a society, where the material and immaterial status of members of the society are acquired via their employment; and where other areas of life - education, free time, family, retirement, etc. - are fitted to the requirements of the labor market (MIKL-HORKE 1991). Therefore, in a working society work is not only labor itself, but also a system of values, attitudes and motivations; it touches the social as well as the economic dimension (WILLKE 1999).

Not only unemployment, but also a fear of unemployment, i.e., a combination of subjective perceptions and expectations of the likelihood of unemployment as well as the assumed impact of that unemployment, that lead an individual to fear this condition, has a number of consequences. High fear of unemployment leads, among other effects, under certain circumstances to decreasing wages. It has a negative effect on consumption, on health, decreases subjective wellbeing and has a negative impact on relationships within a family. Thus, a fear of unemployment may affect the likelihood of unemployment by suppressing job creation, increasing redundancies because less consumption leads to decreasing sales, etc. The highest driver of fear of unemployment is the trend in actual unemployment, even though this is only one of the factors influencing the fear. Others are the individual characteristics of the workers, job-related characteristics and general labor market characteristics (GIMPELSON, OSHCHEPKOV 2012).

Another important aspect of unemployment are health considerations. The relation between health and (un)employment is a two-sided one. While illness can lead to unemployment, unemployment itself is often the cause for ill health. This cause-result-loop is a negative spiral (DGB 2010). A study among Swedish unemployed in the 1980s, for example, showed that job loss leads to a higher mortality risk for men four years after the job loss occurs. This seems mainly due to an about twofold increase in suicides and an increase in deaths caused by abuse of alcohol. These results are especially strong among the youngest (25-34 years) and oldest (55-64) job losers. It is likely that this is due to those groups' difficulties on the labor market (ELIASON, STORRIE 2009). Other studies support those findings. The OECD (2008) states that health problems, physical as well as psychological, are more prevalent among unemployed people than among the employed. This is important, as a higher number of unhealthy people leads to a higher number of people depending on disability and sickness benefits as well as a rise in health spending. Surveys of stress levels among 25 to 40 year olds showed that stress levels decrease with higher education levels. Unemployed participants of the study showed significantly higher stress levels than those with an employment (IGES INSTITUT 2014). The self-assessment of bodily and mental health of unemployed and employed persons differs significantly. With increasing age, the self-evaluated health deteriorates in both groups, but the considerable difference between them remains or even grows in certain age groups. It has to be kept in mind though, that the direction of cause and effect is not clear, i.e., whether unemployment and the drawing of social security lead to less health or whether there is a selection bias and poor health leads to unemployment (EGGS ET AL. 2014). As health problems do not only lead to increased expenses in the health sector, but also to a decrease of human capital and labor resources, this aspect must not be neglected. Policy measures that concentrate on maintaining the employability of unemployed persons therefore must not only concentrate on education and training, but also on health issues. To date, those measures are not federally coordinated, though, and are mostly initiatives of state governments, research institutes and few health insurance companies (DGB 2010). Those topics must be addressed everywhere, but they are crucial in countries, where social security systems are contributions-based and are calculated with the assumption of full employment, so that the social net has difficulties in case of (increasing) unemployment (FÜLLSACK 2009). In many developed countries, this effect is intensified by the current demographic development, which, if combined with the pension scheme of pay-as-you-go financing, e.g., in Germany, will most likely slow economic growth in the long run (BRAUN ET AL. 2014). In the sense of sustainability, this hurts the stipulation of intergenerational justice and is therefore to be prevented.

4.2 Labor Market Policy

Labor is basically an action that is carried out if a situation is unsatisfactory or if resources are scares. In this definition, individuals only work either to prevent scarcity or to shape the world according to our preferences. Labor is purposeful, intentional and usually planned. The scarcity to be prevented or the inadequacy of a situation can lead into a cycle, though. In some cases, the attempt to reduce scarcity generates new possibilities and new scarcities (e.g., in the case of mobility, where dissatisfaction with immobility led to the creation of automobiles which then led to a scarcity of fuel and environmental pollution, both new scarcities to be reduced) (FÜLLSACK 2009). This definition of labor shows that scarcities – whether real and health threatening as in the case of scarcity of health or a scarcity of food, or perceived like in cases of a scarcity of, say, the newest electronic gadget or a bigger car – will necessarily serve to give labor an important place in an individual's life.

The labor market, i.e., the place where the demand for and the supply of labor are matched, and wages, i.e., the price of labor, are negotiated, is, in the economic theory, a regular market. As such, Adam Smith's *invisible hand* (SMITH 1904) would regulate all necessary aspects and governments would not have to interfere. In reality, the labor market is no perfect market in the sense of economic theory. One, it is not homogeneous on both sides of the market. Potential employees have different qualifications, different personal characteristics and abilities, and the potential employers demand different skills and qualifications. In addition, the labor market is not transparent. There are information asymmetries on the demand as well as the supply side. For example, only the potential employee has full knowledge of his or her motivation, skills and attitude; while only the employer has complete information about the job offered. Thirdly, labor is not completely mobile (LAMPERT, ALTHAMMER 2001). The two other assumptions for a perfect market are not met either. Supply and demand on the labor market do not react without delay, and there are personal, temporal, factual and spatial preferences. Therefore, political interventions are justified. In this context, LMP in free market economies or social market economies can be defined as all measures with the aim to influence the labor market in a way that allows all those capable and willing to work to continuously find employment according to their interests and capabilities and to find this employment on the best terms possible for remuneration and working hours (LAMPERT, ALTHAMMER 2001). On the demand side of labor LMP increases a companies' chance to find appropriate labor at the best terms.

Economic theory describes four basic types of unemployment. In the case of *frictional unemployment*, which is caused by job changes and the delays between old and new job, there is no urgent necessity for an intervention of the government, but a possible intervention would be to reduce the time lags between jobs if they are caused, for example, by legal obstacles or other institutional barriers.

Seasonal unemployment, arising because of jobs that are only relevant during parts of the year, e.g., in farming or construction, is usually not one of the main topics of LMP; its reduction is often rather a side effect of LMP measures to reduce structural unemployment.

Cyclical unemployment, developing during a recession, can be tackled by policies to support the economy during recession (usually not by LMP, but rather other measures), but also by supporting individual companies through the reduction of institutional barriers such as the regulations on reduced working hours.

Structural unemployment, on the other hand, is caused by disequilibria between supply and demand for labor, e.g., due to immobility of labor or qualifications that do not match. It is often stable and is the most important type of unemployment for LMP. Its reduction is partly an allocation problem (i.e., LMP must support and improve the process of finding the most suitable employees for existing jobs, e.g., by increasing mobility), and partly a human capital issue, if the skills of potential employees do not match the skills required by potential employers.

Apart from aiming to reduce those four kinds of unemployment, LMP also addresses working conditions, especially work rules and the issue of remuneration. Working conditions will be discussed in more detail in subsection 4.4, as they are relevant for the discussion of sustainability and the labor market. The realities described above are given attention to not only by LMP, but also other political fields. In Germany, for example, health issues are addressed by the Federal Ministry of Health; social aspects are treated in the Federal Ministry for Labor and Social Affairs, as are specific labor topics. The Federal Ministry of Economic Affairs and Energy is concerned with the general economy and therefore also with labor-related topics; as well as green energy and therefore jobs in this area. The Federal Ministry for Family Affairs, Senior Citizens, Women and Youth has their say as well, especially where the labor-environment for families and women are concerned, and the Federal Ministry of Education and Research provides important decisions and programs about the development of human capital. Last but not least, the Federal Ministry of Finance has to approve the budget for the measures decided upon by the respective departments, and the other ministries that have not been mentioned here are likely to treat some labor-related aspects as well. While the competencies for labor-related topics may be assigned differently in other countries, it can be expected that with such a complex topic most countries have a system of widespread responsibilities. With such an abundance of departments responsible, and accordingly many direct, but also indirect influences on the labor market, it is difficult to clearly define LMP measures and to determine its possible influences. In this, LMP is very similar to sustainability with its many responsible institutions (cf. Figure 13). Nevertheless, for the sake of this work it is necessary to have a fairly accurate idea of the possibilities and tasks of this dimension of policy measures. It also has to be kept in mind that there is no monocausal explanation for unemployment. In addition, especially economic and labor market related policy can only be successful if it is continuous and therefore foreseeable, as (private) investments depend a lot on stable future prospects. Therefore, the implementation of reform concepts has to be gradual (VRING 2007) and must be communicated openly and reliably.

To include all aspects in LMP, the following procedure of political reforms of the labor market is suggested: preparation of the reform by a commission consisting of participants from political, scientific and economic backgrounds; followed by a thorough evaluation of the results of the reform; followed by the appropriate adjustments based on the results of the evaluation (HEYER 2006). This procedure takes time, though, and is therefore seldom realized with the necessary thoroughness. On the European Level, the 1994 Essen Summit Meeting of the European Union discussed the increasing unemployment all over Europe in the early and middle 1990s and identified five main causes for its development:

(1) Insufficient investment in vocational training

(2) Low employment intensity of economic growth

(3) High non-wage labor costs

(4) Low effectiveness of labor market policy, and

(5) Long-term unemployment. (EUROPEAN COUNCIL 1994)

The resulting resolutions of the summit were to:

(1) improve employment opportunities for the labor force by promoting investment in vocational training

(2) increase the employment intensity of growth, in particular by encouraging a more flexible organization of work

(3) reduce non-wage labor costs, in particular for low skilled labor

(4) increase the effectiveness of employment policy, in particular by moving from passive to active labor market policies, and

(5) implement selective measures necessary to help the very varied groups of the long-term unemployed (EUROPEAN COUNCIL 1994)

These resolutions shape European labor market policies, the german among them, until today.

4.3 Labor Market Policy Measures

It has been mentioned above that LMP is, directly or indirectly, influenced by several fields of politics. In the next subsections, the measures discussed will be directly linked to LMP. As the indirect impact of other measures is very relevant as well, especially for the evaluation and eventually for the discussion of sustainability and the labor market, this aspect will also be discussed briefly. For all measures to be discussed it is necessary to keep in mind that one and the same policy measure might have positive or negative impact on the labor market, depending on the balance of contradictory effects. The effects might change in the long run from negative to positive or vice versa, but they also might not. Typical examples for this ambivalence are the following:

(1) **Strict employment protection for regular workers**

Positive: workers are committed, incentive to invest in human capital.

Negative: cost of firing increases, quick adaptation not possible, lower flexibility.

(2) **Restrictions on temporary contracts**

Positive: lowers possibility to substitute permanent with temporary workers, higher incentives to train workers, higher incentives for workers to educate.

Negative: reduction of ability to quickly adapt, lowers incentives to educate because there is no impending job search.

(3) **Training programs for the unemployed**

Positive: unemployed persons are able to get higher skilled jobs that have longer duration, direct increase of human stock.

Negative: crowding out of other training programs, reduced incentives for companies to invest in human capital.

(4) **Subsidized employment and work experience programs**

Positive: increases job duration, increased employment of low skilled workers.

Negative: reduces wage difference between low- and high-skilled jobs, thus reducing incentives for workers to invest in skills.

(5) **Generous unemployment benefits**

Positive: increase the time spent looking for work, therefore improving quality of matches and thereby resource allocation, encourages workers to look for higher productivity jobs and firms to create those.

Negative: encourage shirking by existing employees as there is a lower cost of being fired, thus reducing productivity, increases length of unemployment, therefore leading to deprecation of human capital.

(6) **Centralized wage-setting arrangements**

Positive: speed up structural adjustment by making declining industries relatively less profitable and emerging ones more profitable than under decentralized wage-fixing.

Negative: discourage workers from investing in skills (no return on investment via higher wages), weakens link between productivity gains and wage growth.

(7) **High minimum wages**

Positive: compress wage relativities, giving employers incentives to invest in training, substitute low- for high-productivity jobs, increase aggregate productivity levels, reduce demand for low-skilled jobs, give employees incentives to invest in skills.

Negative: lead to downward wage rigidity; reduce incentives for firms to invest in training, compress wage relativities, thereby reducing returns to education and therefore incentives to invest in skills, increase shadow price of labor, leading firms to over-invest in labor-saving innovation.

(8) **Family-friendly politics**

Positive: assist workers with family responsibilities to maintain high-quality job matches, increase available labor force by activating the "hidden reserve"[48].

Negative: induce gender discrimination in hiring processes, leading to sub-optimal allocation of labor resources. (OECD 2007, p. 66)

4.3.1 Measures

Generally, LMP measures are divided into passive and active measures. Passive LMP, also called compensatory, is focused on distribution issues and social aspects. Active LMP (ALMP), in contrast, is employment policy, aiming to secure, improve or increase employment (BLAZEJCZAK 2013). Those two groups of measures will be discussed in the following two subsections.

4.3.1.1 Passive Labor Market Policy Measures

Passive or compensatory labor market policy focuses on distribution issues. It is not aimed at matching supply and demand of labor or at increasing the employability of individuals, but compensates losses of income due to unemployment. Instruments of passive LMP are earnings replacement benefits in cases of short- and middle-term unemployment, social assistance for the long-term unemployed or those not eligible for earnings replacements, insolvency payments or short-time working benefits. As those instruments are a treatment of the symptoms, lessening the negative impact of unemployment and reducing poverty, they are rather a social instrument than an actual instrument to reduce unemployment. The enduring reduction of unemployment is the task of ALMP measures.

48 The hidden reserve comprises persons who would search employment under certain circumstances, e.g., higher wages, more flexible working times, improved day-care for children or the elderly, etc.

4.3.1.2 Active Labor Market Policy Measures

ALMP focuses on actively increasing the employability and the chances to be employed for unemployed persons, i.e., on increasing the likelihood to be employed (KLUVE 2013). Characteristics of active or activating labor market policy are the enforcement of prevention of unemployment, the stipulation of individual responsibility and the creation of more flexibility (BMAS 2006).

BLAZEJCZAK divides ALMP into micro- and macroeconomic aspects (cf. Table 9). The macroeconomic measures will be discussed in subsection 4.3.1.4. Microeconomic policy directly targets the individual level and aims to adjust the supply and demand side of the labor market.

ACTIVE LABOR MARKET POLICY	
Microeconomic policy	**Macroeconomic policy**
- Targets the behavior of market participants and coordination deficits such as asymmetrical information	- Reduction of cyclical unemployment with the help of monetary (Phillips curve) or fiscal policy (increased spending or reduced duties)
- Examples: reduced duties in certain branches, subsidies for companies employing people with impediments, escape clauses in collective labor agreements, advancement of mobility and flexibility, needs-based qualification, conservation of employability, promotion of self-employment	- Starting point for policy measures to increase employment: o Increase growth o Reduce working hours o Dampening the increase of labor productivity

Table 9: Aspects of active labor market policy
(BLAZEJCZAK 2013)

There are various other possibilities to categorize ALMP. BONOLI (2010) identifies four types of ALMP: incentive reinforcement, occupation, human capital investment and employment assistance, while Kluve (2013) finds four different categories:

(1) Supporting job search (e.g., application training, career counseling, monitoring of job search, sanctions as negative incentive)

(2) Training and qualification (i.e., all measures that increase human capital)

a. theoretical vocational training

b. practical vocational training on the job

c. training of basic competences (mathematics, language, etc.)

d. soft skills training

(3) Increase employment in the private sector (financial incentives to influence either the behavior of employers or of the unemployed, e.g., by supporting start-ups)

(4) Increase employment in the public sector (activities that aim at producing public goods and services).

Accordingly, resources for ALMP go to the following sections: job subsidies, reductions in non-wage labor costs, public sector job creation, short time work, job search assistance, training programs, work experience, job-finding and business start-up incentives, training programs for existing workers, and support for apprentices (OECD 2010).

A 2011 report of the ILO[49] found that especially during crises, safeguarding employment measures such as the short working time schemes in Germany are effective. Also, direct political support to companies in labor intensive sectors, such as specific tax reductions, if well targeted, are recommended. Training to maintain skills and adapt (potential) workers' skills to changing demands by employers is a very common measure. It has proven to be successful, as has the improvement of public employment services, which serves to better match potential employers with employees. In addition, the ILO recommends the implementation of programs that target not certain large (age-)groups, but rather more specific groups with precise disadvantages on the labor market (CHARPE ET AL. 2011). The costs for such measures may be considerable, therefore, a thorough evaluation must be conducted to ensure that a measure is appropriate for the realization of targets and that it can positively affect employment. KLUVE gives an overview over four of the most important LMP measures and compares their estimated costs and expected effects (cf. Table 10).

An important aspect of active labor market policy is also the improvement of the placement efforts. This can be done, e.g., with the use of statistical support systems (even though BEHNCKE ET AL. 2007 show that caseworkers tend to be wary of the systems and largely ignore them if the incentives to use it are not strong enough), by assigning a smaller number of cases to a caseworker, by schooling them or by improvements of the matching process in general. An overview over the evaluation of active

49 The International Labour Organization (ILO) has four strategic objectives: "1. Promote and realize standards and fundamental principles and rights at work; 2. Create greater opportunities for women and men to decent employment and income; 3. Enhance the coverage and effectiveness of social protection for all; 4. Strengthen tripartism and social dialogue." (ILO 2014)

labor market policies by MARTIN and GRUBB (2001) suggests that this is one field where efforts usually lead to success in job placements.

EXPECTED COSTS AND EFFECTS OF MEASURES OF ACTIVE LABOR MARKET POLICY				
	Supporting Job-Search	Training and Qualification	Increasing Employment in the Private Sector	Increasing Employment in the Public Sector
Costs	Low	Medium/ high	High	High
Expected short-term effects	Positive	Negative	Positive	Positive
Expected long-term effects (best case)	Positive (small)	Positive (high)	Positive	None
Expected long-term effects (worst case)	Negative (small)	Negative (small)	Negative	Negative (high)
Likelihood of negative indirect effects	Medium	Small	High	High
Suitable for which economic condition	All, increase during recession	All, increase during recession	All	Recession

Table 10: Expected effects of measures of active labor market policy
(KLUVE 2013)

4.3.1.3 Company Measures

Measures of ALMP may also include incentives and support for companies to develop or increase their own measures to decrease the gap between their demand for labor and the qualifications and number of working hours offered. The labor market is very heterogeneous; the bias between supply and demand varies greatly between sectors, but also between regions. While certain sectors complain about a shortage of skilled labor, other sectors are not affected by such a shortage so far. But the differences in the labor market are even greater among regions. While companies in attractive regions, mostly booming cities and/or the corresponding affluent suburbs, are often provided with a large pool of potential employees, companies in rural regions or in declining cities are the first who face the results of demographic changes or migration towards thriving regions. Therefore, it is likely that relevant aspects of labor and the labor market will be in the hands of companies, especially where the skill shortage is concerned. Companies must increase their attractiveness for qualified workers, for example by introducing innovative forms of labor organization, attractive qualifications or certificates or possibilities for an improved work-life-balance. This mainly concerns highly and very highly qualified employers in sectors with a shortage of skills, though. It is not necessarily true for unskilled workers (EICHHORST 2013). This is especially relevant as in the future, the shrinking population in many developed countries automatically leads to a smaller labor force potential, as does the changing structure of the population (BACH ET AL. 2009). It is important to note that the decrease of the labor force potential can be slowed by migration, for example, and the influence on overall economic growth may be highly influenced by technological growth. But for most companies, it is necessary to develop strategies to deal with a decreasing labor force. The challenges of demography can also be addressed on a macro level. Adaptions to the demographic challenges and the changing economic and social realities may demand a newly structured immigration policy; for example a combined point- and quota system for a demand oriented control of immigration. Such a concept for a comprehensive strategy combines long-term immigration and the possibility for short-term migration (HINTE ET AL. 2011).

4.3.1.4 Macroeconomic Measures

The impact of directly labor market related measures depends not only on their design, but also on the economic environment. During a recession measures may lessen the impact of a shrinking economy, and during an economic boom it is possible that no explicit measures are necessary to reduce the unemployment rate, but measures to activate the hidden reserve to fulfill the demand for labor may be in order. As the labor market is highly dependent on the economic situation, measures to influence the labor market can also be taken on a macroeconomic level. In the (macro-) economic theory, there are five elementary instruments to increase employment:

(1) Decrease wages

(2) Increase wages

(3) Decrease interest rates

(4) Decrease taxes

(5) Increase government spending (VRING 2007, p. 11).

Generally, current strategies to realize full employment usually follow either the neo-liberal or the Keynesian approach. The neo-liberal approach is supply-sided and assumes that cost reduction (i.e., decreasing wages, interest rates or taxes) and the improvement of incentives for the supply- as well as the demand side of the labor market will reduce unemployment. The Keynesian side considers the demand-side of the labor market and mostly uses the strategy of increasing public demand (i.e., increase government spending) in down-times to trigger growth (ROGALL 2007).

4.3.2 Labor Market Policy Measures in Germany

In Germany, the labor market policy of the last decade saw many experiments testing new possible methods to fulfill the tasks of said policy (BANGEL ET AL. 2006). On the level of the federal states, model projects and special programs were tested. This was mainly aimed at finding out, which instruments would help to integrate people with lower qualifications or those employed in the low-wage sector into the job market. The tests were to be thoroughly evaluated to provide a basis for informed decisions about LMP (WEINKOPF 2002). This led to a large number of LMP measures. EICHHORST and ZIMMERMANN (2007) for example counted between 60 and 80 measures of labor market policy, depending on the classification chosen.

Current LMP in Germany is mainly based on the Agenda 2010, a plan for Germany aimed at setting a framework to increase growth and employment. In addition, the welfare state was to be restructured and modernized. It was expected to create sustainable growth and employment by combining cyclical incentives with measures on the supply side of the labor- and goods-markets (BACH ET AL. 2009). The German Social Code III, also called the employment promotion law, states the aims of the employment promotion as follows: to prevent the emergence of unemployment; to reduce the duration of unemployment; and to promote the balance between supply and demand on the labor market. Specific goals are the improvement of the individual employability to prevent long term unemployment, equal opportunities for women and men, the realization of a high level of employment and an improved structure of employment (SGB III). The Hartz-IV-Reforms[50] started in 2005, in the middle of an economic stagnation. The core-ideas of the reform were fighting unemployment; reducing labor costs; activating the labor force; and increasing german competitiveness. Secondary aims were the reform of the administration of employment services; and to improve the legitimacy and financing of unemployment insurance. This was to be realized by market-oriented methods and increased personal responsibility and the activation of individuals (HEGELICH ET AL. 2011).

With the start of the reforms, the number of registered unemployed quickly rose from about 4,4 million in 2004 to more than 5 million in the months from January to April 2005, due to a large number of concealed unemployed people (i.e., unemployed persons who are not officially registered) who registered at the government agencies as the change of law made it possible for them to receive basic unemployment benefits due to the combination of unemployment benefits and welfare aid. The economic boom that started in 2006 had an impact on the labor market from the middle of the year 2006. The rising number of employment significantly lowered unemployment till, in 2007, it was down to 3.8 million unemployed persons. For an evaluation of the success of the Hartz-reforms it is necessary to keep in mind that this decrease of unem-

50 The Commission for Modern Services on the Labor Market was colloquially called Hartz-commisson after its head Peter HARTZ.

ployment coincided with an economic boom, and that the correlations must be considered (BACH ET AL. 2009). To institutionalize evaluations, the German Federal Agency for Labor (Bundesagentur für Arbeit, BA) initiated the TrEffeR project, a project to monitor treatment effects and for the prediction of impact and results with the assignment to promptly evaluate the effectivity of the employment promotion for regulation purposes (STEPHAN ET AL. 2006).

STRATEGIES AND MEASURES OF LABOR MARKET POLICY	
Strategy	Possible Policy Measures
Increase the employment of older people	Link the retirement age to life expectancy
	Reform of partial retirement, abandon the block model
	Advancement of (further) qualification of older people
	Temporary wage subsidies
Further the employment of women	(additional) Investments in quantity and quality of child daycare
	Cancelation of child care subsidies (parental care money)
	Reform of married couples tax splitting
Increase the attractiveness of Germany especially for young and qualified immigrants	Public promotion of the EU blue card
	Support of partners of immigrants in their job search
	Point system for the active support of qualified immigration[51]

Table 11: Strategies and measures of labor market policy in Germany
(BRAUN ET AL. 2014)

This project is an important step towards the integration of evaluations into the policy making process. Measures of German LMP have to take into account the propensity to work, the demographic development, and projected migration volume of work. Accordingly, the suggestions for a successful labor market policy include furthering women's and older people's propensity to work or supporting the immigration of qualified workers (cf. Table 11).

51 HINTE ET AL. (2011) suggest a combined point- and quota system for a demand oriented control of immigration such as the one suggested by the IZA (the research institute for the study of labor) is a concept for a comprehensive strategy that combines long-term immigration and the possibility for short-term migration.

4.4 Sustainable Labor Market Policy

So far, there is no exact definition of sustainable labor and the appropriate policy measures to further it; therefore, the following subsection outlines the aspects of sustainable labor. DRAUTZ (2011) states, that individual labor force and collective labor connections must be able to sustain the welfare of a nation in the long run. She stresses that sustainable LMP should include the quality of jobs and shape the work-life-balance. This definition is vague, though, and does not include all dimensions of sustainability as identified in this work. It is impossible to assign LMP or employment policy exclusively to one of the three dimensions of sustainability. It is connected with the ecological dimension, because labor is coupled with the environment: be it that the work is in a field with negative impact on the environment or that environmental rehabilitation and protection create jobs. The economic dimension is affected when long-term economic growth is seen as necessary to ensure a high employment rate, also the full use of the production capital (or in case of employment policy, human capital) is relevant. The social aspects of employment policy are targeted when looking at the improvement of the quality of work and working conditions (e.g., demands for quality standards, compensation, job security, aspects of equality and justice) (BLAZEJCZAK 2013). To gain a general idea over the role of labor in a sustainable society, the following Figure 36 offers an overview.

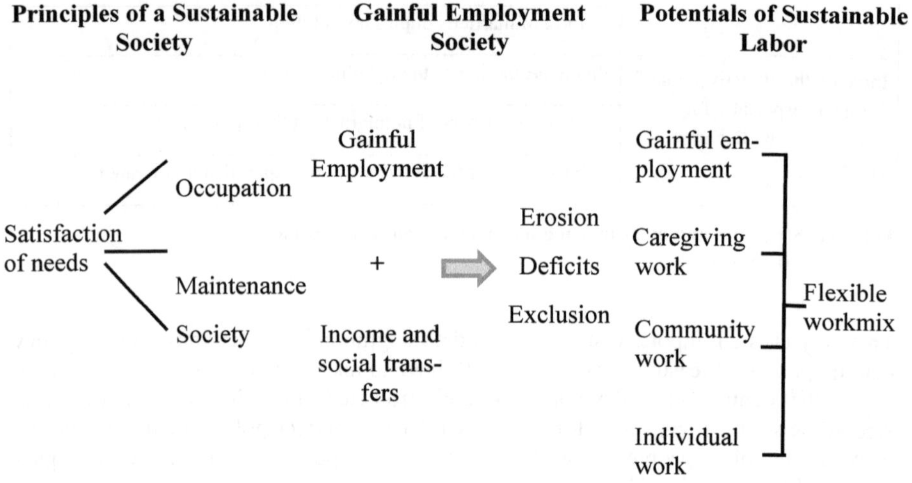

Figure 36: Sustainable societies and sustainable labor
(HILDEBRAND 2003, p. 385)

If one of the principles of a sustainable society is the satisfaction of needs for current and future generations, focusing on occupation rather than labor and stressing the importance of society; and if on the other hand the base of a gainful employment society are gainful employment, but also income- and social transfers, then a combination of both may offer an idea of the potentials of sustainable labor. Sustainable labor would then be not a narrow, but rather a broad definition of labor inasmuch that it does not only consider gainful employment, but also (currently) unpaid labor as part of work, thus discussing a flexible work mix (HILDEBRAND 2003). To analyze LMP measures that are appropriate for the realization of sustainable labor market policy, it is useful to consider once again the dimensions of sustainability.

4.4.1 The Economic Dimension of Sustainable Labor Market Policy

The economic relevance of low unemployment is considerable. A high employment rate means lower payments for unemployment support, higher tax revenues, higher disposable income, thus more buying power, which leads – if marginal consumption is at least in part regional or national – to higher revenues for companies. It also leads to higher tax revenues for municipalities, thus increasing their budget for infrastructural projects, which may in turn improve their attractiveness for companies. Higher tax revenues also mean higher funds, e.g., for education, which could further intragenerational justice and lead to a long-term improvement of the employment situation, thus contributing to the aspect of intergenerational justice. It must be kept in mind though, that one possible strategy for sustainable development is a policy of non-growth. If this is the case, labor market policy becomes more important as this might lead to job-reduction (COSTANZA ET AL. 2012). Its main task would then be the allocation of possibly scarcer jobs, the creation or support of employment in fields that contribute to a sustainable development (e.g., green jobs, cf. subsection 4.4.2) or the support of technological progress and the promotion of possibly following shifts from gainful employment towards individual work, a subsistence economy, and community or educational work (GRUNWALD, KOPFMÜLLER 2006). For companies it is necessary to understand that in a world that supports sustainable development, sustainability is part of corporate responsibility. A strategic vision, by its definition long-term, must include a consistent workforce (PAGNATTARO 2014).

Sustainability in the sense of the social theory of the 19th century means that man should use his qualification and his creativity and his potentials for work, that he should do that self determinedly and that manpower should not be exploited beyond its capacities. Summarized, this is the imagination of a long-term development and use of human resources (HAIPETER, VOSS-DAHM 2002) which is as valid and relevant for a sustainable development as it has been two centuries ago.

4.4.2 The Ecological Dimension of Sustainable Labor Market Policy

The ecological dimension is what likely comes to mind first when considering sustainable LMP. It has been argued before that a certain precedence of environmental concerns is logical, as much irreversible degradation of the natural environment has already taken place, and many theoretically reversible overuses of renewable resources could only be reversed if action is taken swiftly and substantially. It is relevant to keep in mind the interdependencies and possible reciprocal effects of measures on the different dimensions of sustainable development. A typical measure to improve the allocation of jobs, for example, is the support of measures to increase the mobility of individuals[52]. This may lead to regress in the environmental dimension, as such measures may increase exhaust emissions. On the other hand, a job in a "green sector", i.e., a job for the protection of the environment, does not necessarily mean a sustainable job. Working for sustainability or in the environmental protection sector might well mean suboptimal working conditions and therefore not be sustainable itself. In this case, a positive impact on the environmental sector may have negative implications for the social dimension of sustainability (RITT 2007). It is therefore necessary to carefully assess conflicting impacts of measures on the various aims of sustainable labor market policy.

It has been discussed in subsection 2.5 that an equality of dimensions within the limits of regenerability of the natural system is a sensible concept to follow. In this sense, measures affecting the economic or social dimension or, more generally, intra- and intergenerational justice would not be executed if they have a negative impact on the ecological dimension that exceeds the limits of regenerability. Measures to further the ecological aspects of sustainable labor market policy may be realized, though, whenever their positive impact outweighs probable negative effects in other dimensions. One possible approach towards a sustainable labor market is the modernization of the economy by selectively furthering ecological growth (ROGALL 2007). This may for example be done by promoting employment in green jobs. Protecting the environment can create jobs. There is a direct way to do so, by producing goods relevant for environmental protection or offering services directly related to the environment. Indirectly, jobs may be created in sectors providing input for industries or services in the field of environmental protection. Also, jobs may be created by additional foreign demand due to market leadership of successful pioneers in the field, supported by first-mover-advantages (JOHN, RÜBBELKE 2007). The label of "green jobs" must not be confused with the label "sustainable job", though. POSCHEN ET AL. (2012, p. 6) decree that "A green job is any decent job that contributes to preserving or restoring the quality of the environment, be it in agriculture, industry, services or administration.". The purpose of those jobs is to reduce the consumption of energy and raw materials, to limit emissions, waste and pollution in general; but also to protect and restore ecosystems. In ad-

52 E.g., tax-deductible commuting expenses for employed people in Germany.

dition, green jobs may be aimed at enabling institutions to adapt to changes resulting from climate change or irreparable or slowly reparable damage to natural resources.

But jobs do not only have to be green to fulfill the requirements of sustainable development. They must also provide adequate incomes and be "decent jobs" in that they offer a safe working environment, where the rights of workers are respected. Figure 37 shows the relationship between jobs in green industries, green occupations and decent jobs. In a strict sense of sustainability, if all dimensions of sustainability have to be positively affected to make an employment sustainable, the only jobs that are sustainable would be decent jobs in green industries or, at the most, in green occupations. It is highly unlikely that employment mainly in these sections will be realized in the foreseeable future, but sustainable LMP should nevertheless concentrate on furthering the development of legal frameworks for decent jobs as well as employment in green jobs and green industries.

A: decent green jobs in green industries

B: decent non-green jobs in green industries

C: non-decent green jobs in green industries

D: decent green jobs in non-green industries

E: employment in green industries

F: green occupations

G: decent jobs

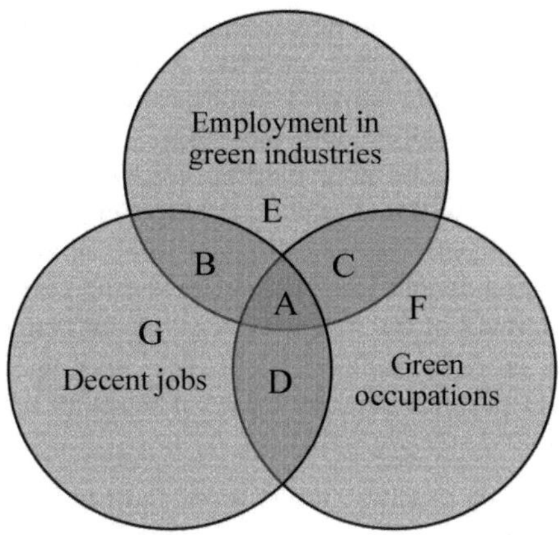

Figure 37: Total employment, green jobs and decent work
(POSCHEN ET AL. 2012, p. 7)

The support of green industries and jobs, for example by efforts to increase the demand for green products and services, is a double-edged sword, though. A growing demand may lead to increased investments in the industries concerned and thereby to a higher labor demand. As the income in green sectors increases, demand for greener goods and services will go up. The eventual impact depends on employment elasticity, the size of demand, therefore size of investment, and the percentage to which demand is met by imports, of course. There is a social aspect to green jobs as well. Employees have reported increased job satisfaction working for companies that embrace or promote sustainability principles (JANN ET AL. 2006). But those positive aspects may be neutralized by the (mostly unintended) side effects. Green goods and services are usually more expensive than their non-green versions; therefore substituting regular goods with green goods will c.p. lead to a reduced budget for other goods and services. Also, green jobs created will likely mean a decrease in non-green jobs, as a rising demand for green goods and services means a lower demand for their non-green substitutes, leading to disinvestment in the sectors affected, and possibly layoffs. Thus, income will decrease, leading to less consumption. It is not clear whether the net effects of greenifying production on labor are positive or negative (POSCHEN ET AL. 2012).

In the 1990s, an often heard argument was that strict rules for environmental protection would hurt the competitiveness of german companies. By now, several studies prove that the environmental protection sector is, at least in Germany, a growth area and even a positive effect on employment was predicted by some scientists[53]. It has to be kept in mind, though, that there are empirical difficulties with the analysis of the sector[54] and that some studies did not find any such effects (HAUFF 2007). The prognoses rely on a number of assumptions about technological changes, customer behavior, flexibility of the workforce, etc. Globally, the net impact of the labor market adjustments necessary for a sustainable development depends on whether the expansion of sustainable production is more labor-intensive than the contraction in unsustainable sectors. Findings of computable general equilibrium models (CGEs) suggest that changes in the sectoral composition will have little impact on the average skill demand; that flexible and adaptable labor markets are key; and that real GDP will decrease and that this decrease will be borne by the workers, if there is no compensatory policy. The net employment effects are estimated to be small (OECD 2012). Accordingly, the OECD recommends that LMP measures should concentrate on ensuring the effectiveness and smoothness of the transition, e.g., by making sure that the jobs created are fair, and that the green economy is inclusive. Labor market institutions, including trade unions, should play an important role in defining and implementing strong employment policies (OECD LEED 2012).

It has been mentioned above that the OECD predicts little impact of the transition towards sustainable production on the job skills demanded, i.e., specific groups with a low, medium or high level of education will not be affected more or less than the others.

53 A comprehensive DIW-study for prognoses of the impact of the German eco-tax and further regulations on employment predicted positive effects (KOHLHAAS 2005). An OECD study of several econometric models and prognostic scenarios for the estimation of economy-wide effects of environmental policy measures found that in all models, the estimated effects are very small. This may vary by country, though (OECD 2004).

54 A big challenge, among others, is the classification of companies into those operating in environmental protection sectors and non-environmental sectors. Data is mostly based on a register where companies can declare themselves as working in the field of environment protection. As the stipulations for working in the environment protection sector are not clearly defined, the data can only be considered a rough estimate. For example, producers of environment protection goods often do not consider themselves as operating in environmental protection. In addition, there is the problem of multi-purpose products, i.e, goods that can be used for environmental protection but also for other purposes (HAUFF 2007).

For Germany, though, data from 1998 shows that jobs in the sector of environmental protection are structured a little differently from jobs in other sectors regarding the education of workers. While the percentage of unskilled labor in the environmental sector is 18.3%, skilled labor accounts for 31.3% of employees, and staff for qualified tasks makes up another 33.6%, companies of other sectors show a percentage of 23.3% for unskilled labor, 27.1% for skilled labor and 30.6% for staff for qualified tasks (HAUFF 2007). This analysis faces the same classification problems that have been described in footnote 54, though, and cannot be used as proof of a different skill structure necessary for sustainable production without further research.

To realize a transition of an economy towards sustainability, it is necessary to have the support of the citizens (cf. subsection 2.7.2.2). Political changes and measures that may reduce (real) wages, limit consumption choices and ask for placing collective over individual rationality, among other impacts, can only be realized if the workers, voters, consumers and stakeholders in general agree on realizing the concept. A 2014 World Value Survey asking "what is more important: the protection of the environment or economic growth and job creation?" showed that on average, in the 56 countries where this survey was conducted 54.6% of those surveyed consider the protection of the environment more important. 40.4% believe that economic growth is more important (WVS 2014).

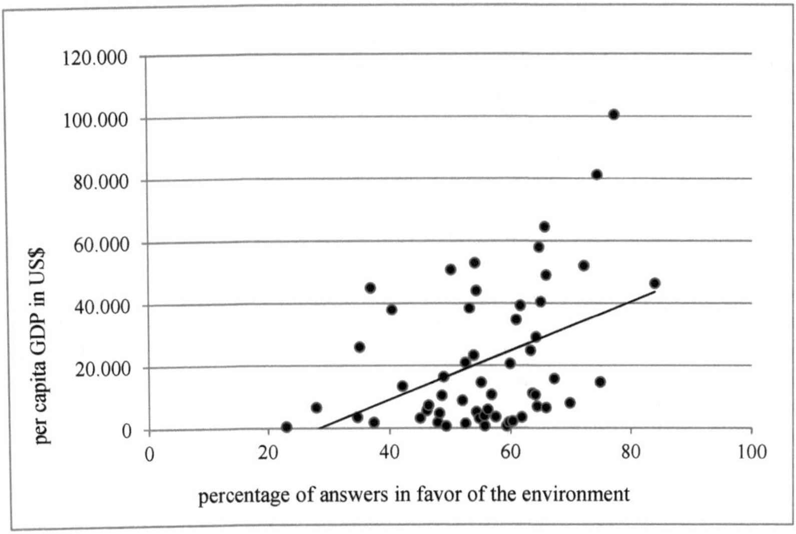

Figure 38: Protection of the environment and GDP
Percentage of answers "protecting the environment" to the question "what is more important: protecting the environment or economic growth?" plotted against per capita GDP in the respective countries (WVS 2014), trend line OLS estimate.

It is interesting to plot the answers against per capita GDP to see whether the importance placed on the environment depends on the income (cf. Figure 38). The analysis of the correlation between the two aspects is significant at the 0,01 level. An increase in GDP leads to an increase of the importance placed on environment protection. The correlation is not very strong, though, with an R^2 of 0.175.

4.4.3 The Social Dimension of Sustainable Labor Market Policy

The social dimension of sustainable LMP concentrates on a new distribution of existing work (e.g., maintaining total working hours, but reducing work hours per person, thus reducing unemployment) and a new organization of working conditions such as flexible working hours, qualification and participation. This comprises interdependencies between ecological, economic and social aims (BLAZEJCZAK, EDLER 2004), but is generally attributed to the social dimension. For a discussion of this dimension, it is helpful to differentiate between an individual and a social context. The individual level focuses on a good quality of life throughout the lifespan of the individual. This includes the right to choose an adequate job, thus unemployment must be prevented. What is "adequate" depends on moral, cultural and technical-economic conditions. The social level concerns a high employment level as well as the quality of work. In the case of sustainable labor, the quality of a job refers to three aspects: the satisfaction of the individual worker, a high creation of value, and the products of the work must meet the requirements of sustainability, i.e. adhere to social, economic and environmental standards. To assess whether labor is satisfactory, three criteria must be met: the labor must contribute to the wellbeing of the individual, it must be qualified to add to the value added, thereby benefitting the society, and the products of the work must be sustainable, i.e., for example, eco-friendly and socio-beneficial (ZINN 2003). Those requirements can be met with the help of a number of measures.

For example, to realize a redistribution of working hours, reduced working hours, more flexible schedules, equal rights for part-time workers and improving options for family time and sabbaticals are adequate measures (COSTANZA ET AL. 2012). Working time measures are also coherent to current measures of family policy that aim at improving the compatibility of caring for a family (including caring for the elderly) and pursuing a career. The normality of a reduced working time would, according to theory and first research results on measures like the german Elterngeld (parents' money)[55], increase intergenerational equality between the sexes by reducing the gender-specific social roles and increasing the freedom of choice between family, career or a combination of both for both sexes. In addition, redistributing the current working

55 The Elterngeld, a german earnings replacement for parents of babies, has been thoroughly researched. It has been found to have several positive influences (in accordance with several aims that the Elterngeld targets), especially on the labor market participation of mothers and the participation in family care of fathers (BUJARD 2013).

hours so that those currently employed work less, but those unemployed (or those working reduced hours but wishing to increase their working hours) can work more, may lead to a reduction of unemployment. The resulting reduction in income for those working full time must not be ignored by politicians, though. It is possible for example that those income effects are softened by an increase in wellbeing, but also that policy measures are necessary to make a redistribution of working hours more attractive. If, as has been discussed before, unemployment leads to worse health, then a decrease of unemployment may lead to better overall health, thus reducing costs for the healthcare system, which would also lessen income effects. Other cause-effect discussions are feasible.

Another important aspect of the social dimension of LMP are working conditions in general. Personal safety, a working environment that does not deteriorate the health of the worker, the right to voice one's opinions and suggestions within the company, the right to a say in the working conditions (e.g., via unions or work councils), and payment that ensures acceptable living conditions, among others, are crucial conditions for the sustainability of jobs. In this context, SAUER (2011) speaks of a humanization of work. It must be kept in mind though, that some policies and programs aiming at the protection of workers or improving working conditions may have a negative impact on the employment rate (VANDENBERG 2010).

4.4.4 Intragenerational Justice and Sustainable Labor Market Policy

Measures undertaken to realize economic, ecological and social sustainability have direct impact on intragenerational justice. In the sense of intragenerational justice, LMP must aim to ensure that employment is possible for anyone who wishes to participate in the labor market. If a redistribution of current working hours as described above was realized, that would be an important step towards more intragenerational justice. The UNITED NATIONS stress that they "recognize that poverty eradication, full and productive employment and decent work for all, and social integration and protection are interrelated and mutually reinforcing, and that enabling environments to promote them need to be created at all levels" and state that this is a global challenge to be targeted "to ensure sustainable and inclusive development and reduce poverty" (UNITED NATIONS 2012, §§ 147-148). As described above, measures toward social sustainability such as reduced or redistributed working hours increase intragenerational justice at least regionally. To realize a global intragenerational justice, global institutions to support such a development are necessary. The UNITED NATIONS are such an institution, but also international associations of trade unions or the ILO play an important role. For example, the members of the EUROPEAN TRADE UNION CONFEDERATION (ETUC) adopted sustainability as one of their guiding principles. They admit, though, that finding a balance between the traditional social topics of trade unions and the pressing ecological matters leads to many conflicts (GABAGLIO 2003).

4.5 Summary

Chapter 3 was aimed at the transfer from the theoretical discussion of sustainable development to the practical topic of labor market policy. After providing a basis by arguing the importance of labor and describing labor market policy and the possible measures to realize it, the transferal to sustainable labor market policy was made. This field is not extensively researched yet, and, to the best knowledge of the author, there is no explicit definition of sustainable labor market policy that includes all dimensions of sustainability. Therefore, labor market policy was discussed for each of the three dimensions as well as in terms of intra- and intergenerational justice. Summarizing these findings, the following definition for sustainable labor market policy is suggested:

Sustainable labor market policy furthers decent jobs that contribute to sustainable development. It must consider possible tradeoffs between the ecological, economic and social dimensions.

It also must regard inter- and intragenerational justice.

This is, of course, a highly theoretical definition and can be specified according to the requirements for the specific aims it is to be used for. It has been discussed in chapters 1 and 2 that the tradeoffs between the dimensions are large and that it is necessary in many cases to prioritize. This prioritization can differ between countries and regions, depending on their individual situations.

5. Indicators

In recent years (and decades) the discussion about political decisions has shifted inasmuch as statistical data is made available for public perusal in many countries, thus enabling people to follow the development of relevant statistics and to draw their own conclusions or ask informed questions. The sheer amount of data made available through statistical agencies, and also polling agencies, research institutes, NGOs and any other single person or group conducting surveys or collecting information and data is overwhelming, though. Most datasets need to be put into a context or be combined with other data to be understood; some require extensive explanations to be intelligible, while others' usefulness may be doubted. Additional problems occur when data from different providers are combined, such as official statistics on European and national level. In those cases it happens that the data of the different data collectors is only vaguely comparable even if they claim to measure the same effects. An often cited example for such a limited comparability is the unemployment rate. Ostensibly, all unemployment statistics report the same information: the rate of unemployed people. Effectively, the definition of an "unemployed person" varies[56], though, thus complicating a comparison of unemployment rates published by different institutions and for different countries.

To make understanding and processing the data easier, thereby simplifying the assessment of situations, measures, etc., it has become more common to present indicators for certain items. Their use has become more popular with the rising obligation to evaluate policy measures or the performance of institutions, among others. Because evaluations are one of the reasons for the growing use of indicators, it is helpful to have an idea of the methods, objects and procedures of evaluations and evaluation processes. Therefore, an overview over the method will be given in chapter 5. Evaluation research is a subdomain of empirical research. It is mainly concerned with the assessment of policy measures or interventions (BORTZ, DÖRING 2006), and within evaluations, indicators are an often used proxy to analyze the effects and impacts of measure, political decisions, company strategies and other possible objects to be assessed. It is important to note that the indicators used in evaluations are not necessarily developed from quantifiable data, but can also contain qualitative information. This will be discussed in subsection 5.4.

---

56 In the case of the unemployment rate, the differences between the rates reported are caused, among other reasons, by different descriptions of unemployed persons. In some statistics, for example, only people who do not work at all may be considered unemployed. Others may count anyone who works up to 15 hours per week, but would like to work more, as unemployed as well. Therefore, even if at a first glance the data reported are comparable between institutions and countries, a closer look at data collection and definitions is necessary.

5.1 Introduction

Indicator, derived from the latin origin *indicare*, meaning to announce, suggest, display, show, is a commonly used word and its related words *to indicate* and *indication* are habitually used in everyday language. The scientific definition is more specific, though. The EUROPEAN COMMISSION describes an indicator as "something that quantifies and simplifies phenomena and helps us understand complex realities or in other words, it acts as a proxy or simplification of more complex information" (EUROPEAN COMMISSION 2007). LUDWIG (2001) adds that an indicator is supposed to inform, an aim that is realized by using quantitative or qualitative descriptors of a situation or a process. Thereby, complex, dynamic situations are made understandable and new or previously concealed information is gained. In summary, indicators are mainly used for:

(1) Improving and simplifying communication (incorporating understandable facts into communication)

(2) Information (made understandable by simplifying and clarifying aggregate data)

(3) Control and evaluation (by measuring and calibrating progress and providing early warning systems)

(4) Planning (and adaption within the process of implementation) (LEÓN 2005; UN DESA 2007).

5.2 Basic Requirements for Indicators

To fulfill the ambitious purposes listed above, it is necessary that the indicators meet certain requirements. Again, the European Commission offers a short overview by stating that overall, the key criteria seem to be that indicators should be relevant, precise, current, comprehensive and comparable (EUROPEAN COMMISSION 2007). The indicators must provide information about the overall viability of the system, must be able to describe changes or change rates and must show the effects of the measure or variable considered on the total system, i.e. sustainable development as a whole (BOSSEL 1999, p. 20). It is therefore helpful to use stock- as well as flow-indicators.

The requirements for indicators can be divided into three different sections: (1) with regard to the content, (2) methodical requirements and (3) organizational. The first section is dominated by two subrequirements. There has to be an agreement on the relation between the key areas the indicator describes[57], and the process of the develop-

57 In the case of sustainability, for example, those key areas would be the economic, ecological and social dimensions. Those key areas need to be clearly defined and distinguishable and their relations and cause and effect relationships known.

ment of an (aggregated) indicator or indicator system has to be open. This shall further social and scientific acceptance of said indicator (system). The second section, the methodical requirements, consist of the postulations that the choice of indicators be transparent (corresponding to the second requirement of the first section that the development of the indicator or indicator system be open); that the indicators be comprehensible and relatable to the aims of the measures; that possible interdependencies between data should be measurable and presentable; that the data necessary for the indicator be available[58]; and lastly, that the indicator be, if at all possible, at least in some measure quantifiable. The latter demand is disputed among scientists, but the requirement that the indicator should be easily communicable implies a certain quantifiability, as qualified data is usually more extensive when analyzed than quantifiable data. Therefore, the requirement is to be supported as far as quantification is at all possible. The organizational section demands that all concerned parties[59] are included in the indicator-choosing-process (DYBE, WEITH 2004, pp. 113-114). The CONSEIL D'ANALYSE ÉCONOMIQUE adds that indicators must be relevant, i.e., suitable to report changes in the area they are designed to describe; consistent, meaning that indicators must really measure what they are supposed to describe (this also requires decisions about the aggregation of heterogenous information. If it is impossible to find an indicator that closely describes the desired topic, a proxy has to be found); and lastly measurable, stating that indicators have to be observable, the cost of data collection has to be adequate and data ascertainment has to observe data protection laws (CONSEIL D'ANALYSE ÉCONOMIQUE, SACHVERSTÄNDIGENRAT ZUR BEGUTACHTUNG DER GESAMTWIRTSCHAFTLICHEN ENTWICKLUNG 2011, p. 12).

FISCHER-KOWALSKI ET AL. (1993, pp. 16-17) also demand that annual data must be available; that the number of indicators in a set must be restricted – thus following the requirement of communicability; and that indicators should be adjusted so that a higher numerical amount means a higher amount of – for example – environmental pollution. Thus, the requirements are targeted on increasing the understanding of the indicators by using consistent measurements and indicators that does enable the users to gather a clear overview over the topic. This restriction does pose a number of problems, though, as a limited number of indicators usually implies to either leave out possibly relevant data for the sake of clarity or that different information has to be aggre-

58 The „availability" of data is a rather broad description. Most data can be collected in some way, but the costs for the collection have to be taken into account. Ideally, the data is already collected and will only be newly interpreted or computed for the formulation of the indicator. For additional data collections that may be necessary for the indicator, the costs of the data collection must be calculated and their financing covered. If that is not the case, the indicator is only of theoretical value but cannot be used in reality and therefore does not help to fill the goals for indicators mentioned above.

59 In those cases where the users of the indicators are the general public, this requirement may be fulfilled by including the users as pretesters during the development of the indicator (set) or by their inclusion in the adaption process of the indicator over time.

gated in order to reduce the number of single indicators. This will be discussed in more detail in subsection 5.3.

The methodical requirements for indicators are strict. Especially for those indicators used as a basis for political decisions with a broad and possibly long lasting impact, it is essential to have a sound and reliable statistical background, but also the interpretation of the data must be as non-ambiguous and relatable as possible. To make sure that indicators are scientifically sound, the OECD, for example, stresses the following points:

(1) *Face validity*

(2) *Focus on summary outcomes*

(3) *Amenable to change and sensitive to policy interventions*

(4) *Commonly used and widely accepted*

(5) *Comparability across countries* (OECD 2011, p. 22).

Point (1) states that an indicator has to encompass all facts intended to be measured.[60] (2) requires indicators to provide easily understood summarized statements that simplify the communication of the indicator results. This requirement is not intangible, though, as will be shown in detail in Figure 40, because different levels of simplification are expedient depending on the target group of communication. Rule (3) demands a finely tuned indicator that really depicts possible changes. For sustainability indicators this is a special challenge as sustainability is a very complex topic and improvements or setbacks of certain indicators measuring sustainability can often hardly be attributed to one specific measure. Therefore, indicators to determine the influence of a certain measure have to take into account the complexity of influences on certain situations. To ensure the fulfillment of requirement (4), it is helpful to use well-known data that has possibly been tested and used for other purposes and has undergone broad scientific discussion so that advantages and disadvantages of the indicator are well-known. To use indicators which have been discussed extensively does not always ensure the common acceptance, though. As will be shown later in this chapter, the assessment of the helpfulness and applicability of data between scientists is not unanimous, so that a wide acceptance is not always the result. Or, to put it differently, the number of widely accepted indicators is likely not sufficient to assess complex measures and situations. Therefore, it is possible that concessions are necessary. Rule (5) is logical and elementary for the evaluation of all topics relevant not only on a regional, but on an international level, such as sustainability. In addition to the five requirements above, the OECD BETTER LIFE INITIATIVE (2011, p. 6) adds another condition:

60 Or, in the case of an indicator set, the indicator has to measure its intended contribution to the intended informational value of the indicator set.

(6) Conceptual soundness.

This stipulates the relevance of the indicator and the high quality of the data used (and therefore encompasses some of the requirements (1) to (5)), but also includes the requirement that a concept exists to adapt the indicator to possible changes or inadequacies in the case of proof that the indicator does not meet other requirements and must be adjusted.

A seventh requirement by the german statistical agency is

(7) Continuity.

While a development and adjustment of indicators might be necessary and sensible, in a longterm assessment of political fields and measures there has to be comparability between the points of time when the data is collected (STATISTISCHES BUNDESAMT 2010b, p. 4). This condition must be regarded when evaluating indicators. It may become necessary to adjust indicators, but this must be done with regard to the comparability to data collected before the adjustment so that comparisons are possible. GÜNTHER and SCHUH offer a more scientific approach to the development of an indicator by stating that to be of use, indicators have to meet the following requirements:

An indicator should be

(1) representative, relevant and accurate
(2) simple and measurable
(3) reliable and reproducible
(4) sensitive for changes over time
(5) controllable
(6) consistent
(7) adaptable to international contexts (where applicable)
(8) clear about the distance of the actual situation to critical limits
(9) *chosen transparently and therefore be communicable and credible* (GÜNTHER, SCHUH 2000).

After the scientific and functional requirements are met, the user-related aspects must be considered. The target group must be identified and indicators must be formulated accordingly. The type of the indicator in accordance with the target group will be discussed in the following subsection 5.3, but all indicators must be understandable, i.e., all target groups must be able to understand and to class the information, the target groups must agree on their relevance, and the indicator must be suitable to provide adequate information for informed decisions, if necessary in combination with other indicators. With such a large number of requirements it clearly is unlikely that all criteria are met, but the deficiencies should be noted and explained to show the difference between the best practical indicator and the best possible indicator (MITCHELL 1996). This is also necessary for a decision on the weighting of the indicator if several indicators are to be used, and to value the explanatory power and reliability of the data – indispensable information if the indicators are to be used as a basis for political decisions. For internationally relevant indicators, the European Commission states a number of requirements that must be fulfilled to be included in EU indicator sets:

i. "an indicator should capture the essence of the problem and have a clear and accepted normative interpretation;
ii. an indicator should be robust and statistically validated;
iii. an indicator should be responsive to policy interventions but not subject to manipulation;
iv. an indicator should be measurable in a sufficiently comparable way across Member States, and comparable as far as practicable with the standards applied internationally;
v. an indicator should be timely and susceptible to revision;
vi. the measurement of an indicator should not impose too large a burden on Member States, on enterprises, nor on the Union's citizens;
vii. the portfolio of indicators should be balanced across different dimensions;
viii. the indicators should be mutually consistent and the weight of single indicators in the portfolio should be proportionate;
ix. the portfolio of indicators should be as transparent and accessible as possible to the citizens of the European Union" (EUROPEAN COMMISSION 2007, p. 18).

In addition, the EEA asks that its indicators meet the following criteria: They

i. must be policy relevant;
ii. should help with monitoring of progress toward the quantified targets (if there are not targets, then use thresholds);
iii. be based on ready available and routinely collected data within specified timescale (to be determined country by country) at reasonable cost-benefit ratio;
iv. be consistent in space coverage and cover all or most EEA countries;
v. must observe time coverage and include sufficient time trends;
vi. primarily be national in scale and representative for countries (to allow for benchmarking);
vii. be understandable and simple;
viii. be conceptually and methodologically well founded and representative (EUROPEAN COMMISSION 2007, p. 18).

If those criteria are met, then a reliable indicator set can be provided. The task of finding indicators that are accepted in every member country (a task that is even more complicated in the case of worldwide organizations) is no small feat.

5.3 Types of Indicators

Indicators are based on statistical data (-sets). In general, three different types of indicators are used: primary data indicators, indicator sets and composite indicators (EUROPEAN COMMISSION 2007). Those shall be discussed in more detail below, as the understanding of advantages and disadvantages of all three types is elementary for the development and discussion of specific labor market and sustainability related indicators in chapter 6.

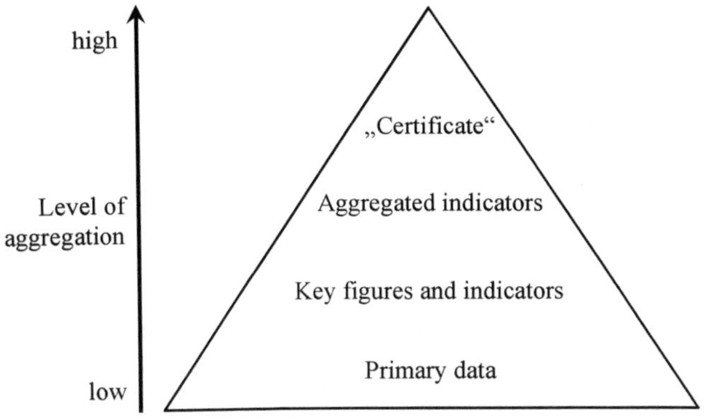

Figure 39: Degree of data aggregation
(GÜNTHER, SCHUH 2000)

GÜNTHER and SCHUH distinguish four different types of indicators (cf. Figure 39): primary, i.e., non-aggregated data, key figures and key indicators, aggregated indicators and certificates. The latter are added to the three types of the EUROPEAN COMMISSION to depict a current trend: the certification of all kinds of standards. To do so, information is gathered, interpreted and rated to deliver a final judgment about the situation. It is of course possible in most cases to get information about the key data included in the rating, but certificates are mainly in existence to give easy assessments.

In general, the difference between the types is the level of aggregation. Less integrated indicators usually provide more detailed information, but require profound knowledge of the subject to weigh and critically assess the information. Integrated indicators consist of very compact information that already includes weightings, but are usually easy to understand even for non-scientists as they contain one single number that can be classified somewhere between the maximum- and minimum value. The latter are usually used for the information of the public or less involved or informed parties, the former are used by experts in the fields concerned, who are able to make their own decisions about the interpretations.

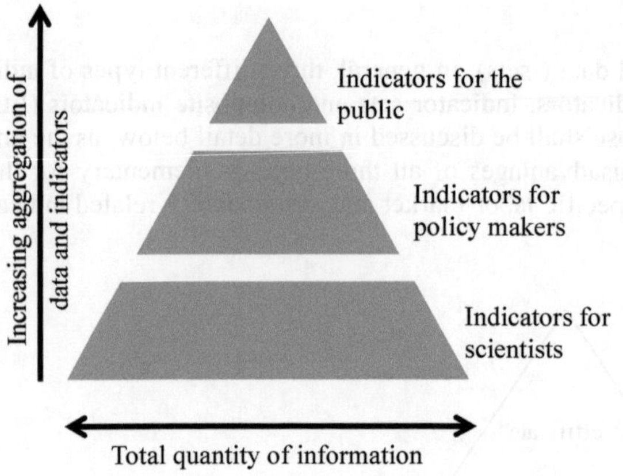

Figure 40: Data, indicators, information and indicator users
(MITCHELL 1996)

The following correlation between the level of data aggregation of the indicator and the quantity of information can be made and attributed to user groups (cf. Figure 40): non-aggregated data that contains a large amount of information is used by scientists, whereas indicators for the public consist of aggregated data that leaves considerably less information to be understood by the addressees. Policy makers, who have an understanding and knowledge of the topic that can be situated between the public and experts, are usually dealing with semi-aggregated indicators that contain a medium amount of information.

5.3.1 Single Primary Data Indicators

Primary indicators are simple statistical data or data series that may have been adjusted, but which have not been interpreted or weighted. As political or societal problems are usually complex, a single measurement or observation will not suffice as a basis for decisions. To only use one indicator would mean to neglect correlations, externalities, conflicting effects on other fields than the one observed, etc. Therefore, if primary data is used as an indicator, it is in almost all cases combined with other primary data sets and the users must decide on the weighting and interpretation of each measurement. This indicator type is only fit for use by informed individuals. This indicator type's advantage is that it does not include potentially biased weightings and contestable interpretations and can be used as basic information for all kinds of situations and research questions. Another advantage is that single observation data is likelier to be available in many countries, whereas it is less likely that all data necessary to calculate an aggregated indicator or even a certificate is available in sufficient quality in all countries.

5.3.2 Indicator Sets

Indicator sets are similar to primary data indicators, but do not consist of one single statistical measure or series, but of several of them. Indicator sets are based on the realization that it is impossible to convey the complex and comprehensive information about, for example, sustainability within one variable. The development of indicator sets is not simple, though. They have to be chosen to be helpful for policy decisions, they are expected to increase transparency and be easy to understand, include qualitative and quantitative information and should be usable even allowing for differences across countries. This leaves three main problems: make a choice out of the endless number of possible indicators, interpreting simple indicators, which are often too general, and observing financial and organizational limits to data collection (OBST 2000). The choice of variables to be included in the data set is also in the danger of being biased or incomplete and must therefore be performed with care and a profound knowledge of the situation to be described or measured. In addition, indicator sets are most helpful and understandable if they include an explanation as to which value would be desirable or critical (MITCHELL 1996). A few simple key indicators included in an indicator set have the advantage of being robust and transparent and easily understandable. But there is a danger of simplification (LUDWIG 2001) and a false implication of completeness due to the numbers of variables included in the set that may give the impression of being all-encompassing.

5.3.3 Aggregated Single Indices

Aggregated single indices (i.e., a set of indicators weighed and subsumed into one variable) that are easily understood by the public and are therefore more often published outside the scientific world, have a certain appeal, as this helps to further the general public acceptance of many topics. The problem with those aggregated single indices, however, is that different interest groups prefer different indicators integrated in the index or, in case they agree on the indicators used, they differ in the weighting coefficients attributed to the indicators (MITCHELL 1996). The aggregation can be spatial or contextual, but also interlinked, i.e., for example in the case of sustainability; more than one dimension is included. Highly aggregated indicators are potentially problematic in a number of ways. For one, the higher the rate of aggregation, the less specific information can be gained from the indicator. It is not clear from the indicator itself, which data has been included, what has been omitted and why, and which importance is placed on every variable. Secondly, the information included must be weighted to form the aggregated indicator. To do so, decisions about the importance of the single variables have to be made, as mentioned above, and those decisions must be based on as objective as possible assumptions. But the assumptions are based on basic values or views that, in the case of sustainability, for example, may consider one dimension as more important as the others or value intragenerational justice higher than intergenerational justice, and ascribe the weightings accordingly. Therefore, a subjective bias is to be expected, however well-founded the assumptions are, and not all user groups will agree on the assumptions (if they are made known) and may therefore challenge the credibility and plausibility of the indicator. Thirdly, with many complex problems or situations, there are trade-offs between different goals. Those have been described for the case of sustainability and sustainable development in chapter 1. Trade-offs between different goals of the underlying system must be considered in the building of a highly aggregated indicator which leads to further adjustments that cause a bias in the final indicator, because one has to decide on priorities – if data from the ecological column suggests an improvement, while in the economic column there seems to be a deterioration, how does one value the situation (DYBE, WEITH 2004)?

Another potential challenge for the creation of an aggregated indicator are the units. It rarely happens that all information to be included in the indicator has the same unit; therefore, again, adjustments have to be made, which might include new assumptions and weightings, thus contributing to a further bias. Still, aggregated indicators are often used due to their specific advantages: they allow a standardization of information and are easily communicable (GRUNWALD, KOPFMÜLLER 2006). The indicators reduce complex and extensive information to a single indicator with a clear statement that can be understood by non-experts. These indicators are often used by politicians as a basis for decisions, for the development of guidelines or for the evaluation of measures (LUDWIG 2001). Aggregated indicators are valued for their seeming simplicity and their clear message. But if they are to be used correctly, it is necessary to be informed about their underlying assumptions, the data used, adjustments to the data, etc., to be able to judge potential biases in the information. Thus, transparency is one of the most important factors for the use of aggregated indicators.

5.4 Building Indicators

The basic features of indicators have been discussed in the subsections above. The following section describes the steps to be followed for the development and application of a system of indicators. When a concept is to be evaluated with the help of indicators, the overall concept that is to be followed has to be specified by a number of guidelines, i.e., action- and target-oriented principles, leading to a first operationalization of the overall concept. This has to be followed by a concretion of clear, quantifiable or qualifiable goals (TILS 2005). Those goals must then be supported by scientifically sound indicators. To make sure the indicators fulfill the requirements, the first step is to define the purpose of the indicators as well as the target user group. This must be followed by a clear definition of the topics to be explained by the indicators, by the goals that shall be reached and controlled by the indicators and by a definition of issues that are to be represented by the indicators. If this step is completed, data suitable for the purpose must be decided on and be collected. The data must then be reviewed, evaluated and assessed (HENSELING ET AL. 1999; LEÓN 2005; MITCHELL 1996).

If data sets or aggregated indicators are the indicator types of choice, the data must then be compiled and represented in a manner adequate to furthering the understanding of the target group. In the case of aggregated indicators, this last step of representation must be preceded by well-founded decisions on the weighting, on adjustments due to unit differences and the handling of trade-offs and conflicting evidence by the data. Variables must be tested for statistical robustness and soundness as well as correlation with other variables used for the indicator to avoid a bias through correlating data. It must be kept in mind that while it is tempting to use a large number of indicators in the set to include most relevant aspects, indicator systems with too many indicators are not suited for practical application (RENN ET AL. 2007). The use of a too large number of indicators reduces the advantages of the indicator type and the understandability and communicability of too many indicators in the set is severely reduced.

5.5 Sustainability Indicators

After the above discussion of basic characteristics and types of indicators, this subsection focusses on indicators to measure sustainability. The scientific nature of data selection and data analysis suggests that scientists or, more generally, experts in the area of sustainability, are responsible for the development of appropriate indicator systems[61]. In the case of sustainability, it may be helpful to create a pool of stakeholders that contribute to the development of indicator sets, that include experts as well as those who have everyday experience of the system and its potential problems, i.e., citizens, corporate representatives, etc., to contribute to the development of indicators. This would be a good way to include best practices, challenges to the implementation and basically applied knowledge about (parts of) the system. This approach has been tried, for example, by the community of Seattle for the evaluation and supervision of their "Sustainable Seattle" program and is rather considered a success (ATKISSON 1996). The UNCED states accordingly, that "In sustainable development, everyone is a user and provider of information considered in the broad sense. That includes data, information, appropriately packaged experience and knowledge. The need for information arises at all levels, from that of senior decision makers at the national and international levels to the grass-roots and individual levels." (UNCED 1992, § 40), thereby strengthening the approach of including data from various sources and levels. The reason for this inclusion of various levels of expertise and applied knowledge is the complexity of the system to be evaluated.

---

61 In this subsection, single indicators will not be discussed as indicator type for sustainable development. Due to the complex and integrated nature of the concept, a single variable will not be able to appropriately describe either the actual situation as a whole nor any changes in the system; therefore they will be left out of the discussion.

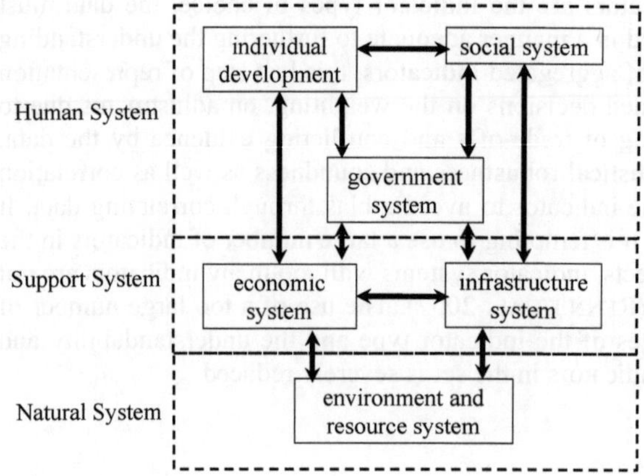

Figure 41: Systems of the anthroposphere
(BOSSEL 1999)

Sustainability as an all-encompassing system in time and space (cf. Figure 31) requires an all-encompassing approach if stocks and flows of the system are to be measured.

The sustainability system consists of three subsystems (cf. Figure 41): the natural system, the human system and, as connection between the first two, the support system. The human system, consisting of the social system, individual development and the government system concerns the superordinate concept of human capital. The natural system, whose parts are resources and the environment, comprise the natural capital. Human capital and natural capital are held together by a support system that includes infrastructure and the economic system (i.e., structural capital or, in other classifications, organizational capital and social capital, cf., e.g., LEANA, VAN BUREN 1999; BOSSEL 1999). Those subsystems influence each other in various ways, so that an evaluation or description of the progress of sustainable development must include not only all systems, but also the links and interactions between them.

The complexity of the general principle makes the development of indicator sets for sustainable development a special challenge. While it has been mentioned before that indicator systems in general should not include more than 30 single indicators if they are to be suited for practical application (RENN ET AL. 2007), 30 indicators seem far too few to describe such a complex system. It is therefore not surprising that most indicator systems for sustainable development include more than 30 variables, and that a very large number of indicator sets have been developed. The database of the International Institute for Sustainable Development (IISD), for example, has a list of more than 600 indicator systems. This list is not exhaustive, but even so, the number is impressive – and it shows that there is no real agreement on the sustainability indicators

(LEÓN 2005). The UNCED (1992, § 40) stated in their 1992 Agenda 21 that "Indicators of sustainable development need to be developed to provide solid bases for decision-making at all levels and to contribute to a self-regulating sustainability of integrated environment and development systems". The European community also claimed, in the year after the adoption of Agenda 21, that "there is presently a serious lack of indicators and environmental assessment material" (MITCHELL 1996, p. 1). Since then, a lot has happened as can be seen by the sheer number of existing indicator sets. The necessary frameworks to:

" (1) place different indicators in context and to organize available information;
(2) assess trade-offs between different dimensions of sustainable development;
(3) help set priorities across different policy areas; and
(4) develop summary or aggregated indicators" (OBST 2000, p. 8)

must be installed, which is a special challenge in an international context. The UN DESA (2007) recommendations for indicators for sustainable development are listed below. Indicators are recommended to be:

(1) Primarily national in scope
(2) Relevant to assessing sustainable development progress
(3) Limited in number, but remaining open-ended and adaptable to future needs
(4) Broad in coverage of Agenda 21 and all aspects of sustainable development
(5) Understandable, clear and unambiguous
(6) Conceptually sound
(7) Representative of an international consensus to the extent possible
(8) Within the capabilities of national governments to develop
(9) Dependent on cost effective data of known quality

Those recommendations are mostly congruent with the general requirements for indicators, but recommendations (1) and (7) are specific for sustainable development indicators. That they should be primarily national in scope is a rather obvious requirement as a reliable data collection will mostly only be possible on a national level. That indicators should be representative of an international consensus is very reasonable, but may be hard to realize because, as has been discussed in several chapters before, the concept of sustainability and sustainable development is interpretable and its realization and interpretations depends on assumptions made and priorities set by those responsible for the implementation. With a concept that is so open to all kinds of interpretations, it is hard to find a consensus about the variables used to measure its success.

One of the indicators that are broadly accepted is the framework of national accounts. It is based on the well-known traditional national accounts, adding environmental resources and assets as well as the idea of human and social capital. The use of national accounts has a number of convincing advantages:

- "It has a long established theoretical structure which has direct links to sustainability;
- Monetary valuation allows comparison of different dimensions of sustainable development and an assessment of their relative importance;
- Its credibility and acceptance make it easier to present sustainable development issues to finance and economics departments in national governments;
- It has well-established links to an existing statistical infrastructure embodying international standards, systems and classifications;
- Its emphasis on internal consistency facilitates the study of policy trade-offs; and
- Its basic structure, and its broad acceptance, limits the need to make normative judgments." (OBST 2000, pp. 8-9)

There are, of course, not only advantages, but also disadvantages of the system that are described as follows:

- "Theoretical accounting difficulties, particularly in the treatment of environmental assets and of human and social capital;
- Practical difficulties in valuing assets and flows which have few relevant markets. More generally, the data needed to estimate environmental and social issues may not exist or be in a useful form;
- The economic perspective on which the national accounts framework builds cannot provide insight into all aspects of sustainable development." (OBST 2000, pp. 8-9)

Despite these objections to the concept, the OECD workshop on sustainability indicators strongly endorsed its use, as it considered its advantages to be convincing. And if the difficulty of finding indicators that fulfill all or at least most of the requirements stated above is taken into account, the acceptance of national accounts as suitable indicators makes even more sense. One must be aware of its shortfalls, though, when valuing the data. Apart from the national accounts, there is also the so-called Pressure-State-Response-Model (PSR), differentiating between Pressure indicators, depicting processes or structures that influence the environment; State indicators describing quality and quantity of natural resources; and Response indicators describing the reaction to environmental problems (HENSELING ET AL. 1999). National accounts and the PSR-model as well as aggregated indicators are the basic forms of sustainability indicators. All indicators must be suitable to control for the effects of measures over time. Short-term impacts on indicators are usually assumed to take place within one to five years after the implementation of a measure. Medium-term impacts are expected within five to ten years, long-term impact is defined as impacts appearing between ten to thirty years after the implementation (TIESSEN ET AL. 2011). This long-term observation is complicated by unpredictable occurrences, and that may distort the results and lead to a wrongly favorable or unfavorable evaluation of the measure. This has to be kept in mind, and a constant review of the variables included in the indicator sets is required.

5.6 The Applied Use of Indicator Systems

After the theoretical discussion of sustainability indicators in subsection 5.5, an incomplete overview over current indicator systems concerning sustainable development shall be given in the following section, with a focus on german and international indicator systems.

5.6.1 Sustainability Indicator Systems in Germany

The official indicators for sustainable development in Germany are the sustainability indicators of the german statistical office. The individual components and their current rating were listed in Table 3. They are divided into four groups: generational justice, quality of life, social cohesion, and international responsibility (STATISTISCHES BUNDESAMT 2012). The indicators for the key thematic fields, combined with target values and time tables assigned to the majority of these indicators, were introduced to measure the effectiveness of policies and strategies towards sustainability (RAT FÜR NACHHALTIGE ENTWICKLUNG 2009). The valuation of the indicators (a target is considered as achieved if the actual value is not more than 5% below target) has been discussed in subsection 3.1. But, even more importantly, the choice of indicators is harshly criticized by some, such as DYBE and WEITH (2004), who state that so far the indicator systems developed in Germany do not fulfil the expectations. The existing indicator systems – as well the ecological as the economic and social indicators – have not much to do with the real social developments. In addition to national indicator sets developed to measure the success of the national sustainability strategy, there are also local indicator sets that were established to measure local Agenda 21 processes. In the first decade after the start of the Agenda 21 process, those indicator sets were developed locally and with more or less expertise. In 2002, a group of regional and national institutions concerned with local Agenda 21 processes has developed a set of 20 indicators that can be used to evaluate the success of the measures implemented. The common indicators have the advantage that they make the results of different communes comparable and simplify the possible transmission of experiences and knowledge from one community to the other. Those indicators are not obligatory and can be supplemented by indicators that are appropriate for specific local or programmatic necessities (AGENDA-TRANSFER AGENTUR FÜR NACHHALTIGKEIT 2003). This indicator set has been continually adapted since its creation in 2000. The adaptation has been furthered by practical experiences of a number of communes (DIEFENBACHER ET AL. 2009).

An alternative concept to measure sustainability in Germany is the HGF-concept that was developed within a project to find reliable indicators to measure sustainable development. The authors participating in the project aimed and still aim to find an integrated concept that analyses strategies and measures not as isolated facts for each dimension, but rather interdisciplinary. The basis for the concept is the four pillar model with institutions/politics as fourth pillar, but the important elements of the models are justice/equality, globality and anthropocentricity. The minimum requirements for the three main aims of sustainable development according to the HGF-concept are:

(1) To secure the human existence
   i. protection of the human health
   ii. ensuring basic services
   iii. ensuring autonomous securing subsistence
   iv. equal possibilities to use the environment
   v. equalizing differences in earnings and wealth
(2) To conserve the societal production potential
   i. sustainable use of renewable resources
   ii. sustainable use of non-renewable resources
   iii. avoiding unjustifiable technical risks
   iv. sustainable development of real, human and knowledge capital
(3) To preserve the possibilities for development and action
   i. equal chances for education, jobs and information
   ii. participation in social decision processes
   iii. sustaining cultural heritage and cultural diversity
   iv. sustaining the cultural function of nature
   v. sustaining social resources" (DIEFENBACHER ET AL. 2009, pp. 34-35).

Another approach to a division of indicators to measure sustainable development in Germany is taken by the official german census report on sustainability that divides the indicators into four groups: generational justice, quality of life, social cohesion, and international responsibility (STATISTISCHES BUNDESAMT 2012). The different approaches to develop indicator sets rely partly on the same data that is usually collected by the federal statistical office of Germany. However, some data is collected independently, and an increasing number of NGOs or other concerned parties collect information with the help of surveys (cf., for example, subsection 5.7).

In summary, the number of measures to determine sustainable development that prominently include social aspects is impressive. Some of the indicator and indicator sets are based on the GDP, using the advantage of a monetary assessment to increase comparability and reduce biases caused by weighting; other indicators are either dimensionless or use a self-created dimension. There is also a group of indicators that abstain from aggregation and let the user of the indicator sets decide on the weight to be placed on every item of the set (cf. Figure 42, where examples for every indicator type are included). Every method has its advantages and disadvantages and it is necessary to decide for every single case of application, whether the advantages outweigh the disadvantages or whether another indicator type should be chosen to correctly assess the result of a measure or the change of the status quo.

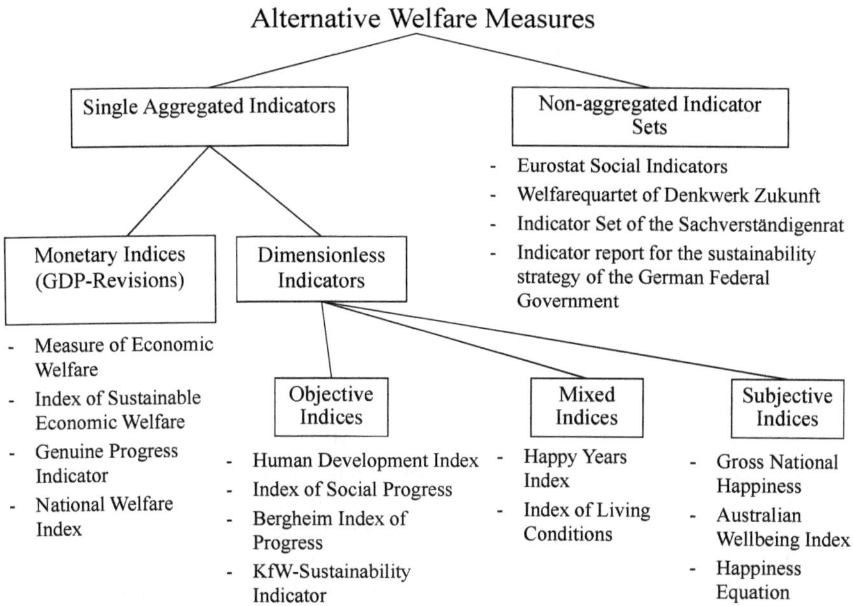

Figure 42: Alternative welfare measures
(ENQUETE-KOMMISSION 2013, p. 299)

5.6.2 International Sustainability Indicator Systems

As discussed in subsection 5.5, the sheer number of existing sustainability indices is overwhelming. Many of the indices are specifically adapted to local or regional sustainability programs, but there is also a large number of international indices – which is commendable as the principle can only be realized on an international level. Internationally used indicators and indicator sets differ strongly from each other, though, depending on the focus of the indicator set (i.e., Ecology, Economy, Industry, etc.). There are indicators that aim at gathering an all-encompassing picture, but most indicators are based on one dimension that is prioritized. On the European level, Sustainable Development Indicators (SDI) as adopted by the European Council are constructed as a three-level pyramid (cf. Figure 43).

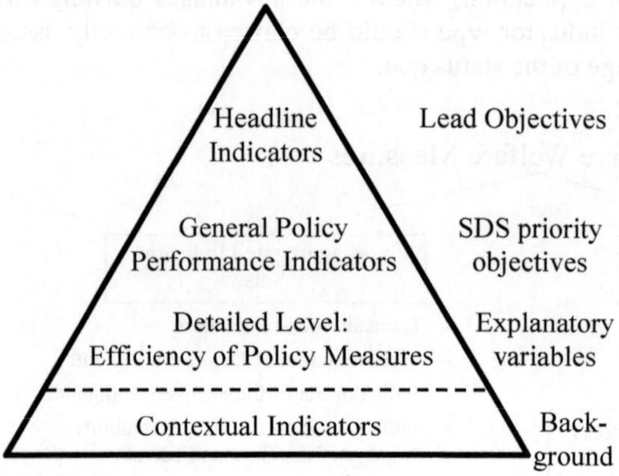

Figure 43: The SDI pyramid of the EU
(WOLFF 2007)

The levels represent the indicator aims specified in the EU Sustainable Development Strategy (SDS), namely overall objectives, operational objectives, and actions. The top of the pyramid depicts the overall objectives, followed by the second level with the indicators to evaluate operational objectives and the third level holds indicators to assess actions taken. Also, contextual indicators are taken into account, but only as background information and as such are not directly represented in the pyramid (EUROPEAN COMMISSION 2007).

Table 12 gives an overview over some of the most commonly used indicators and indices.

The Headline indicators are related to the sustainable development topics of the EU (cf. Table 13). They give an overview over the extent to which the targets for sustainable development have been met in the period of time indicated.

INTERNATIONAL SUSTAINABILITY INDICES		
Indicator Area	**Index**	**Dimensions**
Innovation, Knowledge, Technology	Summary innovation index	Human Resources; Knowledge creation, transmission and application; innovation finance
Development	Human Development Index (HDI)	Health; Knowledge; GDP
	Index of sustainable and economic welfare	Economics; Welfare
Market, Economy	Green Net National Product (EDP) and System of integrated Environmental and Economic Accounting (SEEA)	Natural Resources; Economics; Environment
Eco-system	Sustainability performance index (SPI)	Technical; Ecological, Human Resources
	Eco-index methodology	Economics; Life cycle impact
	Living Planet Index (LPI)	Biodiversity; Ecosystem
	Ecological Footprint (EF)	Natural Resources; National consumption
Environment (policies, nations, regions)	Environmental Sustainability Index	Environmental systems; Stresses; Human vulnerability; Societal and institutional capacity; Global stewardship
	Environmental Quality Index	Environment
	Environmental Performance Index	Policy categories
	Environmental Vulnerability Index	Hazards; Resistance; Damage measurement
Environment (industries)	Eco-indicator	Human health; Ecosystem quality; resources, minerals and fossil fuels
	Green Pro-1	Environmental; Technological; Economical
Industries	Composite Sustainable Development Index (CSDI)	Economics; Environment; Social performance
	Composite Sustainable Performance Index (CSPI)	Corporate citizenship; Environment; Economics
	G score method	Voluntary environment; Health; Safety
	ITT Flygt Sustainability Index	Corporate contribution; Sustainable policies and commitment
Products	Life Cycle Index (LInx)	Environment; Cost; Technology; Socio-political

Table 12: International sustainability indices
(WAHEED ET AL. 2009)

THE EU SUSTAINABILITY INDICATOR SET	
Theme	**Headline Indicator**
Socio-economic development	Growth rate of real GDP per capita
Sustainable consumption and production	Resource productivity
Social inclusion	People at -risk-of-poverty or social exclusion
Demographic changes	Employment rate of older workers
Public health	Healthy life years and life expectancy at birth, by sex
Climate change and energy	Greenhouse gas emissions; share of renewable energy in gross final energy consumption; primary energy consumption
Sustainable transport	Energy consumption of transport relative to GDP
Natural resources	Common bird index; fish catches taken from stocks outside safe biological limits: status of fish stocks managed by the EU in the North-East Atlantic
Global partnership	Official development assistance as share of gross national income
Good governance	n.a.

Table 13: Themes and indicators of the EU sustainability indicator set
(EUROSTAT 2013)

This information is supported by information on the adaptability of the indicators to specific purposes, provided for example by the UN DESA (2007).

The composite sustainable development index by the UN DESA contains topics similar to those cited above. The indicators are divided into 14 groups[62] that used to be allocated to the corresponding dimension of sustainable development. This division is no longer an explicit part of the set though, due to the integrated and multi-dimensional nature of the indicators and the concept of sustainable development (UN DESA 2007). There are not only indices to measure the performance of sustainability indicators, but also indicator sets that aim to measure the success of policies to implement and further sustainable development. The Sustainable Governance Indicators, for instance, aim to measure whether sustainable governing is realized. Therefore, data for 41 countries from the OECD and EU are collected and grouped into three dimensions: the Policy Performance Index, the Quality of Democracy Index, and the Governance Index

62 The indicator groups of the CSDI are the following: poverty, governance, health, education, demographics, natural hazards, atmosphere, land, oceans, seas and coasts, freshwater, biodiversity, economic development, global economic partnership, and consumption and production patterns (UN DESA 2007).

(SCHRAAD-TISCHLER 2014). The EU is working on improving the indicators to make sure they meet the requirements for useful indicators (cf. subsection 5.2) Especially, working groups of the EU, but also cooperating organizations, are concentrating on developing composite indicators, monetary weighting for indicators, improved indicators of sustainable development, environmentally extended Input-Output tables, and, in general, new concepts that might replace GDP as a key indicator and global monitor for environment and security. Those are many fields of work and it is hoped that there are synergies between the different fields (EUROPEAN COMMISSION 2007).

5.7 Wellbeing and Indicator Systems

The previous analysis shall be illustrated by the insertion of an example of a well-researched field of importance to the human existence: wellbeing. This topic is directly related to sustainability inasmuch as the often-cited definition by the BRUNDTLAND COMMISSION that "sustainable development, which implies meeting the needs of the present without compromising the ability of future generations to meet their own needs, should become a central guiding principle of the United Nations, governments and private institutions, organizations and enterprises" (WCED 1987b) refers to the rather broadly interpretable concept of *human needs*. Wellbeing and its measurement are also relevant to the labor market, as a large part of an individual's life is spent working, thus labor has a significant effect on wellbeing. In addition, wellbeing in the work environment is an increasingly important topic in labor-related research (cf. subsection 4.4).

The discussion of wellbeing instead of monetary wealth is also advantageous with regard to the preferences and perceived importance of several factors influencing welfare by citizens. An example for developed countries, where survival or the basic physiological and safety needs are met (cf., for example, MASLOW's *hierarchy of needs* later in this chapter; cf. Figure 45) is cited by JACKSON (2011), who shows the factors influencing subjective wellbeing and happiness as evaluated by a survey in Great Britain in 2011. The most important factor for subjective wellbeing are partners and family, ranked by 47% of the surveyed as the most important factor (cf. Figure 44).

Health is also considered very important, other influences are rated as less influential. Many of the factors do depend on the monetary affluence of the country or the individual. But the survey shows that at least in rather affluent countries, social aspects play a very important role in the assessment of individual wellbeing.

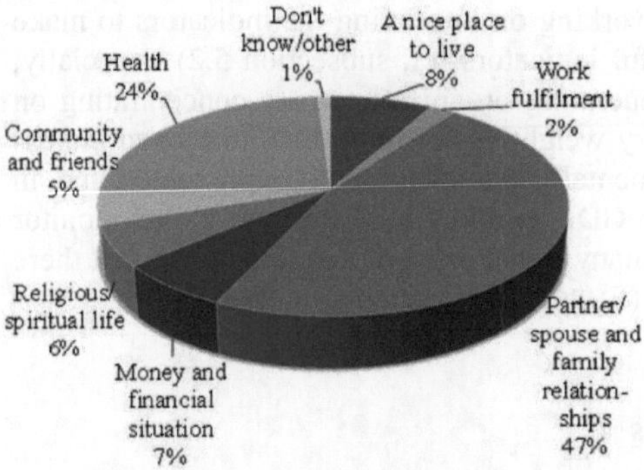

Figure 44: Factors influencing subjective wellbeing and happiness
Data for Great Britain (JACKSON 2011, p. 62)

The results for Great Britain are not transferable internationally or even for all developed nations. But they do offer an indication for the importance of factors other than monetary considerations for wellbeing. The discussion of Wealth and Wellbeing is nothing new for economists as well as philosophers and sociologists. Adam Smith's œuvre *An Inquiry into the Nature and Causes of the Wealth of Nations* (SMITH 1904) is still basic literature for anyone studying economics. The interpretation of the title is a monetary, materialistic approach to wealth, a typical approach to economic topics as well as everyday life that is still very common among scientists today. This is, up to a certain point, plausible, as material wealth and perceived quality of life are closely related. But this postulate of "more is better" is only true at lower levels of material wealth. After a certain point growth does not increase happiness (or wellbeing or utility) (DALY 2007). This can be explained, for example, with the help of MASLOW's hierarchy of needs (cf. Figure 45).

Figure 45: Hierarchy of needs
(MASLOW 1943)

MASLOW (1943) explains that the first needs to be satisfied are the physiological needs that are necessary to maintain the physical integrity. Once those needs are fulfilled, safety needs, such as material safety and professional safety are to be satisfied. The needs that MASLOW argues to become relevant after the fulfillment of the material needs are the immaterial needs, such as friendship and love, but also respect and, finally, self-actualization. The two bottom steps of the pyramid are closely correlated to the income level of the person or, in case of a more generalized view, of a society. The latter three steps are less dependent on the income level.

The theory of the pyramid can be criticized, because in many cases, social needs, for example, already arise when safety needs are not yet satisfied. But the principal idea remains valid, however temporarily interconnected the single steps may be. There is a lack of close correlation between income and happiness, especially in comparisons between countries, independent of their level of fulfilment of needs; even though current measurements of wellbeing, especially monetary indicators, suggest otherwise. The idea that higher income does not mean a higher level of wellbeing or happiness is called the EASTERLIN PARADOXON, after RICHARD EASTERLIN, who in 1974 showed that the association of income and happiness is rather strong on an intranational level (most likely because people tend to consider their relative status in comparison with their immediate environment), but cannot be proven on an international level. This is another reason why wellbeing and happiness must be measured in other terms than the simple aggregation of monetary units in the GDP.

In short, wellbeing is a very complex and multidimensional construct. POLLARD and LEE (2003, p. 59) state that "There are five distinct domains of [...] well-being: physical, psychological, cognitive, social and economic" or a balance between the domains (DODGE ET AL. 2012, p. 230). Apart from the economic domain, the aspects are not measureable in any of the current physical or monetary units, and researcher's attempts to measure it have been sketchy and experimental. The most common measure for wellbeing is the GDP, mainly because of its quantifiability and comparability. However, it is lacking in some very crucial aspects:

(1) Changes in quality are not or only partially incorporated
(2) Public goods and services are included inadequately
(3) Domestic labor, honorary labor and the value of leisure time are not included
(4) Negative external effects of economic activities or natural disasters are included disproportionately and distortingly[63]
(5) Immaterial wealth is not included

63 A typical example for the lack of applicability of the GDP in case of negative externalities is the flood of the river Elbe in 2002: this natural disaster contributed to an increase of 3% of the GDP, caused by the rebuilding of houses, companies and infrastructure. The substantial economic and environmental losses are not included in this indicator (ANGRES 2005).

(6) The distribution of wealth is not considered
(7) The GDP is an aggregated indicator
(8) GDP only includes flows, not stocks
(ENQUETE-KOMMISSION 2013; STIGLITZ ET AL. 2009).

Therefore, new measures for wellbeing have been developed. The 1980s saw a new field of research: happiness economics and happiness research, a socioeconomic approach to measuring welfare and wellbeing.[64] Following the ideas of MASLOW's theory of needs, countries, where the basic needs are fulfilled, should rather focus on policy measures that increase wellbeing instead of measures to increase GDP growth. If the main focus of economic policy was to improve well-being instead of increasing GDP, measures would change radically. For example, more efforts would be bestowed on meaningful employment, reducing poverty and inequality (COSTANZA ET AL. 2012).

Most alternative indicators for wellbeing lack the comparability and the easy quantification of the GDP, though and have not been established as generally renowned measures. Many of them have been tested and adjusted over many years and decades. Some of them are merely theoretical, though, due to difficulties in the data collection or with the weighting. To solve those challenges for the actual utilization of the indicators, which could contribute to a more comprehensive measurement of sustainable development, further research is necessary. There are many monetary indices, but also immaterial indicator sets, the latter usually being more inclusive of the dimensions of sustainability. But the information to be gained from those indicators, and the ensuing valuation of the single indicators in the set or, in the case of composite indicators, the weighting used to transform single indicators with different unities into one indicator, is biased according to the user's values, experiences, preferences and intentions. The factors used to assess the social aspects of sustainability (e.g., wellbeing) also vary between cultures; it is therefore almost impossible to find a generally accepted measure as a base for international political decisions. Those difficulties should not hinder the development of national or regional indicators, though. To assess the progress in sustainable development, it is necessary to rely on dependable information from all dimensions of sustainability. In addition, the development of an indicator or indicator system can give useful insights into the aims that are to be reached and into the importance placed on single aspects.

---

64 Happiness has been a topic of contemplation and research in both oriental and occidental philosophy for millennia, but in philosophy, the aim was the concept itself and the pursuit of happiness. In contrast, socioeconomic happiness research aims to quantify and thereby compare happiness levels and to utilize the findings to implement measures to increase wellbeing.

5.8 Summary

This chapter dealt with the indicators, especially with the basic requirements for building indicators and the conditions that must be fulfilled to make an indicator a "good" indicator, i.e., one that fulfills the informational purpose it is intended for. In order to do so, types of indicators were discussed, the necessary data quality necessary for each type and their advantages and disadvantages were discussed. To illustrate the use of indicators, indicators to measure sustainable development were introduced and indicator use to assess sustainable development in Germany and on an international level were described. As wellbeing is one of the fields were indicators are methodologically on a very high level, and as it is also a relevant aspect for labor market policy, a short introduction into indicator systems measuring wellbeing was made.

6. Evaluation

Evaluation is one area of application for which indicators are indispensable. To assess certain aspects of policy measures, e.g., the success, the requirements, possible challenges, hindrances, the opinions of stakeholders, etc., the method of choice usually is evaluation. To develop indicators and indicator systems, one must be informed about their use and application and the answers the indicator is supposed to provide. It is therefore fundamental to have an insight into the method, which will be given in the following chapter.

6.1 Introduction and Definition

Evaluation or evaluation research is a subdomain of empirical research. It is mainly concerned with the assessment of policy measures or interventions (BORTZ, DÖRING 2006). BUSHNELL, a New Zealand politician, uses "the term evaluation to refer to empirical testing of the strength of the linkage between the outputs (policy) and the outcomes (results) as well as the relationship between inputs and outputs (i.e., testing the technical efficiency of production)" (BUSHNELL 1998). It can be considered a scientific service, and its purpose is to systematically and transparently review a topic. Evaluation aims to assess certain characteristics of an object or program according to a number of criteria (WIDMER 2008) and is often used as a controlling or management tool.

It does have some functions of a subsequent controlling tool, inasmuch that its objective is to provide an analysis of the effectiveness and efficiency of the implementation of a measure. Evaluation can be used for a large number of objects: projects, programs, strategies, initiatives, organizations, institutions, products or persons (WIDMER 2008). It is used to accompany changes and expansions, but also new projects in three main areas: The ex ante analysis of strengths and weaknesses and a projection of the effectiveness of the available methods and processes and their components allows the choice of an appropriate method. The accompanying evaluation aims at detecting possible room for improvement during the implementation of a measure or during a period of change. The ex post analysis aims at evaluating the success and effectiveness of the object. All three include a comprehensive study of possible causes for (in-) efficiencies and successes or failures (ANT 2008a). While evaluation belongs to the methods of the social sciences and has many common features with empirical research in economics, there are also distinct differences. Both approaches aim to explain social phenomena and do so using a combination of theories and observation. Both also share the general aims, namely influencing decisions and decision making through observation, description and recommendations. But evaluation is not an explicit element of economics. Economic recommendations are usually based on predictions derived from models or doctrines, whereas evaluators concentrate mainly on empirical evidence and use techniques from all social sciences to assess and evaluate. PICCIOTTO (1999) describes this difference as the "use of different lenses" for the examination of policy measures.

Evaluation has been around for a long time. In the case of LMP, for example, proofs of early attempts to gather knowledge about the effects and impacts of policy measures in Germany dates back to the early 1930s, where measures used to lessen the impact of the economic crisis of the 1920s were analyzed. Similar analyses can be found in other political fields. Those attempts were not systematical, though, and a solid base for policy research and success controls for policy measures did not develop until the end of the 1960s. Systematic Evaluation of the labor market only developed in the early 1980s. This was due to an increase of unemployment, the according increase of measures to reduce unemployment and the subsequent necessity to gather information on the success of those measures and their efficiency (BRINKMANN ET AL. 2006) to efficiently allocate scarce funds for political interventions. HECKMAN ET AL. (1999) see a strong correlation between the elevated interest in evaluations and the escalation of the costs for welfare states.

The beginnings of the discussion about "good evaluation" date back to the 1960s. The U.S. Evaluation Research Society (ERS) published the renowned "Standards for Program Evaluation" in 1982, while the Committee on Standards for Educational Evaluation based in the U.S. and Canada published their "Standards for Evaluations of Educational Programs, Projects, Materials" that were focused on evaluation in education but were based on a more open methodological approach in 1981. Europe saw a rising importance of evaluation and evaluation standards in the 1990s, the Swiss and German societies for Evaluation (SEVAL, DeGEval) published an adapted and revised version of the American standards for program evaluation published by the Joint Committee in 1999 and 2000, respectively. Other European countries developed their own standards that were not based on the American guidelines (WIDMER 2008). It must be noted that the original conception of an evaluation in the US of the 1960s and 1970 was a basic "knowledge leads to action"-model. The idea was that a policy maker identifies a specific problem that requires solution. He or she lacks the understanding and/or information to decide on an appropriate solution; therefore independent researchers are called in to provide the missing knowledge, which the policymaker then uses to reach a solution (ALBAEK 1995). The problems with the simple "knowledge leads to action" evaluation model are the underlying assumptions: one, that policy making is an accumulation of discrete decisions based only on rationality; and two, that the researchers' knowledge and information is easily available and objectively interpreted (ALBAEK

1995). Both assumptions are arguable[65], thus the simple model is usually abandoned and the more sophisticated models of later decades are commonly used.

6.2 The Tasks of Evaluation

As mentioned above, evaluation is used to precede, accompany and ex post-evaluate programs, standards, measures, etc. Independent of the time of implementation that is chosen for evaluation, the main tasks of evaluation and evaluators can be categorized as follows:

(1) *Perception:* Evaluators collect data on whether the measure was adapted to the target group, about the implementation of the measure, changes in general conditions, causal relations, etc.

(2) *Control:* While aiming to control the implementation of the program to allow for in-time corrections of the process, the data collected also enables evaluators to control the performance of persons engaged in the process.

(3) *Learning:* Evaluation provides information necessary to enhance the dialogue between the different stakeholders of a program or measure by improving transparency.

(4) *Legitimation:* The data collected allows the control for efficiency of the program. (STOCKMANN 2006).

An alternative list is proposed by CHELIMSKY, who states that the purposes of evaluations are the following:

(1) "Measure and account for the results of public policies and programs;

(2) determine the efficiency of programs, projects and their component processes;

(3) gain insights into public problems and into past or present efforts to address them;

(4) understand how organizations work and how they learn;

(5) strengthen institutions and improve managerial performance;

(6) increase agency responsiveness to the public;

(7) reform governments th[r]ough the free flow of evaluative information; and

(8) expand the measurement of results or efficiency from the national to the international scale" (CHELIMSKY 1997).

Many of those tasks are very similar to other methods of social, economic, or socioeconomic research. The methodical approaches of evaluation differ from other socioeconomic test and research methods in the following aspects. Other methods aim to falsify

65 For a discussion of politics and influences on policymakers' decisions see, e.g., chapter 2. A discussion of possible biases and challenges in evaluations follows later in this chapter.

or prove theories or hypotheses. In contrast, an evaluator's objective is to find action alternatives for existing problems, either before the implementation of a measure or during the implementation process in case of occurrence. Instead of the research questions of the evaluator, the information needs of the target group are the focus of the evaluation process. In addition, the strict division between researcher and the object of research that constitutes a necessity in (objective) research is not exercised during an evaluation, thereby rendering the evaluator an active partner in the implementation process. This is inevitable as the evaluators research should directly result in an adaption of the process. Therefore, it is not an object of evaluation to offer a non-judgmental result; rather, a judgment is explicitly demanded. There is also a distinct difference in the primary quality criteria of evaluation: not validity, reliability and objectivity are the most important criteria, but rather communication, intervention, transparency and relevance (STOCKMANN 2006). Nevertheless, the basic rules of research and data collection must be observed, especially if the conclusions of an evaluation are used in political processes, company decisions, etc. In those cases, evaluation will have an extensive impact, so results must be scientific and correct, if significant and helpful for the decisions. Therefore, standards applying to scientific research have been broadened and completed to form standards for evaluation (STOCKMANN 2006). The German Society for Evaluation (DeGEval), for example, maintains that evaluation should be guided by the aim to realize the following attributes: utility, feasibility, propriety and accuracy (BEYWL 2002). Those attributes are specified in 25 standards for good evaluation (cf. Table 14). Those are a combination of STOCKMANN's description of the evaluation framework above, and the rules for sound empirical work.

The use of the evaluations' results can be categorized in three different areas that STAMM (2008) calls *blockade, innovation*, and *alibi*. The *blockade* occurs when a number of reasons prevent a direct use or implementation of the evaluation results. This may be due to mistakes in the evaluation itself, but also due to unexpected results and possibly stakeholders who object to an implementation of the results. A positive and often hoped for, outcome is the *innovation*. This occurs if the aim of the evaluation was to not only assess, but to also concentrate on the implementation of the results. In this case, evaluations might lead to improvements of the object analyzed. In the case of program evaluation, evaluation studies that are expected to control and revise the evaluation object sometimes lead to an obvious use of the results: the implementation of program changes. A suboptimal, but not rare, result is what STAMM (2008) calls the *alibi*, referring to evaluation studies that are only conducted because they are supposed to legitimate a project or program. In this case, unwanted results are simply not published, whereas favorable results (whether they are achieved straightforwardly or whether their outcome is influenced by a bias towards the expectations of the initiator of the evaluation, deliberately or not) are published prominently. This, among other things, prompted the DeGEval to include the "disclosure of findings" (cf. Table 14) as a mandatory rule into their *Evaluation Standards*.

Evaluation Standards			
Utility	**Feasibility**	**Propriety**	**Accuracy**
Stakeholder identification	Appropriate procedures	Formal agreement	Description of the evaluand
Clarification of the purposes of the evaluation	Diplomatic conduct	Protection of individual rights	Context analysis
Evaluator credibility and competence	Evaluation efficiency	Complete and fair investigation	Described purposes and procedures
Information scope and selection		Unbiased conduct and reporting	Disclosure of information sources
Transparency of values		Disclosure of findings	Valid and reliable information
Report comprehensiveness and clarity			Systematic data review
Evaluation timeliness			Analysis of qualitative and quantitative information
Evaluation utilization and use			Justified conclusions
			Meta-evaluation

Table 14: The DeGEval standards
(Beywl 2002)

6.3 Basic Principles of Evaluation

To conduct a successful evaluation that is consistent with the standards for a successful evaluation, it is necessary to meet a number of requirements. It is

(1) Necessary to clearly define the objectives of the measure or the program; and the objectives must be at least partly measurable.
(2) The components of the evaluation must be included in all activities from the beginning.
(3) Precise objectives (cf. (1)) and the content of the evaluation have to be decided on to provide a basis for the choice of adequate methodology of the evaluation.

(4) Adequate and appropriate instruments for the purpose of the evaluation must be applied, their choice and application must observe the rules of transparency and thereby facilitate duplication.

(5) The evaluation process should not only contain quantitative data, but ensure the inclusion of qualitative data such as observations of qualified stakeholders or experts (ANT 2008a, pp. 58-60).

It is essential to note that the consideration of isolated empirical or statistical data is not sufficient when assessing the efficiency of a policy measure. Expert knowledge has to be taken into account to ensure the validity of the results. It is also necessary to conduct follow-up studies to assess long term effects of measures and programs (ANT 2008a).

Evaluators of programs and measures are necessarily dealing with a large number of stakeholders. Their needs and wishes may influence the design and results of the evaluations (cf. subsections 6.7 and 6.8), so it must be clear who they are. ROSSI and FREEMAN (1993) identify ten types of stakeholders in policy evaluations: policy makers, decision makers, sponsors of the evaluation, target participants, program management, program staff, evaluators, program competitors, contextual stakeholders and the evaluation community. All of those have a stake in the evaluation and must be taken into account when conducting an evaluation.

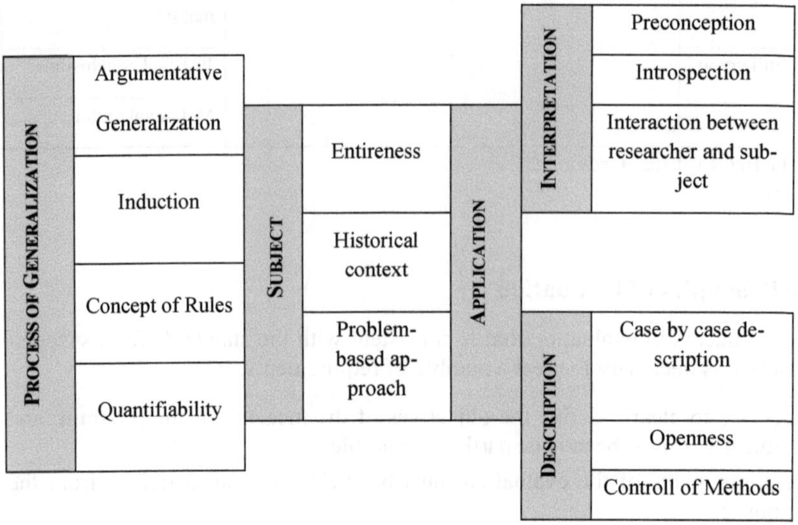

Figure 46: Pillars of qualitative thinking
(MAYRING 1990, p. 14)

A typical way to approach an analysis such as an evaluation is the following: in qualitative thinking, there are three main pillars: the process of generalization, where the overall concept, e.g., the rules or the general quantifiability of the data, is decided on. The second pillar is the subject that must be studied in its historical context and with all its problems. The third pillar consists of the application of the former findings, i.e., the description of the topic or situation to be researched, and the interpretation of the results (cf. Figure 46) (MAYRING 1990).

It is also essential to keep in mind that interpretation of data can vary considerably due to political or social bias. The case of labor market policy provides many such cases and scope for interpretation. If, for example, it is stated that a family is poor, even though the father is full-time employed, different interest groups will draw different conclusions from the situation or assume different possible reasons that need to be approached. A unionist might blame low wages, the feminist may blame a lack of appropriate employment for women, family politicians may assume that the wife is not working because of a lack of daycare for the children; others may blame the inadequate education of the father, etc. (ROCHEFORT, COBB 1993).

If all possible reasons were researched, the bias would be rather low. It is likely that in many cases not only one reason caused a certain result. Research, or in the case of measures or programs, evaluation, must therefore include an overall analysis of possible interpretations. In reality, this is often either prevented by the bias mentioned above or monetary or spatial restrictions. Evaluation of policy measures and programs is complicated by such complex situations with manifold influences, as a single defect may be caused by numerous reasons and can thereby not be corrected with the help of only one measure. Evaluation must therefore always take into account which other measures or influences may have caused a change in the situation the measure to be evaluated is or was to have an effect on. It is, in short, necessary to detect spurious correlations between measure and effect. Traditional evaluation of political programs does not observe this requirement. It rather assumes that a program takes place, then something happens within a black box; afterwards there are some effects which can be analyzed within a cost-benefit analysis, followed by the abortion or repetition of the program (SCHMID ET AL. 1997). This approach may support programs that were not successful, but where the impact of other circumstances, such as other programs that were not considered or an economic boom, led to a favorable result of the cost-benefit analysis; but also to the abortion of programs that do not yield a favorable result of the analysis, but where the non-favorable results were, e.g., caused by a regression, and where without the program, the effects of the regression would have been worse.

Another factor to be considered is the time span of the evaluation. There are measures that only take effect after years, while others might work a lot faster (STEPHAN ET AL. 2006). Evaluation research must therefore also include the dimension of time and take into account that results may only occur long after the assumed completion of a measure. This aspect does not only concern the time span until the final effects of a program or measure are visible and measurable, i.e., in the case of summative evaluation.

It is also relevant in the case of formative evaluation, i.e., evaluation during a measure with the aim to improve the program during its implementation. In this case especially, the evaluator must keep in mind that some effects need time to be measurable, and that some problems during the implementation stage may disappear once a habituation of stakeholders to certain forms of organization or processes has taken place, even without external interventions. In addition, the case of formative evaluation is facing another spatial problem: if there is a large number of participating stakeholders, which is often the case with sustainability programs, a timely adaption is hard or even impossible, if the individual groups or participants may have started the implementation at different times or have planned a time frame for implementation that is not in accordance with that of other similar programs (HEISTER 2008).

When planning an evaluation, it is also necessary to define whether it is to be an Input-Evaluation, a Process-Evaluation, an Output-Evaluation, an Outcome-Evaluation (BLASCHKE, PLATH 2000) or a combination of the four. Input evaluations assess the status quo before the implementation of a measure or the start of a program. Process-Evaluations accompany the implementation or execution of a program, whereas Output-Evaluations assess the status quo after the implementation or execution of the program or measure, referencing it to the results of the Input-Evaluation, if available. The Outcome- or Impact-Evaluation takes a look at the long-term changes resulting from the measure evaluated, including not only direct, but also indirect impact. The latter is especially important to a concept like sustainability, where complexity and long-term consideration are essential. It is also necessary to keep in mind that, apart from the evaluation of intended, expected or anticipated impact of a program, an evaluator should also consider a broader view including unintended and unexpected impacts. In a very complex and interdependent world the narrow view of only assessing intended impacts and results will most likely significantly reduce the validity of the evaluation (WIDMER 2008).

Generally, the self-conception and the standards for evaluations proposed by the evaluation societies in different countries demand certain ethical standards. The guiding principles for evaluators can be summarized as "systematic inquiry, competence, integrity/honesty, respect for people, responsibilities for general and public welfare" (MORRIS 2011). They imply that professional ethics must be followed if the results of the evaluation are to be helpful. Ethics, a concept that applies to all acts and decisions, is as important in evaluation as in other areas of research or politics. Ethics in evaluations can be discussed on three levels: the basic principles of moral behavior, the principles of conduct for members of a profession, and the (scientific) study of values, beliefs and actions connected with moral concerns (MORRIS 2011). To make the standards and guiding principles applicable for most if not all situations that may arise in evaluations, they are rather general. This poses new difficulties, though, as universally valid principles and standards are necessarily open to interpretation, thus inviting the projection of a wide range of values, preferences and opinions onto them (DATTA 2002).

6.4 The Evaluation Process

Usually, an evaluation follows the steps of any assessment or social research. The problem and accordingly the research question(s) are phrased, the research is conducted, the researched data is analyzed and the results are then used (ATTESLANDER, CROMM 2003, p. 22). Transferred to the process of an evaluation, this can be remodeled into a planning level, an execution level, a management level and a use-of-evaluation level (cf. Figure 47).

Those levels are connected, and many aspects belonging to different levels must be conducted at the same time. For example, during the planning stage of the evaluation, it is also necessary to decide about the selection of the evaluator and determining the intended use of the evaluation. During the execution of the evaluation, monitoring is necessary on the management level.

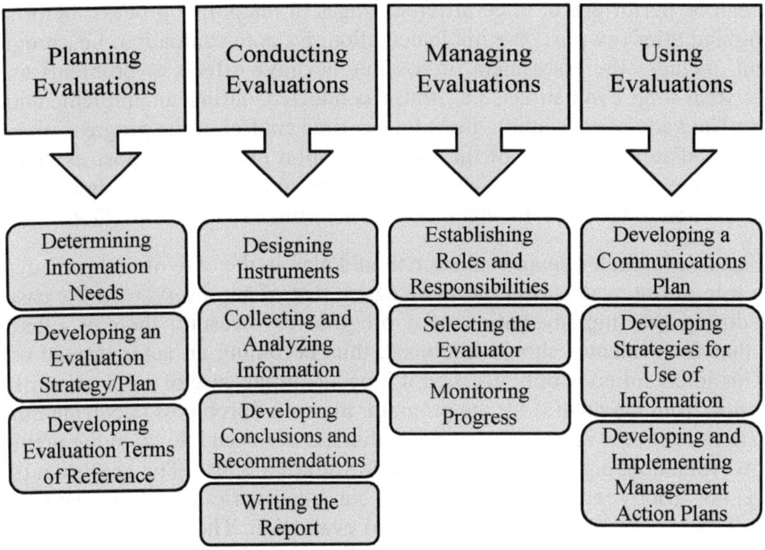

Figure 47: Steps of an evaluation
(SECRETARIAT DU CONSEIL DU TRESOR DU CANADA 2012)

A similarly detailed suggestion for the steps to prepare and conduct an evaluation is given by ANT, who lists the phases as follows:

(1) "setting up the working methodology, procedures, programming and planning
(2) describing the precise objectives of the procedure

(3) choosing and validating the methodology
(4) developing the methodological tools (observation plans, questionnaires, interviews)
(5) executing field analyses
(6) collecting and exploiting data for quantitative and qualitative analysis (general and specific, internal and external)
(7) selecting and establishing the links with the population concerned
(8) writing the reports (conclusions and recommendations)
(9) executing all tasks which are relevant to the project (project management, reporting and suggestions for future improvement)" (ANT 2008a, p. 68).

It must be noted that the above steps are not necessarily consecutive.

Evaluation can be performed at three different stages of the policy process: before (ex ante), during and after (ex post) the implementation. Ex ante evaluation, i.e., program development, includes the assessment of possible negative effects or problems as far as possible. Real-time evaluations, i.e., those conducted during an implementation, have a control and advisory function, including in-time control of the progress, thereby permitting immediate corrections of the implementation process. Ex post evaluation, i.e., the summative evaluation of the effects of the program or measure, is conducted after the completion of the implementation or the measure (STOCKMANN 2006).

It is often discussed which role an evaluator should play in the case of real-time evaluations. The role of the evaluator is, in many cases, that of an observer. In the case of evaluation during the implementation of a program or measure, there is often an agreement that the evaluator should intervene, thus becoming an actor instead of an observer. This intervention is only justified if it occurs in the case of a deviation of the implementation from the goal(s) for the program, in case of problems occurring during implementation, or if new information appears that has not been known in the previous stages of the evaluation, e.g., hidden agendas (HANBERGER 2001). The execution of an evaluation is not strictly regulated and uniform, but rather varies greatly in accordance with the aims and specifications of the object of evaluation. There is a certain framework, though, that includes choices about the different methods and types of evaluation to be chosen. An example for such a framework can be found in Figure 48. The elements of the different steps and principles of an evaluation will be discussed in the following sections.

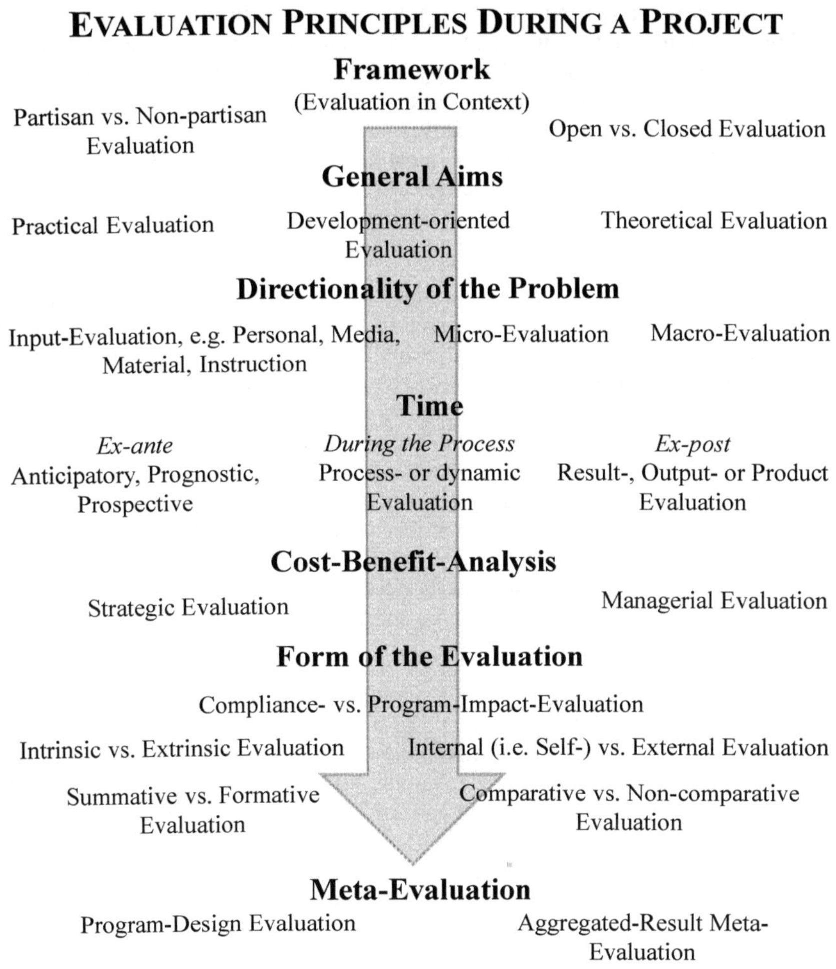

Figure 48: Evaluation principles
(WOTTAWA, THIERAU 1998, p. 32)

6.5 Evaluation Methods

Evaluation as a meta-discipline consists of many sub-disciplines. In the planning phase of an evaluation, the key questions to be answered have to be defined and the appropriate methods have to be chosen. For a success-control, for example, there are four methods possible: micro-econometric evaluation that measures direct effects of the measure on the participating individuals, leaving the possibility to identify effects on an individual, regional or measure-specific base; macro-econometric evaluation that includes indirect effects on non-participating individuals and the economy and is particularly useful when evaluating large programs with expected spillover-effects; efficiency analysis by comparing cost and utility; and implementation analysis. For bigger projects a mix of the methods is likely the most appropriate choice. The evaluator has to keep in mind the possibility that the results of the micro- and macroeconomic evaluations are completely due to negative or positive externalities or spillover effects and include such analyses in the evaluation (BRINKMANN ET AL. 2006).

Within the micro- and macroeconometric methods, it is usually necessary to collect numeric data. Key statistical descriptors have to be described and individual and informed observations have to be made and accumulated to implement both a quantitative and a qualitative approach (ANT 2008a). The proportion of quantitative and qualitative data necessary for a successful completion of the evaluation depends on the specific aims of the project. As a typical trend, social sciences tend to apply the rigid criteria and methods of the natural sciences to their research. That often leads to an unnecessary quantification, or the requirement of quantifiable data in this field of research (ATTESLANDER, CROMM 2003), possibly even in cases where qualitative data would provide much better information. A method that offers an alternative to the commonly used cost-benefit analysis and its necessary monetization of all aspects is multicriteria evaluation (MCE), which can be applied when the monetization is impossible, pointless or undesired (STAGL 2004).

The discussion about the appropriate use of quantitative and qualitative data is one carried out between the so-called positivist and post-positivist evaluators. Positivism assumes that there is a possibility of objective interpretation of reality by using scientific methods, observations and cause-effect-relations. Post-positivism stresses that reality needs more than observation to be understood, and that more theory is needed to interpret possibly diverse cause-effect-relations (KHAKEE 2003). In short, post-positivist evaluators challenge the assumption that a scientific approach to evaluation using scientific methods and logic is more accurate when analyzing socio-political issues than the use of multi-methodological approaches. This does not necessarily imply that positivist, i.e., technocratic, methods must not be used, but that qualitative and quantitative methods must be combined and the assumption of scientific objectivism should still be striven for but with the knowledge that it is unlikely to be realized and the according allowances made (HANBERGER 2001).

It also has to be decided early in the project whether the evaluation should be partisan. DATTA defines a non-partisan evaluation as referring to "(…) an evaluation that is and is regarded by partisans of all persuasions as balanced, fair, and faithful, so that *if methodological quality is high*, debates focus on the implications of the findings for practice or policy, not on the credibility of the findings themselves" (DATTA 2000). A partisan evaluation, in contrast, is therefore an evaluation carried out in the interests of a specific lobby, sponsor or interest group. This is to be avoided as it implicitly means that the evaluation is not balanced and fair and not conducted to meet the standards of evaluation. Partisan evaluations are expected to support a certain view or justify specific programs or measures or to validate catering to a certain interest group. If it is done transparently, then users could integrate the knowledge about the view with which the evaluation is carried out into their assessment and, eventually, their use or non-use of the results. In many cases, though, it is not apparent or only discernible after thorough research, whether the evaluators carried out a non-partisan (and thus, if carried out with the appropriate methodological correctness, trustworthy) or a partisan evaluation. It is important to note that an evaluation can also be partisan without an explicit mandate from a stakeholder. If the evaluator neglects important facts, be it from oversight or on purpose, the evaluation results will be biased and thus only partially useful, if at all.

Another decision to be made is whether the evaluation should be internal or external. These two options are used in different ways by various scientists. ANT explains internal evaluation as evaluation of the internal efficiency of administration and institutions and focuses on the methods, instruments, quality of staff, etc.; thus it is rather a management tool. Accordingly, external evaluation is an evaluation that measures whether a program fulfills its purpose[66] (ANT 2008a). Another use of internal vs. external in evaluations is the decision whether the evaluators are stakeholders, e.g., an official in a ministry who evaluates programs initiated by the ministry itself or an employee in a company who evaluates processes within the company. In contrast, an external evaluation is one that is conducted by professionals who are not stakeholders. A special version of the internal evaluation in the latter sense is empowerment evaluation, defined as "(…) the use of evaluation concepts and techniques to foster self-determination. The focus is on helping people help themselves. This evaluation approach focuses on improvement, is collaborative, and requires both qualitative and quantitative methodologies. It is also highly flexible and can be applied to evaluation in any area, (...)" (FETTERMAN 1994). This approach has the advantage that program staff has the chance of devolving some of the responsibility for the evaluation, and that it empowers program staff to evaluate their own program. But this advantage can also be seen very critically, and it is necessary to keep in mind that program staff is biased. It is therefore only justified to use the results of empowerment evaluation if the bias is strongly controlled and complemented with third-party, i.e., external evaluation (SCRIVEN 1997).

Evaluation is usually a time-consuming process, as the clarification of the goals, the definition of the stakeholders, the collection of the data, etc., are extensive. There are cases though, where a rapid provision of reliable information is necessary, e.g., in cases

66 If an institution or system is internally efficient, a likewise external efficiency is not a given. For example a course for adult education of unemployed people can be well conducted, positively evaluated by the participants, i.e., be internally efficient - and then do nothing to fulfill the actual aim of the program because its content does not meet the requirements of the labor market, i.e., is externally inefficient (ANT 2008).

of humanitarian emergencies, natural disasters, etc. In those cases, real-time evaluations (RTE) or rapid evaluation and assessment methods (REAM) are called for. The REAM and RTE were developed to rapidly evaluate effectiveness and impact of disaster relief (MCNALL, FOSTER-FISHMAN 2007). Those methods are especially challenging, as they are conducted during dynamic processes, often under time pressure and other stress factors. HANBERGER (2001) for example describes RTE as a game where the evaluator knows only that there will be players on the field, but not how the game will be executed, who will win and who will score; and to make things harder the rules of the game may change at any time during the game. Those evaluation situations are therefore to be conducted with a careful consideration for possible bias and errors, and prognoses or several scenarios based on possible developments within the process must be developed. In addition, it is necessary that the continuing process is accompanied by further evaluations to enable timely reactions to changes.

6.6 Types and Models of Evaluation

Models for evaluation are manifold, as is the case with most social research methods. The choice of method depends on the questions of the planned evaluation and on the goals that have been determined. The methods used are well-known in the social sciences, some quantitative, some qualitative, some experimental, others observant, etc., and their use is adapted to the specific evaluation, e.g., by combining the methods. The goals and questions of the evaluation therefore need to be determined as first step of the evaluation, to permit an informed decision on the methods to be applied. CHELIMSKY (1997) divides the evaluation goals into evaluation for accountability, evaluation for development, and evaluation for knowledge.

Evaluation for accountability is expected to answer cause-effect questions, therefore the use of methods needs to take into account the need to link findings to interventions. This can be done by using randomized controlled clinical trials, quasi-experimental methods, controlled or cost/effectiveness approaches or research synthesis, among others. The suggested methods for *evaluation for development* are, e.g., case studies, research synthesis, internal or empowerment evaluations, cluster evaluation, performance measurement and monitoring and stakeholder evaluation. *Evaluation for knowledge* can use any of the above methods or a combination thereof, depending on the research questions. It is necessary to note that all three perspectives could justify the use of all the methods mentioned above, but that different purposes often call for the use of different methods (CHELIMSKY 1997).

A similar approach is used by FOSS HANSEN who sorts evaluation models according to the questions asked. She also differentiates between the goals to be achieved by the evaluation – researching the results, testing for efficiency and effectiveness or whether stakeholders in the program or measure are satisfied, among others (cf. Table 15).

A TYPOLOGY OF EVALUATION MODELS		
Evaluation Models	Questions	Criteria for Evaluation
Result models		
• Goal-attainment model	To what degree has/have the goal(s) been realized?	Derived from goal(s)
• Effects model	Which effects can be uncovered?	Open, all consequences should be uncovered
Explanatory process model	Is the level of activity satisfactory? Are there implementation problems?	Performance is analyzed from idea to decision and implementation and to the reaction of the addressees
System model	How has performance functioned as a whole?	Realized input, process, structure and outcome assessed either in relation to objectives in same dimensions or comparatively
Economic model		
• Cost-efficiency	Is productivity satisfactory?	Output measured in relation to expenses
• Cost-effectiveness	Is effectiveness satisfactory?	Effect measured in relation to expenses
• Cost-benefit	Is utility satisfactory?	Utility measured in relation to expenses
Actor model		
• Client-oriented model	Are clients satisfied?	Formulated by clients
• Stakeholder model	Are stakeholders satisfied?	Formulated by stakeholders
• Peer review model	Is professional quality in order?	Formulated by peers
Program theory model (theory based evaluation)	What works for whom in which context? Is it possible to ascertain errors in program theory?	Program theory is reconstructed and assessed via empirical analysis

Table 15: A typology of evaluation Models
(FOSS HANSEN 2005)

Another approach for a classification of evaluations is suggested by CONTANDRIOPOULOUS and BROUSSELLE (2012) who develop a method to contrast evaluation models using two dimensions: the cost-sharing equilibrium and the level of issue polarization. The first dimension refers to a possible bias caused by the financiers of the evaluation. In theory, this should not make a difference in the conduction and use of an evaluation. In reality, though, commissioners of evaluations are often given more influence, thus possibly creating a bias (HANBERGER 2001). The second dimension refers to the level of interest the topic provokes in stakeholders and other groups. If, for example, an issue is not rousing much discussion or interest outside the small world of the program, company or measure evaluated, then the level of polarization is rather low. If the topic is relevant for others outside the program, then it is not unlikely that they will try to use the results of the evaluation.

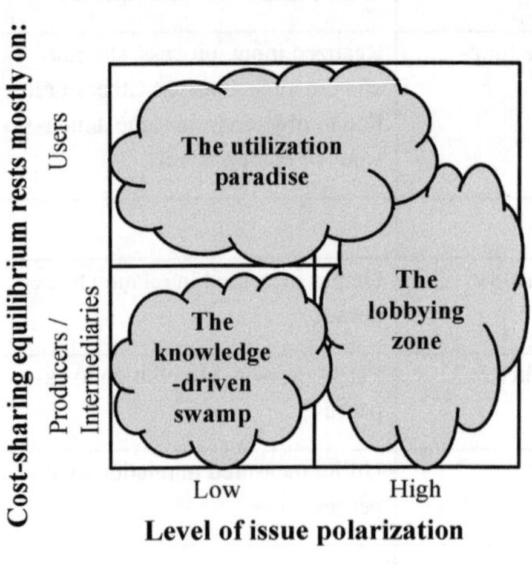

Figure 49: Classification of evaluations
(CONTANDRIOPOULOS, BROUSELLE 2012)

The combination of the two dimensions then provides four possible outcomes (cf. Figure 49): (1) the cost-sharing equilibrium mainly rests on the producers of the evaluation and the level of polarization is low; (2) the cost-sharing equilibrium mainly rests on the producers of the evaluation and the level of polarization is high; (3) the cost-sharing equilibrium mainly rests on the users and the level of polarization is low; and (4) the cost-sharing equilibrium mainly rests on the users and the level of polarization is high.

(1) is described by CONTANDRIOPOULOUS and BROUSSELLE as the "knowledge driven swamp", (3) and (4) are considered the "utilization paradise", and (2) and partly (3) are the lobbying zone. This classification of evaluations is especially relevant for evalua-

tions of policy measures and programs, as it gives an idea of the possible use of the outcome.

CHELIMSKY (1997) points out that the evaluations that are conducted with the goal of gaining knowledge, i.e., for example, part of the knowledge-driven swamp, are those that are usually conducted without much hope of use. They are nonetheless very important as those evaluations are the ones that are the most likely to eventually cause democratic reform.

6.7 Challenges to Evaluation

Evaluations are an established instrument for the assessment, but also the preparation and supervision of programs and measures. As those measures and programs are not conducted in a vacuum, they are facing the problems of all social research projects: a complex, interdependent, ever-changing world with external effects, actors with self-interests, etc. In addition, evaluators usually face situations where the interests of all stakeholders do not coincide. The suggestion that all stakeholders should reach a consensus implies that there is one single truth or reality of the problem treated - which is not always the case (PALUMBO, HALLET 1993). Those two kinds of challenges – the methodical and the individual/human factors – shall be discussed in the following sections.

6.7.1 Methodical Challenges

The methodical challenges for evaluations are, as mentioned above, those that every social science research project faces. There are the statistical problems accompanying every analysis of data, and the difficulties of the data collection itself. Depending on the kind of evaluation conducted, experiments and comparative tests may be a method chosen to conduct the evaluation. One of the basic problems of microeconomic counterfactuality, i.e., that one individual cannot be participant and non-participant in a measure at the same time (BLASCHKE, PLATH 2000). This problem is often eliminated by choosing a control group of non-participants (FITZENBERGER, SPECKESSER 2000). In the case of many policy measures, this poses another difficulty, though: the selection bias or „creaming“[67], as it is called in the case of labor market policy, for example. This selection bias is caused by the selection criteria for participants that may lead to an inclusion of those that are more likely to succeed with the help of the program,

67 Creaming effects are selection effects or biases caused by administrative selection, because the participants for a measure may be chosen on a subjective expectation of who is best suited for a successful reintegration in the labor market, thus causing a self-fulfilling prophecy. This must be considered when evaluating measures (LUSCHEI, TRUBE 2000). In addition, creaming occurs when participants for a measure or program are chosen based on particular criteria.

thus leading to exaggerated positive results of the comparison. On a macro-level, for example in the case of estimating the reference value by doing a before- and after-the-program evaluation, the possibility of exogenous influences must be considered, i.e., the occurrence of external effects that may lead to an improvement or degradation in the assessment of an individual but that are not causally related to the program (POTIER 1998). The latter difficulty is aggravated by the time-ranges that are typical with policy measures. Time ranges considered in forecasting and trying to determine future developments range between a few months to four or five years (which usually corresponds to a policy cycle) or, in some cases, up to 20 or 30 years. All predictions and forecasts are either very fragile and prone to errors due to unexpected events changing the original condition (e.g., natural disasters, wars, changes of political systems, behavioral changes of the society, etc.) if they are too long-ranging; or of limited informational value, if they are too short-ranging. With political measures, there is also a risk of a substitution effect (i.e., beneficiaries of a subsidy abandon activities on the free market) or crowding out, i.e., the government providing services that the market would have provided without their interference (STEPHAN ET AL. 2006).

6.7.2 Human Challenges

Apart from the methodical challenges that every evaluation faces, there are also a number of human aspects that need to be considered. It can often be observed that planners and regulators fail, even if a large and possible sufficient amount of information is available to them. This is often the case not only because of their own failures in predicting the consequences of their policies or projects. They are also dealing with a target group that is difficult to predict, but also reflective and responding intelligently to planning and predictions, thereby creating self-fulfilling or self-confounding "prophesies", especially in those cases where the policymakers attempt to push society and citizens in a particular direction, i.e., for example, altering their habits or behavior (DRESNER 2008). This unpredictable reaction to measures is only one aspect of the challenge and is not directly related to the evaluation, but rather to the project and its planning, implementation and outcomes itself. There is also another dimension, though – influences on the evaluation itself. Those are especially interesting because they must be acknowledged and, if possible, eliminated to ensure a valid and reliable evaluation. There are three groups of stakeholders that can complicate the execution of an evaluation: the program staff, the financiers/clients and the evaluators themselves. The program staff may resist the evaluation, or, in the worst case, make it more difficult by holding back information. This can be due to a fear that the results of the evaluation may lead to a non-continuation of the program, thus endangering the jobs of the program staff. But resistance to evaluation may also partly be due to a general psychological anxiety to be evaluated (DONALDSON ET AL. 2002), however unsubstantiated that fear may be. This opposition can be reduced by a very open communication of the aims of the evaluation or by demonstrating fairness and impartiality.

The second group of stakeholders is the financiers or clients. It has been discussed in former chapters that politicians can be described as parts of a principal-agent system, where they are the agents that should fulfill their principals' assignment, but have their own agenda. They may therefore try to bias the evaluation towards their own interests to make sure that unwanted results are either not reached or not published. Another aspect of the financier's influence on evaluations are the time frames. A measure may only show its full impact after a longer period of time, but as political cycles are short[68], there is a risk that evaluations take place before the full impact of a program is observable, thus possibly leading to a discontinuance of effective programs or the continuance of ineffective ones.

The third group that may influence the outcome of evaluations are the evaluators themselves. If they are consciously or unconsciously influencing the results of their evaluation, the evaluator bias can be considerable. This is the case, for example, if important stakeholders are not taken into account, if relevant data is neglected or if unrealistically positive or negative estimations of further development are included in predicting future outcomes. In addition, to successfully conduct an evaluation, an evaluator needs sound knowledge of quantitative and qualitative methods, but also of the project to be evaluated to make sure that no complex connections and correlations are overlooked. The standards for good evaluation practice of several national organizations for evaluation aim at reducing the evaluator's bias, and the continual reviewing of evaluations and evaluators by their peers also serves to secure and improve the quality of evaluations.

6.8 Policy Evaluation

Policy evaluations should not differ much from any other evaluation. But the evaluation of policy measures and programs faces a number of challenges and characteristics. Some of them have been discussed above, for example the time-frame for the evaluations and the possible self-interest of policymakers. It has to be kept in mind that politics usually are a multi-actor game. Therefore, evaluation should include all actors, active or passive (HANBERGER 2001). The job of an evaluation is not only to uncover the effects and efficiency of policy measures, but also to inform. As PICCIOTTO (1999) states, "Public policy is informed both by economics - the queen of the social sciences - and by evaluation - the overarching meta-discipline." He concludes that evaluations should serve to decrease information asymmetries between principals (i.e., in the case

68 If an election takes place every four years, for example, then evaluations would be needed in advance of the end of the election period, as they may be used in election campaigns – either in favor of the ruling party(s) or to criticize them. Taking into account the duration of a methodically sound evaluation, if a measure is implemented at the beginning of the political cycle and shall then be evaluated in time for the election campaigns, it is obvious that an evaluation often only considers short- and, if at all, medium-term impact of measures and programs.

of policy evaluation: the people) and agents (i.e., the state). The questions that politicians may ask are, for example, the following: "How will pursuing this outcome affect the others we are interested in? What effect does this output have on the desired outcomes? What would be the cost of the output in the future? How can we get more output for the same level of inputs? How should our agencies be organized?" (BUSHNELL 1998) The questions do not differ greatly from those asked from program managers or other institutions that look to evaluation to answer their questions about effects and efficiency of programs and measures. In politics, though, the playing field is far larger, the intended and unintended effects usually affect a larger group, and the dimension of measures is far greater in financial as well as personal and institutional aspects. At the same time, an evaluation is complicated by the large number of concurrent measures that may or may not have an impact on the subject to be evaluated, the number of possible external shocks that may occur, etc.

Another specific element for policy measures are the two levels of program or policy implementation: the political, administrative and financial implementation; and the 'street level' implementation. The former is often called the managerial level implementation (BARBIER, SIMONIN 1997). Evaluations must therefore include both levels. In addition, evaluations of policy measures are often a combination of all three types of evaluations: ex ante, ex post and accompanying the implementation. A general model of target-oriented policy evaluation is the one below (cf. Figure 50).

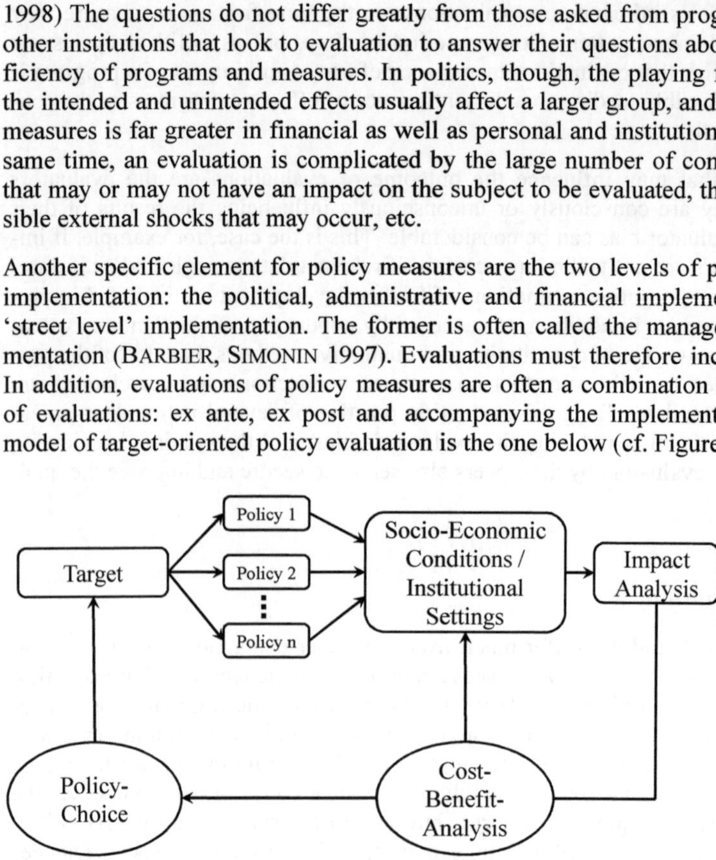

Figure 50: Target-oriented policy evaluation
(SCHMID 1997)

The first step is the (1) identification of the target(s). This is to be done on the basis of an analysis of market failures. Then (2) the policy measures are decided upon, their impact and the implementation process itself being influenced by the (3) socio-economic and institutional conditions. This includes the organizations involved in administering the programs, but also network structures (internal as well as external) and feedback loops concerning the outcomes. This is followed by an (4) impact analysis, i.e., the analysis of policy adoption by observing financial and physical flows that are immediately recognizable and a (5) cost-benefit-analysis that must include opportunity costs[69]. SCHMID concludes the cycle with the final (6) policy choice and the assessment whether the (1) target has been reached.

This cycle can be adapted for ex ante, accompanying and ex post analyses. In the case of ex ante evaluations, (2) is simply the number of possible measures that are assessed and whose impact is to be predicted; (3) are predicted conditions or, in the case of the institutional aspects possibly known conditions; the analyses (4) and (5) are estimates that are the basis for the final policy choice (6). For an accompanying evaluation, the policy measure must be chosen in the second step, but the cycle can be repeated as often as the budget and time frame allow: in theory, the chosen policy is adapted or, in the most extreme case, even changed if the analyses show that the measure chosen was not appropriate or useful. In practice, this is a highly unlikely course. Policy measures have been decided upon in an often time-consuming and predetermined decision process and it is improbable that a measure can be easily adapted. Secondly, as mentioned above, there is the aspect of time. If the impact of a measure is only observable after a certain length of time, then an accompanying evaluation may rule out policy measures that would have been effective. Therefore, accompanying evaluations will usually only evaluate the implementation and such measures as are easily adaptable. Ex post evaluation leaves out step (2), as this has been predetermined. Step (6) may include recommendations for future choices of policy measures.

HANBERGER (2001) claims that the relevant questions to be asked in the evaluation of policy measures are the following: "What is the context? Who are the key actors and other stakeholder? What is the policy problem? What are the relevant variables and outcome criteria?" During the decades, several recommendations for politically relevant evaluations have been made: in the 1970s, BANNER ET AL. (1975) recommended that the evaluator should be completely independent and that the evaluator(s) should be well-trained and able to draw from an "invulnerable source of adequate funds". They also support a very open approach to the evaluation and the communication and discussion of possible outcomes of the evaluation as well as the corresponding implications. In the 1980s, PALUMBO (1987) stresses the importance of recognizing the "different information needs by different stakeholders at different times in the policy cycle" when conducting an evaluation with political relevance. HEDRICK (1988) suggests specifying the full scope of issues to be considered, even if it is impossible to include everything in the actual evaluation. He also stresses that limitations to the evaluation must be stated clearly and that the presentation of the results must include non-technical statements to make sure they are understood by all stakeholders. In the same vein, TURPIN (1989) reminds evaluators to always discover which stakeholder has

69 Opportunity cost is the utility of the best alternative that has been forgone in favor of the chosen option.

which motivation and to make sure that all stakeholders are included in some way to prevent a biased evaluation. He also agrees with HEDRICK in his recommendation of an open discussion of limitations and difficult decisions.

6.9 Evaluating Labor Market Policies

The evaluation of policies and political measures has been discussed in general in subsection 6.8 above. The example of the evaluation of labor market policy and the according measures shall be discussed a little more detailed, as it is one of the basic utilizations for labor market indicators.

6.9.1 Labor Market Policy Evaluation

The approach to labor market policy and its evaluation is similar to the approaches discussed in the chapter above. A certain target is set; an appropriate policy is chosen which is then implemented. The effected measures then lead to the take-up of the policy, i.e., specific actions are carried out within the program or measure. This affects the labor market and therefore the target which can, in turn, be evaluated (cf. Figure 51). This proceeding is simplified, though. It neglects, for example, exogenous influences that may have an impact on the target.

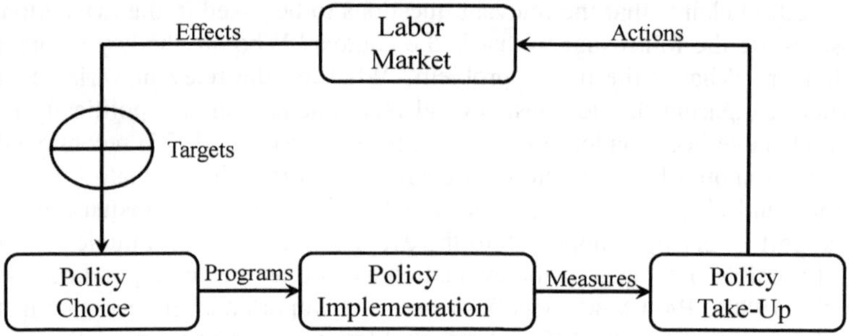

Figure 51: The policy evaluation cycle
(SCHMID 1997)

The simplified approach to labor market policy evaluation is the goal- or target-oriented evaluation described in subsection 6.8. This method adds to the traditional, program oriented evaluation the possibility to include processes of the political development of the measure as well as the socioeconomic context and the conditions of the implementation, allowing the inclusion of secondary objects into to the evaluation process (BANGEL ET AL. 2006).

But even in the first step, the setting of the target, evaluation is relevant. It must not only assess ex post whether targets have been reached, it must also discuss ex ante, whether the targets are appropriate and clearly defined. This includes the discussion whether there is a plurality of measures that may influence the same issue in opposed ways (BLASCHKE, PLATH 2000). To better understand the process of the implementation and evaluation of labor market policy measures, it is helpful to gain an overview over the organization, i.e., the institutional basics, of labor market policy. Generally, there are three elements of institutional frameworks for individual policies (cf. Figure 52).

(1) Policy regimes, i.e., the policy outcome of the different campaigns of the groups involved;
(2) Organizational regimes, i.e., the element providing the financial framework and the administrative infrastructure necessary for the implementation of programs and measures; and
(3) Incentive regimes, i.e., context conditions influencing the "adoption of policies in the target area" (SCHMID 1997).

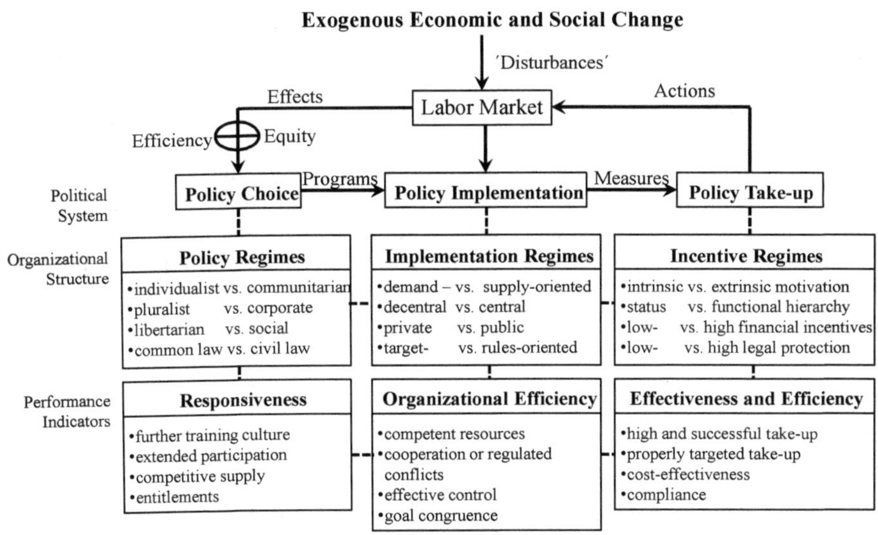

Figure 52: Analytic framework for the evaluation of labor market policy organization
(SCHMID 1997)

For each of the elements there are a number of organizational structures. Policy regimes, for example, can be individualist or communitarian, libertarian or social etc; whereas implementation regimes can be, e.g., demand- or supply-oriented, private or public, or target- or rule oriented. Incentive regimes aim for example at either intrinsic or extrinsic motivation, high or low financial incentives or concentrate on status hierarchies or functional hierarchies. Depending on the regime, there are different performance indicators. For policy regimes, the responsiveness is monitored, implementation regimes are assessed by their organizational efficiency; and incentive regimes can be evaluated for their effectiveness and efficiency. The questions regarding LMP and the according policy measures which evaluation is expected to answer concern, for example, the effectiveness and efficiency of the programs and measures. To determine those dimensions, the impact and the costs (including opportunity costs as well as the costs for possible external effects) must be measured. The measurment of impacts proves a formidable challenge, though. Traditional LMP evaluation focused on individual policy instruments and programs; mostly by comparing the goals of the programs with the outcomes. In those traditional evaluations, the formation of the policies and the process of implementation are treated, as SCHMID (1997) calls it, as a black box. The comparison of goals with outcomes is often conducted as a basic cost-benefit analysis. If costs are higher than the benefits, then the project is considered as not successful. If the benefits are higher than the costs, the project was successful, but can still be less successful than a different measure with an even better cost-benefit balance. In theory, it would also be necessary to measure whether the non-execution of a program or measure would have led to even higher costs through inaction. If this were the case, then a measure that has higher costs than benefits, but a better balance than that of the non-program case, may still be continued for a certain time. But cost-benefit analysis has a distinct disadvantage: it assumes that costs and benefits are measurable in a common unit (preferably monetary). As has been discussed in subsection 4.1, benefits of labor market policy do not only regard direct influences on individual and national income, but also on individual wellbeing (cf. subsection 5.7), an aspect that is only measurable in some of its direct results (e.g., better health, thus lessening the costs for the health system), but not in its entirety and not in monetary units.

In addition, there are other risks of traditional evaluation concepts. First of all, success indicators tend to concentrate on the supply side of the measure, i.e., on the continuance of participants and the incorporation rate into the first labor market, thereby ignoring possible changes on the demand side, namely the regional labor market situation or socioeconomic determinants of the labor market development. Secondly, to compare the impact of different policy measures, evaluators tend to concentrate on a number of basic quantifiable indicators, thereby neglecting special characteristics of the particular program. Thirdly, there is a danger of confusing financial control, evaluation and monitoring. Fourthly, the risk of counterproductive impact of evaluation has to be kept in mind. This is, in general language, often called "learning for the test", i.e., figuratively the tailoring of projects and measures to meet the targets for evaluated indicators (e.g., by constructing measures only for the unemployed most capable of competing on the job market), thereby risking the neglect of other dimensions or aspects that have been overlooked in the choice of indicators. Fifthly, there is a risk of neglecting complex interwoven institutional situations (e.g., competition with other labor market programs, difficult implementation, etc.) as well as risk of neglecting superior purposes while concentrating on minor, attributable targets (BANGEL ET AL. 2006).

In summary, it is necessary to acknowledge that the evaluation of active labor market policies is not comprehensive; and that it is impossible to draw absolute conclusions from the data researched. What evaluation can do, for example, is to show that policies can have a positive impact; labor market policy is therefore not useless. Also, it can show that a well-chosen combination of measures leads to the best results (IMMERVOLL, SCARPETTA 2012). As for the actual execution of labor market policy in Germany, it can be said that in general, it does not differ much from the development of evaluation as a whole. Starting from the 1980s, the German Institute for Employment Research (IAB), for example, conducted studies to evaluate immediate and continuing effects based on data accrued in the process of administration (BLASCHKE, PLATH 2000). In 2003, the German Ministry for Economy and Labor (BMWA) authorized a project group for evaluations in the Ministry. The group was expected to assess previous evaluations realized in the ministry and to compare them with international evaluation standards; with the aim to know how a good evaluation should be performed and which expectations the ordering party may have (LORENZEN 2008). This project was a considerable step towards an institutionalization of evaluations, as in the beginning of the 1990s evaluation was not utilized in the Ministry at all. For laws and measures to be passed there were impact assessments; but those were not universally structured after objective, general criteria. This changed, though, and by now all laws and labor market programs have to be evaluated independently (WEILAND 2008).

6.9.2 Challenges for the Evaluation of Labor Market Policy

The evaluation of labor market issues faces the same procedural challenges as other evaluations. But the organization and institutional conditions of the labor market lead to a number of aspects that must be considered when assessing the effects of labor market measures and programs. The aspects to be considered are methodical, but also spatial and political. It is also necessary to consider information- and complexity challenges. The assessment of labor market policy impacts is often done in the conventional approach, i.e., in the form of measuring the number of participants who find employment after the program or measure, or in the form of earning effects for participants. This approach neglects the evaluation of wider policy impacts on the whole labor market. Issues to be addressed in this context are creaming effects, deadweight effects/windfall profits[70], substitution effects[71], unintended side-effects, for example

70 Deadweight effects or windfall profits occur, e.g., when subsidized persons that would also have been hired without the subsidies, are hired.

through crowding out[72] or market distortions by supporting certain industries with subsidized employees, creating an advantage over companies not benefiting from subsidies; and last but not least the consideration of opportunity costs (SCHMID 1997). Opportunity costs are often neglected as the determination whether the money spent would have been more effective in a different project, i.e., if a different measure would have had a bigger impact (HUJER ET AL. 2000), is often neither politically desirable nor statistically realizable, as the potential impact of other measures that could have been conducted but were decided against cannot be put in numbers.

Another methodical challenge is the analysis of causalities. A typical example in labor market discussion is the analysis of well-being in connection with unemployment rates: does unemployment make unhappy? Or do unhappy people tend to become unemployed because of their unhappiness (OESCH, LIPPS 2011)? The same goes for the impact of measures. To offer reliable results to policy makers it is necessary to determine whether a program or measure was responsible for the results measured. This is made difficult by the fact that there is no monocausal explanation for unemployment; and usually no monocausal explanation for the transition from unemployment into employment (WEINBERG 1999). The elimination of counterfactuality, i.e., the fact that one individual cannot be participant and non-participant in a measure at the same time, can usually be accomplished by using a control or comparison group (BLASCHKE, PLATH 2000). The organization of programs and measures as experiments implies the random choice of participants and non-participants out of a group of potential participants. Experiments are the simplest option for an evaluation with a control group, because the random choice of participants and control group prevent systematic differences between the two groups. The difficulty with experiments is, though, that they are politically not feasible, because the random assignment of participation in measures can hardly be communicated to voters (EICHHORST, ZIMMERMANN 2007). In addition, the results of singular or isolated experiments are not necessarily transferable to other regions or situations. Depending on the size of the experiment, the specific situations in different regions, different times (e.g., different stages of the economic cycle) or different groups of participants, the results are not conferrable.

An alternative to experiments is the creation of artificial control groups by using matching-methods. Choosing a control group that is as similar to the participants as possible is a more feasible option, but does have the disadvantage that the artificial control group corresponds with the participants only in some observable characteristics. This may lead to the oversight of potentially relevant explanatory characteristics, and thus to non-reliable results. The evaluation of both methods, experiments and matching, are often also complicated by a small number of cases. This makes it harder

71 Substitution effects are the effects of participants being hired instead of non-participants, but the total number of employees has not changed, thus simply causing redistribution, not an increase in employment.

72 Crowding out can occur for example by using taxes that companies may have put to better use.

to draw reliable conclusions as to the effectiveness of a measure (WEINKOPF 2002). If neither matching nor an experimental design can be applied, then the efficacy of the measure in terms of differences in the outcome between participation and non-participation cannot be evaluated (EICHHORST, ZIMMERMANN 2007). All methods of labor market evaluations also face a different problem: much time was and is spent on finding the perfect estimators and methods of measurement; but too little time is spent on considering the quality of the data used as a base for the estimators and measures. This neglects the fact that even an almost perfect econometric model cannot compensate inadequate and unreliable data (SMITH 2000). It is therefore necessary to define the data necessary to measure impacts, effectiveness and efficacy and to collect this data in the necessary quality.

A second aspect of labor market policy that complicates the evaluation of the measures is the number of stakeholders and their specific interests. As financiers as well as project workers and "clients", i.e., the intended beneficiaries of the measures, but also supervisors and scientists have an explicit stake in the success of a program, their information and impressions must be considered in an evaluation. But as every stakeholders' interest in a program differs from that of the other stakeholders (a financier may be interested in an optimal rate of transmission into regular employment or low costs, instructors may be interested in being considered successful to ensure their employment be securing future students, etc.), their own interests and the possible bias through their priorities must be included in the evaluation. The next aspect to be considered is the complexity not only of measures, but also of the evaluator groups. In the first case, if the measures are composed as network of measures, an evaluation is often complicated by the sheer size of the network. In the case of EQUAL, for example, a community initiative that supported innovative, transnational projects that were aimed at reducing discrimination and disadvantages in the labor market[73] (EUROPEAN COMMISSION EQUAL 2008), 129 partnerships were included, and each partnership had an evaluator. In addition, there was an evaluation to oversee the single evaluators. The third assessment level in this project network was an evaluation on the european level that included the results of the national evaluators. On every level, evaluators did not only evaluate the evaluators on the lower levels, but also conducted their own evaluation of the projects (HEISTER 2008). This is without doubt an extreme example, but it is not rare that evaluators from different institutions have to work together to conduct a very complex evaluation, such as in the case of the Hartz-Evaluations in Germany, where different research institutions worked together on a joint report, and the outcomes do not only depend on their expertise, but also on their cooperation. Evaluations where a number of evaluators work together are usually fulfilling what can be called the joint venture between science and praxis for the evaluation of labor market policy. Often, the methodical specialty of one evaluator and the experience of a second one

73 EQUAL's main topics were increasing employability, encouraging inclusive entrepreneurship, facilitating adaptability, promoting gender equality, integrating asylum seekers (EUROPEAN COMMISSION EQUAL 2008).

complement one another and increase the reliability of the results. This is often necessary in the case of labor market policy, as the system is complex; and measure and target groups are very heterogeneous (BRINKMANN, WIEßNER 2002).

The third challenge that evaluators of labor market measures face are time aspects. Many programs are developed and funded for only a certain period, and their continuation depends on the results of an evaluation. But results of measures are often only visible sometime after the completion (BOUIS ET AL. 2012); and long-term impacts cannot be assessed until a few years at least after the conclusion of a measure. As the allocation of funds of programs of the European Social Fund (ESF) programs, for example, where funding periods usually last six years, is partly based on the results of programs in the preceding funding period, evaluations must often be conducted before the program is completed or before at least medium-term conclusions can be drawn. Summative evaluations are therefore often too late to influence the decisions and are rather academic research than evaluations with impact on decisions (HEISTER 2008). A similar schedule occurred with the evaluation of the Hartz reforms in Germany. The substantial labor market reform dubbed after one of its drafters was to be thoroughly evaluated; therefore an evaluation was commissioned in November 2002 and was expected to be completed four years later. In 2005, there was to be an interim report (HEYER 2006). This was a very extensive evaluation, but the time frame shows that it was impossible to draw reliable long-term conclusions from the results of the evaluation. The Four Laws for Modern Services in the Labor Market, as the four parts of the Hartz reform are called were passed in December 2002 (First and Second Law) and December 2003 (Third and Fourth Law). The First and Second Law came into effect in January 2003 (BGBL. I 2002). The Third Law came into effect in January 2004, and the Fourth Law in January 2005 (BGBL. I 2003a, 2003b). The laws include an obligation to scientifically evaluate all measures of the activating labor market policy. In compliance with this obligation, a comprehensive data base was developed that also takes into account the heterogeneity of the participating groups (CALIENDO, STEINER 2005). In short, the laws came into effect in 2003, 2004 and 2005 with an interim report due in 2005 and the final report in 2006. Considering that measures do not have their full impact right away, and that there are usually teething problems in the implementation and that data collection and the writing of a substantial report take their time, an evaluation with such time pressure faces almost insurmountable challenges. The Hartz-evaluations were also a combined evaluation project. Due to the insight that prerequisites for large evaluation projects with considerable time pressure are

(1) institutions with the relevant know-how,
(2) the readiness for cooperation between the institutions, as the commission for such large projects cannot be fulfilled by one institution only,
(3) the willingness to be part of a systematic, administrative part of the research process, and
(4) the availability of a sufficient and as actual as possible amount of data and datasets,

the evaluation project was assigned to almost 20 research institutes, where about 100 scientists worked on the report (HEYER 2006).

The time frames are often politically motivated. It has been discussed in subsection 3.3.4 that politicians have their own interests, and their foremost interest is often their reelection. If the next election is close, then either positive results are needed for the incumbents, or negative information is hoped for by the opposition. In both cases, information has to be made available as quickly as possible, in many cases preventing a long-term evaluation. In addition, the results of evaluations are not always used by politicians in their decisions, especially if they are not the clients. Scientific research that was not prompted by policy-makers is often not directly useful or usable for politics. In addition, evidence research needs independence, time and qualified scientists. As qualified scientists are usually identified by the number of journal articles they publish, gaining a reputation as qualified scientists needs time as well. Also, data is not always available in the quality and quantity necessary for a thorough analysis. In addition, in some cases it is doubtful whether it is possible at all to detect clear causalities. Those are all aspects that complicate political consulting, and they are reasons for a development in German labor market policy that ZIMMERMANN (2014) considers a shift from evidence-based policy to a politics-oriented approach. Scientific evidence means proving something by using statistically sound results. Policy-oriented evidence making, i.e., research that was ordered by policy-makers, in itself is not untrustworthy or biased; it is necessary though to carefully study possible influence by the sponsor(s) and the compliance of the research with the rules of good scientific work.

6.10 Evaluating Sustainability

Evaluating sustainability is rather a slogan than a realized concept. This is due to a number of specifics of sustainability that must be considered in case of an evaluation. So far, sustainability is usually connected with the aspect of longevity and is only discussed as such in evaluations (ANT 2008b), neglecting the other dimensions. Generally, for political decisions, there are two aspects of sustainable development: prevention/provision, i.e., acting with regard to avoidance of future damage or inequalities, and aftercare or the repair of damages already occurred (BRAND, JOCHUM 2000). The steps and considerations of an evaluation of sustainability are very similar to the steps of most evaluations that deal with political topics. But they are different inasmuch that in every step of the evaluation, the dimensions of sustainability – ecological, economic and social as well as institutional, intragenerational and intergenerational – must be considered. The interlinkages between the environmental, social and economic issues are so strong that separate analyses might falsify the results of an evaluation. The dimensions are often analyzed separately, though, because of the type of information to be gathered in the different areas. Environmental data might be more scientifically based and acknowledged, whereas data on social performance has a tendency to be more subjective (BENNETT, JAMES 1999). This does not justify the neglect of links between the dimensions, though, as ignoring them would rule out the evaluation of spill-overs and external or unintended effects as well as make the finding of reliable causalities almost impossible.

In the case of Germany, a number of pre-set indicators for key thematic fields were introduced, and target values and time tables assigned to the majority of these indicators (RAT FÜR NACHHALTIGE ENTWICKLUNG 2009). Those indicators can mostly be assigned to one of the dimensions of sustainable development, but many of them can be related to two or more dimensions. An evaluation including those indicators with the aim of making a clear statement on the state of sustainable development in Germany requires the setting of priorities, though. It has been discussed in subsection 3.3.3.1 that many aspects have to be treated with opposite measures. Therefore, an assessment of results in sustainable development that includes, for example, an increase in a certain variable, may well be judged favorable from an economic point of view, for example, but unfavorable from a social or ecological point of view; or a development may be judged positively in relation to intragenerational equality, but negatively in its effect on intergenerational justice. Those aspects have to be considered by evaluators of sustainable development, and the complexity and partly inverse effects of changes, make it almost impossible to offer a clear judgment without setting priorities. The latter is politically not feasible, though, therefore the results of evaluations are often rather an overview over the development of a number of indices, thus avoiding the subjective decisions necessary for a prioritization.

6.11 Summary

Chapter 4 discussed indicators and indicator systems. One of their most important utilizations is in evaluations, which were discussed in this chapter. After an introduction and a description of the tasks of an evaluation, the basic principles to be followed and typical steps of evaluations processes, evaluation methods and types of evaluations were presented. Evaluations, especially policy evaluations, face a large number of challenges. Therefore, one subsection discussed methodical, but also human challenges to evaluations and evaluators. To make the transfer to labor market policy and sustainability, a general overview of policy evaluations was given. Finally, the evaluation of labor market policy was described and challenges for this field of evaluation were discussed. The final subsection then offered details on the evaluation of sustainable development, with a focus on Germany.

7. Indicators for the Evaluation of Sustainable Labor Market Policy

The theories and discussions in the preceding chapters were aimed at developing an understanding of sustainability and its application to the labor market. To pursue a sustainability strategy that comprises policies to further sustainable labor, tools for the evaluation of said policies with regard to their contribution to a sustainable development must be provided. So far, without a comprehensive definition of sustainable labor, the assessment of the success of measures with regard to sustainable development was impossible. Chapter 3.4 provides an overview over the areas of labor and labor market policy that must be included in an evaluation of sustainable labor market policy and suggests a basic definition for sustainable labor market policy. In this chapter, criteria that must be fulfilled if an indicator is to be helpful in assessing the sustainability of a certain measure will be discussed. These criteria will then be applied to indicators that are currently used as well as suggestions for indicators that should be used when evaluating labor market policy. For the sake clarity, the indicators are divided into macro- and micro-level indicators.

7.1 Criteria for Sustainability Indicators

When developing an indicator or indicator set, a number of criteria have to be fulfilled to make sure the indicator is suited to the intended purpose. The requirements for good indicators have been discussed in chapter 4, and can be roughly divided into two parts: technical details and explanatory aspects, which shall be detailed in the following sections.

7.1.1 Explanatory Aspects

To clearly identify an indicator and to make sure that there is no ambiguity inasmuch that several stakeholders or user groups may use different data for what is intended to be one and the same indicator, a clear definition, even if the indicator name seems to be explicit, is necessary. This can also include a description of the target values or qualitative target to be met so that the indicator can be classified in terms of success in reaching the goals set. This definition should be followed by the placement of the indicator in its policy context. This includes the dimension(s) of sustainability the indicator covers, linkages to other relevant indicators, but also an analysis of underlying concepts and definitions that are relevant for the indicator. To offer a reliable indicator set, a definition of the indicator is necessary. The utilization of most indicators has advantages and disadvantages which must be discussed openly to make sure that they are considered in the interpretation of the indicator. Therefore, the description of the indicator must also include the limitations of the indicator as well as possible alternative interpretations and definitions or other indicators that could be used as an alternative. An overview over the explanatory aspects that a thorough description of an indicator must include is given below.

(1) Indicator name

(2) Indicator definition

(3) Goal

(4) Policy relevance

a) Underlying definitions and concepts

b) Sustainability dimension(s) covered

c) Linkages to other indicators

(5) Limitations of the indicator

a) Limitations in explanatory power

b) Limitations in informational value

c) Alternative definitions

d) Alternative indicators

7.1.2 Technical Aspects

The explanatory aspects must be supported by a number of technical details that are necessary to appraise the indicator and to decide on the indicator's practicability. This includes a qualification or quantification of the target including the unit of measurement, but also an assessment of the methodology of the indicator, i.e., a description of the method of collection, a statement about the international renown of the method in the scientific community as well as with the user groups, and a short review whether the recommended standards for the building of good indicators are met. The third aspect is a detailed examination of the data itself. This comprises the data source, i.e., the organizations or institutions collecting the data, its reliability, and its availability on an individual, regional, national or international level to facilitate comparability – an important consideration when evaluating sustainability. In addition, the periodicity of the data (e.g., monthly, annually, biannually, etc.) must be stated, and, if applicable, possible time lags between the fact to be measured and the availability of the data (c.f. for example the collection of the data for the Hartz-evaluations in Germany in subsection

5.9). Lastly, an overview over the quality of the data must be given. An overview is given below:

(1) Quantification of the goal (cf. explanatory aspects) and unit of measurement

(2) Methodology

  a) Method of collection

  b) International acknowledgement of method

  c) Recommended standards

(3) Data source and availability

  a) Regional level

  b) Periodicity

  c) Time lags in availability

  d) Data source

    a. Contributing organizations

    b. Reliability

    c. Comparability within regions

(4) Quality of the data

  a) Seasonal adjustment

  b) Level of aggregation, data included in the indicator (if applicable)

7.2 Micro-level Indicators

Microeconomic Evaluation considers the effects of a measure in terms of difference between an output variable for an individual who took part in a program or measure, and the output variable for the same person without participation in the program. This *potential outcome approach* poses a number of challenges, namely the prediction of the potential outcome for a person for the option (participation/non-participation) not chosen (HUJER, FITZENBERGER 2013). Data for microeconomic indicators is usually only available in small numbers, the variability between measures within regions and nations makes a comparison between outcomes almost impossible. Therefore, the following micro-level indicators shall be discussed for the case of Germany. Data for the indicators is usually collected directly from the participants in a measure, the control-group, if applicable, and the experts (e.g., trainers, employment agency staff, and evaluators) involved in the measure. Data is also available from microeconomic panels such as the german socio-economic panel (SOEP) or the labor market monitor for eastern Germany. On the micro-level, three types of indicators are usually used: input indicators, output indicators and outcome/effect indicators (BRINKMANN 2000). The indicators discussed in the next two chapters are chosen for their importance in measuring sustainability. They are not exhaustive, and there are many more indicators, especially on the level of single measures, that could go deeper into the effects of the programs. However, the latter will not be discussed in this context, as this work aims at a rather general overview. The indicators suggested here are a basis for further research and discussion. Most of the indicators are already used and data is available at least in most countries, but are not interpreted yet in terms of sustainable development. Some other indicators are suggested even though the collection of the data necessary is costly and complicated, and the methodology is disputed. Still, they are deemed important by the author, and may be useful for evaluations.

7.2.1 Net-Costs of the Measure

Indicator Definition: Net-costs are the balance between costs and benefits of the measure. This must include an assessment of opportunity costs, i.e., an analysis whether the same benefits could have been realized with lower costs or whether with the same costs, higher benefits could have been reached.

Goal: To choose measures that yield higher benefits to at least equal the costs they cause.

Policy Relevance: With scarce funds to be allocated, spending on specific measures must be justified. Therefore, the costs for a measure must be compared to the benefits of the measure. The indicator is relevant for the economic dimension of sustainable development, but also for the ecological and social aspects.

Limitations of the indicator: While the calculation of costs is rather straightforward, the estimation of benefits is not. The calculation of benefits is more complicated. For a reliable cost-benefit analysis, benefits must be explicitly attributed the measure. It has been discussed in chapters 3 and 5 that this is not always possible due to the complexity of the relations between various fields of policy and between the dimensions of sustainability. In addition, BROMLEY (1990) criticizes cost-benefit paradigms because they most likely cannot include all relevant information.

Methodology: In most cases, the method of choice to determine net-costs of a measure is a cost-benefit analysis. This is a widely used and widely researched analytical tool. The assessment of social benefits is not undisputed, as many aspects cannot be described in monetary terms, making a comparison more complicated. This is an area of ongoing research. Nevertheless, the indicator provides basic information about the program or measure and offers an approximation of at least some aspects of the benefits.

Data source and availability: The indicator depends on a number of data from different areas. The costs of the measure should be documented by the executing institution, for the benefits data must be drawn from various sources. Those include data from statistics agencies, but also from surveys. The net-cost of measures should be calculated after every measure, but as many benefits may only occur years after the completion of the measure, calculation should be repeated in specified periods of time.

Quality of the data: The indicator is highly aggregated and includes many aspects that may be subject to interpretation.

7.2.2 Integration of Participants into the Formal Labor Market

Indicator definition: Percentage of participants in a measure that transferred into the formal labor market after participation. This percentage must be compared to the projected transferal into the formal labor market for individuals who did not participate in the measure.

Goal: Increase the number of participants in measures who find regular employment after the program.

Policy Relevance: One of the main goals of active LMP is to include unemployed or precariously employed persons into the formal labor market (cf. chapter 4 for the importance of employment). In terms of sustainability, this is especially relevant for the social and economic dimensions.

Limitations of the indicator: It is necessary to compare the percentage of those employed after the measure with the employment rate of those who did not participate but had preconditions similar to those of the participants before the measure. This is essential to assess the benefit of the measure and to distinguish effects of the measure from other influences. Possible challenges in finding such a control group are discussed in subsection 6.9.2, but without such a control group the explanatory power of the indicator is very low. In some cases, the number of participants in a measure is too low to yield statistically reliable results of the analysis.

Methodology: Data is collected by statistic agencies or labor market agencies, but also by the institutions responsible for the measure. The methods are similar to those of the data collection for unemployment rates, but the data sets must be individualized to follow the employment history of participants or members of the control group. A thorough analysis of this indicator demands an assessment of success immediately after the measure and then repeatedly in specified periods of time (e.g., one year, three years, five years after the measure, etc.).

Data source and availability: Data should be available on an individual level to measure the impact of the measure. Data can then be aggregated to measure the overall effect of the measure. Reliable data is only available in specified periods of time after the conclusion of the measure.

Quality of the data: Low level of aggregation, seasonal adjustment may be necessary depending on the time spans considered.

7.2.3 Quality-of-Job Indicators

An important factor to determine the sustainability of a job is the quality attributed to the job. This is a stipulation of the social dimension of sustainability, but can also influence the economic and ecological dimensions (e.g., where mobility is concerned).

7.2.3.1 Long Working Hours

Indicator Definition: The indicator measures the percentage of workers who work more than 50 hours (in some countries: 48 hours) per week.

Goal: Especially a reduction of involuntary long working hours, but also reduction of long working hours in general.

Policy relevance: The assumed mechanism is that financial stress among breadwinners leads to economic vulnerability, and therefore an acceptance of poor working conditions. Those poor working conditions, e.g., long working hours, lead to poor health, which often leads to more financial stress, possibly leading to the necessity of even longer working hours (ARTAZCOZ ET AL. 2009). In addition, long working hours are, on average, not beneficial, either to employees or the efficiency of the organization as a whole (SPURGEON ET AL. 1997). VIRTANEN ET AL. 2008 found that long working hours can lead to a decline in cognitive functions, especially among the middle aged. Therefore, the indicator is connected to the social, but also the economic dimension of sustainability.

Limitations of the indicator: It is not possible to determine how many hours people should be required to work if they are to remain safe and healthy, because currently available data is insufficient. Therefore, the determination of, e.g., 48 or 50 hours per week as long working hours is an arbitrary assumption. Finally, there is only anecdotal evidence for the suspected effects of long working hours on the quality of life, therefore, the explanatory power of the indicator is limited (SPURGEON ET AL. 1997). In addition, the Working Time Directive of the EU (EUROPEAN PARLIAMENT 2003) demands that member states must provide legislation to ensure that the average working time per week, including overtime, is not more than 48 hours. If legislation prohibits working hours over 48 hours per week, then it is unlikely that individuals working more than that will admit it officially. This leads to a bias in the data collection. The indicator does not differentiate between voluntary and involuntary excessive hours.

Methodology: Data on working hours is collected in the Labour Force Survey by Eurostat for European countries, and the OECD worldwide. Data is based on household surveys. Comparability is made difficult by different measurements of the indicator, e.g., "hours usually worked" vs. "hours actually worked", the latter including holidays, illnesses and other temporary reductions in working hours.

Data source and availability: Data is available on a regional level and is usually collected annually or with larger time periods between data collection. Comparability between regions is made difficult by the limitations of the indicator described above.

Quality of the data: The level of aggregation is low, seasonal adjustment is necessary.

7.2.3.2 Commuting Time

Indicator Definition: The average time necessary for the trip from work to home and back.

Goal: To reduce commuting time (measured in minutes).

Policy Relevance: Commuting time is a relevant factor for wellbeing and the quality of life. It is usually considered a mental and physical burden (STUTZER, FREY 2008). It is also directly linked to the ecological dimension of sustainable development depending on the method of transportation chosen.

Limitations of the indicator: From an economic point of view, commuting should not lead to a decrease in perceived quality of life compared with other individuals, because it is considered a simple optimization problem, where commuting is compensated, e.g., by higher incomes. Therefore, the relationship between commuting time and quality of life needs to be studied more intensively (STUTZER, FREY 2008).

Methodology: Data is derived from time use surveys, e.g., by the OECD or Eurostat. Survey methods are advanced. Comparability is reduced by biases in the surveyed groups.

Data source and availability: Data is theoretically available on a regional level, but is more reliable on the national level, due to a small number of survey participants in some regions. The periodicity of the data collection is low and data availability is time-lagged.

Quality of the data: Seasonal adjustment is not necessary, the level of aggregation is low.

7.2.3.3 Quality of Work Life

Indicator Definition: "[Q]uality of work life [QWL] is a way of thinking about people, work, and organizations. Its distinctive elements are (1) a concern about the impact of work on people as well as on organizational effectiveness, and (2) the idea of participation in organizational problem solving and decision making" (NADLER, LAWLER 1983).

Goal: To increase the QWL.

Policy Relevance: QWL affects job satisfaction, but also other aspects of life. In order to promote "good jobs", the perceived quality of the working environment and of working life in general must be improved. This affects the social dimension of sustainability, but indirectly also the economic dimension, because increased wellbeing improves health, and often the productivity of workers (SIRGY ET AL. 2001).

Limitations of the indicator: Value patterns related to work and quality of life in general vary greatly between countries and regions (HOFSTEDE 1984). The indicator is aggregated; therefore, priority setting and weighting of basic data may differ between regions. In addition, QWL is based on the perception of those surveyed, therefore it is not objective.

Methodology: There are various measures of QWL; all of them are aggregated indicators. SIRGY ET AL. (2001) suggest the inclusion seven main aspects: health and safety needs, economic and family needs, social needs, esteem needs, actualization needs, knowledge needs and aesthetic needs. Data is collected with the help of surveys. There is no method that is internationally agreed on; therefore, comparability is only partially possible.

Data source and availability: Data availability depends on the conduction of surveys. Data is usually collected on a company level; therefore, the choice of companies included in the survey can significantly influence the outcome for a region.

Quality of the data: The level of aggregation is high, biases through weightings are possible.

7.3 Macro-level Indicators

Microeconomic evaluation is partial analytical and only studies the direct influences of a measure on an individual. Influences on non-participants or for the whole economy are not considered. Therefore, it is possible that participants in a measure improve their relative competitive position in comparison to non-participants, but the overall effect on the economy is negative (HUJER, FITZENBERGER 2013). The linkages between labor market policy and other policy fields are manifold. Therefore, indicators attempting to measure the impact of a measure on a macro-level are inevitably incomplete due to exogenous influences, but also due to cross-impacts due to other policy measures. Still, there are methods to identify and single out influences, even if the results are rather approximations. It must also be kept in mind that many macro-level indicators are only helpful for extensive measures that concern many individuals, because measures with a smaller sphere of influence will, at least in most cases, not have significant impact on macro-level indicators. The following macro-level indicators are mostly taken from several renown indicator sets, e.g., of the ASIAN DEVELOPMENT BANK (2011), the CONSEIL D'ANALYSE ÉCONOMIQUE, SACHVERSTÄNDIGENRAT ZUR BEGUTACHTUNG DER GESAMTWIRTSCHAFTLICHEN ENTWICKLUNG (2011), MITCHELL (1996), the german statistical office (STATISTISCHES BUNDESAMT 2008, 2010, 2012, 2013), the UN DESA (2007), EUROSTAT (2013), and the AGENDA-TRANSFER FOR THE LOCAL AGENDA 21 (2003) in Germany. For the sake of readability and to avoid redundancies, some subsections include various indicators for the same field.

7.3.1 Influence of LMP on Labor Productivity

Indicator Definition: Labor productivity is the volume measure of output (GDP or GVA) divided by the measure of input use (total number of hours worked or total employment) (Freeman 2008).

Goal: Increasing Labor Productivity by using effective LMP, quantification depends on goals of the nation and the importance placed on economic growth.

Policy Relevance: Labor Productivity is a key factor for economic growth. The idea of the application of this indicator to the evaluation of sustainable labor market policy is that high productivity leads to economic growth, thus enabling countries to further intragenerational justice (e.g., through redistribution of income or wealth) and furthering the economic dimension of sustainable development. The indicator can be directly linked to GDP growth.

Limitations of the indicator: There are various interpretations and, accordingly, measurement options for the indicator. Increased labor productivity does not imply impact on individuals.

Methodology: Labor productivity is widely discussed and researched. BASSANINI and VENN (2007), for example, use a difference-in-differences approach to research effects in different industries, while ACEMOGLU and SHIMER (2000) prefer a general equilibrium model. The OECD (2003) bases its measure of labor productivity on human capital growth (labor input as sum of shares of workers with different educational levels weighted by relative wage) as a proxy. There are no generally recommended standards, but the OECD method has been applied to various OECD members and enables comparisons between nations.

Data source and availability: Annual OECD data available on national level. Time lag between availability of the data and period of measurement of about one year. The reliability of the data depends highly on the contributing national statistical offices. Comparability between nations is possible.

Quality of the data: Seasonal adjustment is not necessary. The level of aggregation is low, but measurement of human capital is only approximate and GDP as component of the indicator is medium aggregated.

7.3.2 Influence of LMP on GDP per Capita

Indicator Definition: The GDP is “an aggregate measure of production equal to the sum of the gross values added of all resident, institutional units engaged in production (plus any taxes, and minus any subsidies, on products not included in the value of their outputs)” (OECD 2002), per capita or per person employed to ensure comparability between countries of different sizes. Growth in GDP per capita has two components: labor utilization[74] and labor productivity (BASSANINI, VENN 2008), and can be calculated as the sum of changes in hourly GDP per efficient unit of labor, changes in average hours worked and changes in human capital (OECD 2003). The influence of LMP on GDP per capita is measured using the indicator “labor productivity” (cf. chapter 7.3.1.).

Goal: Increase GDP by using efficient LMP. Quantification of the goal varies among countries, with large differences between developed and developing countries. GDP is measured in monetary units, GDP-growth as ratio.

Policy Relevance: GDP is used as global measure for economic growth, often used to measure the economic dimension of sustainability. Indicators attempting to reduce the shortcomings of the GDP as indicator[75] are, e.g., the green GDP or the Natural Resource Accounting (NRA). The influence of increased labor productivity can also be measured on alternative indicators.

Limitations of the indicator: Environmental or social costs for economic growth as well as costs for future generations are not accounted for in GDP. Aspects of wellbeing, as an alternative concept of welfare in contrast to the GDP, such as free time or standards of living, are not included.

Methodology: Method for GDP is internationally acknowledged, even if shortcomings of the indicator GDP (growth) are discussed vividly.

---

74 Labor utilization is defined as quotient of total hours worked and total population.

75 The GDP has been widely criticized as an indicator, but is still often used as it is fully monetised and therefore easy to compare, it contains information about production of goods and services and the use of incomes. In addition, it is well-known (EUROPEAN COMMISSION 2007).

Data source and availability: GDP Collected on national level, in some countries on the level of federal states. Usually updated annually, but quarterly data published by some statistical offices. Data is usually published about six months after the end of the period considered. Collected by the statistical offices of the countries, comparability is great, even if for some countries, doubts exist about the reliability of the data. Labor productivity data collected annually (cf. chapter 7.3.1).

Quality of the data: Seasonal adjustments not necessary in cases of annual collection, only in case of quarterly publication. High level of aggregation for final indicator, but the data basis used is usually easily available.

Conclusion: The GDP, but also the green GDP and other measures of national accounting are only slightly useful to measure sustainable development, as the dimension of a measure must be considerable to have measurable impact on national accounting. In addition, other measures or international influences may contort the measurement and the attribution of effects to just one set of measures is almost impossible.[76]

7.3.3 Employment Indicators

To assess the success of labor market policy, employment indicators are the first choice. This includes employment rates (e.g., for selected age or education groups), precarious employment and long-term unemployment.

7.3.3.1 Employment Rate

Indicator definition: An employment rate measures the percentage of the labor force that is actually employed. The labor force is usually defined as population of working age, but can also refer to certain age groups (e.g., young workers or senior workers) or a sex (e.g., employment rate of women), people in certain social conditions (e.g., young mothers or fathers, labor force with a certain school leaving certificate) or a combination of the above.

Goal: Measuring participation of people willing and able to work in the labor market. The usual aim is to have full employment or only voluntary and frictional unemployment and to eliminate structural and cyclical unemployment. Due to information asymmetries and transaction costs, the aim is usually the natural rate of unemployment

76 A study on the macroeconomic results of the Hartz-reforms in Germany found mainly positive effects but warned that cyclical effects on GDP must be isolated to measure the impact of measures (KLINGER, ROTHE, WEBER 2013).

(NRU)[77], even if the quantification of the latter goal is disputed (STAIGER ET AL. 1997).

Policy relevance: The indicator is suitable to contribute to measuring the social and economic aspects of sustainable development. Related indicators are mainly on the micro-level, e.g., number of jobs in green jobs or working conditions.

Limitations of the indicator: As with all indicators on a macro-level, complicated estimations are necessary to isolate the influence of one measure on a certain indicator. In addition, international comparability of the indicator is limited due to different definitions of unemployment (c.f. chapter 3) in different countries, even if institutions such as the ILO aim at equalizing the measurements. Comparability between countries can be complicated by varying definitions of unemployment (BRANDOLINI ET AL. 2006).

Methodology: Indicator internationally acknowledged, even if different definitions of unemployment exist.

Data source and availability: Data available on a regional level and on a monthly basis. Time lags in availability are small (in the case of Germany, e.g., not more than a month (BUNDESAGENTUR FÜR ARBEIT 2015b)). Data sources vary within countries, for Germany, e.g., the labor agency is responsible for the collection of data from companies, but also their own agencies. Comparability within nations is possible if, e.g., the ILO data that is based at a standard definition of unemployment is used. Comparability within regions of the same country is possible. Data reliability depends on the system of collection, reliability for Germany is high.

Quality of the data: Unemployment rates are usually seasonally adjusted to detect underlying trends in the development of the unemployment rate. The level of aggregation is low.

7.3.3.2 Precarious Employment

Indicator Definition: The proportion of employees in precarious employment, i.e., in jobs that are not permanent or not subject to social insurance contribution or jobs that are felt to be precarious by the employee (KROLL, LAMPERT 2012).

Goal: To reduce the percentage of precarious jobs. Quantification of the goal depends on total unemployment rate in the country concerned.

Policy Relevance: Precarious employment has negative effects on health, but also on further employment. It is, according to the definition of sustainable jobs, unsustainable, especially where social sustainability and intragenerational justice are concerned.

---

77 For details on the NRU cf. for example SALOP (1979) or BLANCHARD (1997).

Increased health-costs caused by precarious employment also affect the economic dimension. Linked indicators are total employment, and precarious employment in age groups or by sex.

Limitations of the indicator: Precarious employment may be rated differently depending on the nation. Therefore, negative effects of precarious employment may vary greatly, making the indicator more or less relevant. In the case of Germany, for example, it can be considered relevant (KROLL, LAMPERT 2012).

Methodology: Data is collected by national employment or statistical agencies. Due to the differences in the interpretation and definition of the indicator, international comparability is a methodical challenge.

Data source and availability: Data is available on a regional level and in most cases collected monthly, with small time lags for the availability of the data. In some cases (especially where the self-assessment of workers is concerned) data stems from national censuses and is therefore only available every ten years.

Quality of the data: Seasonal adjustment is usual for data based on employment statistics. The level of aggregation is low.

7.3.3.3 Long-term Unemployment Rate

Indicator Definition: Long-term unemployment is the percentage of people with continuous unemployment for a year or longer in the total unemployed (THE WORLD BANK 2015).

Goal: Reduction of long-term unemployment.

Policy Relevance: Long-term unemployment especially affects older individuals and individuals without formal training (BUNDESAGENTUR FÜR ARBEIT 2014). To realize intragenerational justice, a reduction of solidified structural unemployment is necessary. This concerns the social dimension of sustainability as well as the economic dimension. The indicator is closely linked to other employment indicators, but also education indicators.

Limitations of the indicator: The reasons for long-term unemployment are manifold and the indicator does not differentiate between them. In the case of Germany, for example, data may be distorted due to the regulation that unemployed persons who take part in an active LMP measure of more than 15 hours per week are not considered unemployed (BUNDESAGENTUR FÜR ARBEIT 2004).

Methodology, Data source and availability, and quality of the data: Cf. indicator "Precarious Employment".

7.3.4 Income Poverty

Definition: Proportion of population living below national poverty line.[78]

Goal: The reduction of poverty. In the case of relative income poverty, this also means that the lower incomes are more equalized. Quantification of the goal varying greatly among the countries.

Policy relevance: The concept of poverty describes a situation where basic needs cannot be satisfied[79]. This concept is closely related to economic growth and income indicators. The sustainability dimensions covered are social and economic sustainability, but also the aspect of intragenerational justice.

Limitations of the indicator: Income poverty and its interpretation depend crucially on its definition. In the case of an absolute poverty threshold, the indicator can easily be misused by lowering the threshold and thus "improving" the indicator. In addition, comparability between countries is not given with this indicator. The indicator must be adjusted based on purchasing power parity (PPP). The indicator only considers income, not fortunes. An alternative is the consideration of income inequality (ratio of the share in national income of highest to lowest quintile) and indicators including fortunes.

Methodology: Data on poverty is collected with the national income data. The calculation of the income poverty ratio is disputed, though, as there is no clear and unambiguous definition of poverty and accordingly, the ratio is calculated differently by different authorities.

Data source: Data is usually easily available on a monthly basis, as wages are often the basis for taxes and are therefore monitored closely. Time lags between the period measured and the availability of the data are small. Comparability is only possible with adjusted data or if the same interpretation of poverty and the same measurement of the poverty threshold are applied, and in case of PPP-adjustment.

Quality of the data: This aspect depends highly on the truth of reported incomes, a low level of illicit employment and a non-biased setting of the threshold. The level of aggregation is low.

---

78 The poverty line can be measured relatively (e.g., in the case of Germany, anyone with an income of less than 60% of the median income is considered poor (SCHRÖDER, RÖHL 2014) or absolutely (with a fixed standard that is adjusted regularly). Most countries chose the latter approach (FENG, NGUYEN 2014)

79 The discussion about „basic needs“ is ongoing, though, therefore, the definition of who is poor varies widely (HAGENAARS, VOS 1988)

7.3.5 Education Indicators

Education is a crucial aspect for sustainable development. Better education increases the awareness of environmental challenges, but also the ability to provide better living conditions by finding better jobs. In addition, education is essential for furthering technical development, which may help to meet many of the challenges for sustainable development.

7.3.5.1 Adult Secondary/Tertiary Schooling Attainment Level

Indicator definition: Adult secondary (tertiary) schooling attainment level: proportion of the population of working age with completed secondary (tertiary) education (UNESCO 2015).

Goal: Increase the percentage of the population with completed education. Quantification of the goal depends on status quo in the countries; generally the goal is to reduce the percentage of adults without secondary schooling attainment as far as possible. In addition, the schooling attainment level of women is often made a priority to increase intragenerational justice.

Policy Relevance: Human resources are key factors for the development of a nation, as well in economic terms as in social and, ultimately, also ecological aspects. Studies show that education is highly correlated to employment (OECD 2011), and some evidence suggests that higher education levels lead to an improved awareness about environmental and social concerns. The indicator is linked to other education indicators, but over education's impact on employment, labor productivity, innovation, etc., also to economic indicators.

Limitations of the indicator: Data on schooling attainment is often criticized for a possible lack of reliability, because data collection is often based on self-declaration. In addition, data sometimes combines studying at a given level and the completion of the level, thus reducing the comparability.

Methodology: Various methods for the estimation of educational attainment where data is not fully available have been developed[80]. The methodology is internationally recommended by the UNESCO and therefore broadly acknowledged.

Data source and availability: Data is based on national censuses. This leads to large time lags between data collections, because in many countries, censuses are only conducted every ten years.

---

80 C.f. BARRO, LEE 1993, 1996; LAU ET AL. 1991; NEHRU ET AL. 1995; PSACHAROPOULOS, ARRIAGADA 1986

Quality of the data: Seasonal adjustments are not necessary, the level of aggregation is very low. Data should include statistics about gender and age-group to offer reliable information.

7.3.5.2 Life-long Learning

Indicator definition: The quota of the population aged 25 to 64 currently in education or training (UN DESA 2003).

Goal: Measurement of education and training after primary/secondary/tertiary education, often during employment. Quantification of the goal varies between nations.

Policy Relevance: Cf. indicator "Adult secondary/tertiary schooling attainment level". Life-long learning can increase the flexibility of workers and therefore improve adaption to new technologies or behavior to further sustainable development. Relevant for economic, social and ecological sustainability, and intragenerational justice.

Limitations of the indicator: Data is usually based on samples or census data. Biases are possible, as are unreliable results due to small sample sizes. The term life-long learning is not unambiguously defined yet (ASPIN, CHAPMAN 2000), leaving room for interpretation, and reducing comparability between countries.

Methodology: Cf. limitations of the indicator. It is recommended to implement basic guidelines to ensure comparability between regions and nations. There are no international standards yet.

Data source and availability: Data usually only available on national levels, data collected during censuses (i.e., often only every ten years) or via surveys, therefore, data is only available in long intervals.

Quality of the data: No seasonal adjustment necessary, level of aggregation low.

7.3.6 Work Accidents and Occupational Illnesses

Indicator Definition: Work accidents occur during the execution of work and lead to health damage or loss of life (OECD 2007b).

Goal: Elimination of work accidents, at least considerable reduction. Quantification of the goal varies between countries; indicator unit is number of cases per 100.000 workers.

Policy Relevance: Work accidents and occupational illnesses are visible evidence for work hazards. They cause high costs for workers, but also companies and communities[81]. With an increasing likelihood for work accidents and occupational illnesses, the job satisfaction decreases. Sustainability dimensions covered are social and economic aspects.

Limitations of the indicator: The definition of work accidents vary between countries. In some statistics, only major injuries are collected, in others, only injuries that were compensated are recorded. The attribution of the label "occupational illness" is also disputed. The distinct correlation between an illness and the job the patient was employed is hard to prove and remains a cause for negotiations and disputes between insurance companies, patients, and companies.

Methodology: Due to different methods of collection in, but also within the nations, comparisons are difficult. But the ILO Resolution on "Statistics on occupational injuries resulting from accidents at work" (ILO 1998) became a basis for data collection for this indicator and improved comparability considerably. In addition, the 2001 methodology recommendations of the European Statistics on Accidents at Work (ESAW) of the European Commission offered further assistance for an increased comparability of the indicator between nations.

Data source and availability: Data is collected by insurance companies, labor bureaus, social security registers, censuses, and via specific surveys (OECD 2006). Data is usually available on a regional level, is collected at regular intervals (one month to one year, depending on the data source), and is available with moderate time lags.

Quality of the data: Seasonal adjustment is not necessary, data is only lowly aggregated.

7.3.7 Income Inequality

Indicator Definition: JENKINS (1991) considers the study of economic inequality as "the analysis of differences across the population in *access to, and control over, economic resources.*"

Goal: To reduce income inequality as far as possible. The most common measure for the indicator is the Gini-coefficient with possible values between 0 (i.e., full equality in the distribution of incomes) and 1 (maximum inequality in the distribution of incomes).

---

81 Costs for those accidents and illnesses are estimated between 0.4 and 4% of GDP in various countries (EASHW 1998; TAKALA 2002).

Policy Relevance: The renowned KUZNETS' curve (1955) was one of the first descriptions of the correlation between inequality in the distribution of incomes and a country's economic growth. Kuznets discussed the growth process as exogenous. Newer studies attribute the potential effects of inequality on growth to a variety of reasons (DEININGER, SQUIRE 1996). The indicator is especially relevant for the economic and social dimensions of sustainability and for intragenerational justice.

Limitations of the indicator: The Gini-coefficient is aggregated, and it is impossible to attribute changes in the indicator to a specific redistribution, e.g., between the richest and the middle-income group or between the middle-income and low-income groups.

Methodology: JENKINS (1991) distinguishes between ordinal and cardinal inequality measures. He states that "all inequality measures, even ones related to apparently objective diagrams, inevitably involve value judgments of various kinds" (JENKINS 1991, p. 19). Nevertheless, due to the availability of the primary data necessary for the Gini-coefficient and due to the fact that studies found the indicator's explanatory power to be similar to that of other, more complicated and less common measures, the Gini-coefficient remains the indicator of choice.

Data source and availability: Primary data for the Gini-coefficient (i.e., the distribution of income in the population) is collected by statistical agencies, but also fiscal authorities and censuses. Data is usually available on an annual level, in many countries more often.

Quality of the data: Due to the level of aggregation, the interpretation of the Gini-coefficient must be accompanied by further information (e.g., quintile-specific data).

7.3.8 Number of Decent Green Jobs in Green Industries

Indicator definition: Percentage of jobs in total jobs that can be classified as a) decent jobs, b) green occupations, c) jobs in green industries, or a combination of two or all three of the above (cf. figure 37).

Goal: To increase the number of decent green jobs in green industries, i.e., employment in those sectors and preparing potential employees for work in them. As an intermediate step, an increase of jobs that fulfill at least one or two of the three aspects above is aimed at.

Policy Relevance: To realize sustainable LMP, the jobs created or the jobs that formerly unemployed individuals are placed in should meet at least some of the requirements for sustainable jobs. It has been discussed in chapter 3 that not all requirements are likely to be met in one job at once. But to realize sustainable development with the help of LMP, it is necessary to increase the number of at least partly sustainable jobs. This indicator is relevant for all dimensions of sustainable development.

Limitations of the indicator: The biggest challenge is the classification of jobs and companies into the aspects of sustainable jobs. As described in chapter 3, the self-registration and -classification of companies can lead to distortions in the data.

Methodology: There is no internationally acknowledged method of data collection yet; standards for the classification of the jobs have to be developed.

Data source and availability: Data can only be collected by either surveys or through (self-) classification by employees, employers or labor agencies. With the data bases existing so far, only rough estimates of the indicator are possible, and comparability between regions or nations is impossible.

Quality of the data: No reliable data collection yet.

7.4 Summary

This chapter introduced a number of indicators that are either already used to assess the effects of LMP or should be included in evaluations to consider the aspect of sustainability in the measures. Each indicator was discussed according to the criteria necessary for analyzing the content and quality of an indicator. Special attention was given to the measurement of sustainability, including the policy relevance and the dimensions of sustainability concerned. To structure the choice of indicators, a classification into macro- and micro-level indicators was made.

8. Conclusion

This work aimed at evaluating sustainable LMP. A thorough analysis of the literature on the topic yielded the result that, while publications and discussions about sustainability in general and the ecological dimension in specific are abundant, there is a lack of research on the transfer between sustainability and LMP, and publications by institutions of the executive and legislative mention LMP in passing, but do neither specify what sustainable labor market policy is, nor do they propose concrete measures to realize it.

The research done for this work therefore concentrated on two main areas: sustainability and its implementation, and, secondly, sustainable LMP and the possibilities to evaluate and measure the sustainability of a measure.

The first part aimed at structuring the manifold theories, models and interpretations of sustainability. It can be shown that the model became more and more complicated and integrated over time. This is very helpful especially for understanding the complexity of the concept and to show the connections and interdependencies between its dimensions. However, the more and more complex (and realistic) models prove that to take measures towards the realization of sustainable development, a prioritization among the aims for sustainable development is inevitable. Therefore, the author went on to discuss the implementation of sustainable development in general, and the political feasibility of realizing such a complex concept. The analysis shows that progress towards a sustainable development has been made. Nevertheless, scientists note that the progress is still insufficient on a global level, especially in the ecological dimensions. This is interesting, because the awareness of ecological, social and economic challenges as well as international agreement on the importance of the concept are high.

To find an explanation for the hesitance to make bigger steps to realize sustainable development, the second chapter analyzed possible obstacles for the implementation of the guiding principle. It was shown that some of those challenges are institutional, and many are on an individual level. One of the most common problems is the difference in individually rational behavior and the behavior that would be rational from a collective perspective. In addition, information asymmetries and the ensuing principal-agent issues, e.g., between voters and the legislative or between the legislative and the executive, pose a challenge to the realization of sustainable development. It can be concluded that better information of all stakeholders and clear signaling on all sides may reduce these problems, especially on a regional or national level. However, the difficulty to find a solution increases with an increasing number of stakeholders. The knowledge about the challenges and possibilities to mainstream the general principle helps to understand the process of implementing sustainability. It puts the scientific understanding of the necessity to realize sustainable development into a broader context of political feasibility and the public support required for the necessary actions.

Chapter 3 then aimed at transferring the general principle and models introduced in the first two chapters to LMP. In a first step, the importance of work was analyzed. This was used later on to discuss the connection between labor market policy measures and the dimensions of sustainability. This transfer is not common yet, but it is necessary. Work, and accordingly LMP, influences (and is influenced by) many areas of everyday life, but also many fields of policy. It is therefore a very complex and multilayered field of research that poses a large number of challenges. Its interwovenness makes it a very rewarding, but also complicated area of research that combines many methodical approaches. The basis for research in this area is a sound definition. In the course of this work, a working definition was suggested.

One of the tools to make informed policy decisions for LMP measures is evaluation. Evaluations of labor market measures that have been conducted so far did not specifically include an analysis of the influence of the measure on sustainable development and on the sustainability of the measure's outcome. Therefore, chapter 4 and 5 detailed how indicators are used in evaluations and how they can be applied to sustainable development and the labor market.

The last chapter then merged the three topics sustainability, LMP and indicators. A number of indicators for LMP measures are examined with the help of criteria for good indicators as discussed in the methodical chapters. Those indicators were specifically chosen for their importance in measuring sustainability. It is detailed for each indicator which dimensions of sustainability it concerns, but also which limitations in methodology and explanatory power exist.

Essentially, the following conclusions can be drawn from this work:

1. Sustainable development is an established guiding principle and the implementation of the theoretical idea is in progress.
2. There are many challenges for the implementation of the principle into everyday life and into policymaking. Those obstacles can be overcome by a reduction of information asymmetries.
3. Labor market policy is interlinked with all dimensions of sustainability and is an important policy field. To realize sustainable development, it is therefore necessary to incorporate sustainability requirements into labor market policy.
4. To assess whether labor market policy measures are sustainable, it is essential to conduct evaluations that include indicators that consider the impact of measures on the dimensions of sustainability. A set of indicators is suggested in this work.

9. Publication Bibliography

ABRAHAM, MARTIN; HINZ, THOMAS (Eds.) (2008): Arbeitsmarktsoziologie. Probleme, Theorien, empirische Befunde. 2. Auflage. Wiesbaden: VS Verlag für Sozialwissenschaften / GWV Fachverlage GmbH Wiesbaden.

ABRAHAM, M.; HINZ, T. (2008): Wozu Arbeitsmarktsoziologie? In M. ABRAHAM, T. HINZ (EDS.): Arbeitsmarktsoziologie. Probleme, Theorien, empirische Befunde. 2. Auflage. Wiesbaden: VS Verlag für Sozialwissenschaften / GWV Fachverlage GmbH Wiesbaden, pp. 11–16.

ABRAMOVITZ, MOSES; DAVID, PAUL A.; REDER, MELVIN WARREN (Eds.) (1974): Nations and households in economic growth. Essays in honor of Moses Abramovitz. New York: Academic Press.

ACEMOGLU, D.; SHIMER, R. (2000): Productivity Gains from Unemployment Insurance. In *European Economic Review* 44 (7), pp. 1195–1224.

AGENDA-TRANSFER AGENTUR FÜR NACHHALTIGKEIT (2003): Gemeinsam empfohlene Indikatoren zur kommunalen Nachhaltigkeit. Bonn.

AKERLOF, G. A. (1970): The Market for "Lemons": Quality Uncertainty and the Market Mechanism. In *The Quarterly Journal of Economics* (Vol. 84 No.3), pp. 488–500.

ALBAEK, E. (1995): Policy Evaluation: Design and Utilization. In R. C. RIST (ED.): Policy evaluation. Linking theory to practice. Aldershot: Elgar (An Elgar reference collection, 3), pp. 5–18.

ANGRES, V. (2005): Zum Einstieg in die Welt der Indikatoren: Der DUX - ein persönlicher Denkanstoß. In R. BÖCKER, C.-P. HUTTER (EDS.): Umweltindikatoren - Mythos oder Wirklichkeit? Was wissen wir wirklich über unsere Umwelt? Stuttgart: Wiss. Verl.-Ges. (Beiträge der Akademie für Natur- und Umweltschutz Baden-Württemberg, 39), pp. 11–13.

ANT, M. (2008): A Framework for Implementing Evaluation and Assessment Strategies in Social Policy. In M. ANT (ED.): Nachhaltiger Mehrwert von Evaluation. Bielefeld: Bertelsmann-Verl., pp. 55–72.

ANT, M. (2008): Die Dimensionen der Evaluation im Nachhaltigkeitsmanagement. In M. ANT (ED.): Nachhaltiger Mehrwert von Evaluation. Bielefeld: Bertelsmann-Verl., pp. 159–170.

ANT, M. (Ed.) (2008): Nachhaltiger Mehrwert von Evaluation. Bielefeld: Bertelsmann-Verl. Available online at http://deposit.d-nb.de/cgi-bin/dokserv?id=3105427&prov=M&dok_var= 1&dok_ext=htm, checked on 12/9/2013.

ARBEITSGEMEINSCHAFT ENERGIEBILANZEN (2013): Auswertungstabellen zur Energiebilanz für die Bundesrepublik Deutschland 1990 bis 2012. Berechnungen auf Basis des Wirkungsgradansatzes. Edited by DIW Berlin, Energy Environment Forecast Analysis. Berlin. Available online at ag-energiebilanzen.de/index.php?article_id=29&fileName= ausw_06082013ov.pdf, checked on 4/8/2015.

ARROW, K. J. (1984): The Economics of Agency. Edited by Institute for Mathematical Studies in the Social Sciences. Stanford (Economic Series, 451).

ARROW, K. J.; FISHER, A. C. (1974): Environmental preservation, unsertainty, and irreversibility. In *Quarterly Journal of Economics* (Vol. 88 No. 2), pp. 312–319.

ARTAZCOZ, L.; CORTÈS, I.; ESCRIBÀ-AGÜIR, V.; CASCANT, LORENA, VILLEGAS, RODRIGO (2009): Understanding the relationship of long working hours with health status and health-related behaviours. In *Journal of Epidemiology and Community Health* 63 (7), pp. 521–527.

ASHENFELTER, ORLEY; CARD, DAVID (Eds.) (1999): Handbook of labor economics. Amsterdam: North-Holland (Handbooks in economics, 3).

ASIAN DEVELOPMENT BANK (Ed.) (2011): Framework of Inclusive Growth Indicators. Key Indicators for Asia and the Pacific 2011. Key Indicators for Asia and the Pacific 2011. Manila.

Aspin, David N.; Chapman, Judith D. (2000): Lifelong learning: concepts and conceptions. In: *International Journal of Lifelong Education* 19 (1), S. 2–19.

ATKISSON, A. (1996): Developing indicators of sustainable community: lessons from sustainable Seattle. In *Environmental Impact Assessment Review* (16 (4)), pp. 337–350.

ATTESLANDER, P.; CROMM, J. (2003): Methoden der empirischen Sozialforschung. 10., neu bearb. und erw. Aufl., 104. - 111. Tsd. Berlin: de Gruyter (De-Gruyter-Studienbuch).

BACH, H.-U.; FEIL, M.; FUCHS, J.; GARTNER, H.; KLINGER, S.; OTTO, A. ET AL. (2009): Der deutsche Arbeitsmarkt - Entwicklung und Perspektiven. In J. MÖLLER, U. WALWEI (EDS.): Handbuch Arbeitsmarkt 2009. Analysen, Daten, Fakten. Nürnberg: Institut für Arbeitsmarkt- und Berufsforschung (IAB-Bibliothek, 314), pp. 11–78.

BACHMANN, G. (2002): Nachhaltigkeit: Politik mit gesellschaftlicher Perspektive. In Bundeszentrale für politische Bildung (Ed.): Die Diskussion um Nachhaltigkeit. Bonn, pp. 8–18.

BAECHLER, L. (2012): Bridging the gap between the short run and the long run in sustainable development strategies. In M. MEIMETH, J. D. ROBERTSON (EDS.): Sustainable Development - how to Bridge the Knowledge-Action Gap? Exploring the added value of social and cultural perspectives. 1. ed. Baden-Baden: Nomos (Denkart Europa. Schriften zur europäischen Politik, Wirtschaft und Kultur, 18), pp. 27–46.

BANGEL, B.; BRINKMANN, C.; DEEKE, A. (2006): Evaluation von Arbeitsmarktpolitik. In R. STOCKMANN (ED.): Evaluationsforschung. Grundlagen und ausgewählte Forschungsfelder. 3. Aufl. Münster, New York, München, Wien: Waxmann (Sozialwissenschaftliche Evaluationsforschung, Bd. 1), pp. 311–344.

BANNER, D. K.; DOCTORS, S. I.; GORDON, A. C. (1975): The politics of social program evaluation. Cambridge, Mass: Ballinger.

BARBIER, J.-C.; SIMONIN, B. (1997): European Social Programmes: Can Evaluation of Implementation Increase the Appropriateness of Findings? In *Evaluation* 3 (4), pp. 391–407.

Barro, Robert J.; Lee, Jong-Wha (1993): International Comparisons of Educational Attainment. In: *NBER Working Paper Series* (4349).

Barro, Robert J.; Lee, Jong-Wha (1996): International Measures of Schooling Years and Schooling Quality. In: *The American Economic Review* 86 (2), S. 218–223.

Barro, Robert J.; Lee, Jong-Wha (2001): International data on educational attainment: updates and implications. In: *Oxford Economic Papers* (3), S. 541–563.

BASSANINI, A.; VENN, D. (2007): Assessing the Impact of Labour Market Policies on Productivity: A Difference-in-Differences Approach. In *OECD Social, Employment and Migration Working Papers* (54).

BASSANINI, A.; VENN, D. (2008): The Impact of Labour Market Policies on Productivity in OECD countries. In *International Productivity Monitor* (17).

BATT, F. R. (1929): The law of master and servant. London: Pitman.

BAYER, S. (2004): Nachhaltigkeitskonforme Diskontierung. Das Konzept des "Generation Adjusted Discounting". In *Vierteljahrshefte zur Wirtschaftsforschung* (73 (2004), 1), pp. 142–157.

BECKENBACH, FRANK (Ed.) (2007): Soziale Nachhaltigkeit. Marburg: Metropolis-Verl. (Jahrbuch Ökologische Ökonomik, 5).

BEHNCKE, S.; FRÖLICH, M.; LECHNER, M. (2007): Targeting labour market programmes. Results from a randomised experiment. London: Centre for Economic Policy Research (Discussion paper series / Centre for Economic Policy Research, 6537: Labour economics).

BENNETT, M.; JAMES, P. (1999): Key Themes in Environmental, Social and Sustainability Performance Evaluation and Reporting. In M. BENNETT, P. JAMES (EDS.): Sustainable measures. Evaluation and reporting of environmental and social performance. Sheffield: Greenleaf Publ., pp. 29–74.

BENNETT, MARTIN; JAMES, PETER (Eds.) (1999): Sustainable measures. Evaluation and reporting of environmental and social performance. Sheffield: Greenleaf Publ.

BERGHEIM, S.; BOECKERS, M. C. (2010): Building Blocks for Ethical Market Economies in the 21st Century. A background paper on qualitative growth. Edited by International Cultural Dialogue and Sustainable Development. BERTELSMANN STIFTUNG. Gütersloh.

BERTELSMANN STIFTUNG (Ed.) (2009): Jugend und die Zukunft der Welt. Ergebnis einer repräsentativen Umfrage in Deutschland und Österreich "Jugend und Nachhaltigkeit". Bertelsmann Stiftung. Gütersloh.

BEYWL, W. (2002): Standards für Evaluation. Köln: Geschäftsstelle DeGEval.

BGBL. I: Erstes Gesetz für moderne Dienstleistungen am Arbeitsmarkt 2002 (Teil I Nr. 87), pp. 4607–4620.

BGBL. I: Zweites Gesetz für moderne Dienstleistungen am Arbeitsmarkt 2002 (Teil I Nr. 87), pp. 4621–4636.

BGBL. I: Drittes Gesetz für moderne Dienstleistungen am Arbeitsmarkt 2003 (Teil I Nr. 65), pp. 2848–2918.

BGBL. I: Viertes Gesetz für moderne Dienstleistungen am Arbeitsmarkt 2003 (Teil I Nr. 66), pp. 2954–3000.

BIRD, R.C; CAHOY, DANIEL R.; PRENKERT, JAMIE D. (Eds.) (2014): Law, Business and Human Rights. Bridging the Gap. Cheltenham: Edward Elgar Publishing.

BLANCHARD, O.; KATZ, L. F. (1997): What We Know and Do Not Know About the Natural Rate of Unemployment. In *The Journal of Economic Perspectives* 11 (1), pp. 51–72.

BLASCHKE, D.; PLATH, H. E. (2000): Möglichkeiten und Grenzen des Erkenntnisgewinns durch Evaluation aktiver Arbeitsmarktpolitik. In *MittAB* 33 (3), pp. 462–482.

BLAZEJCZAK, J. (2013): Nachhaltige Beschäftigungspolitik. In M. VON HAUFF, T. NGUYEN (EDS.): Nachhaltige Wirtschaftspolitik. 1. Aufl. Baden-Baden: Nomos (Bd. 5), pp. 153–171.

BLAZEJCZAK, J.; EDLER, D. (2004): Nachhaltigkeitskriterien aus ökologischer, ökonomischer und sozialer Perspektive - Ein interdisziplinärer Ansatz. In *Vierteljahrshefte zur Wirtschaftsforschung* (73/1), pp. 10–30.

BMAS (2006): Die Wirksamkeit moderner Dienstleistungen am Arbeitsmarkt. Bericht 2006 des Bundesministeriums für Arbeit und Soziales zur Wirkung der Umsetzung der Vorschläge der Kommission Moderne Dienstleistungen am Arbeitsmarkt (ohne Grundsicherung für Arbeitssuchende). Kurzfassung der Ergebnisse, 12/20/2006.

BMU; UMWELTBUNDESAMT (2010): Umweltbewusstsein in Deutschland 2010. Ergebnisse einer repräsentativen Bevölkerungsumfrage. Edited by Bundesministerium für Umwelt, Naturschutz und Reaktorsicherheit, Umweltbundesamt. Heidelberg, Potsdam. Available online at http://www.umweltdaten.de/publikationen/fpdf-l/4045.pdf, checked on 7/12/2013.

BÖCKER, REINHARD; HUTTER, CLAUS-PETER (Eds.) (2005): Umweltindikatoren - Mythos oder Wirklichkeit? Was wissen wir wirklich über unsere Umwelt? HOHENHEIMER UMWELTTAGUNG; INSTITUT FÜR LANDSCHAFTS- UND PFLANZENÖKOLOGIE. Stuttgart: Wiss. Verl.-Ges. (Beiträge der Akademie für Natur- und Umweltschutz Baden-Württemberg, 39).

BÖHRINGER, C.; LÖSCHEL, A. (2004): Die Messung nachhaltiger Entwicklung mithilfe numerischer Gleichgewichtsmodelle. In *Vierteljahrshefte zur Wirtschaftsforschung* (73 (2004), 1), pp. 31–52.

BONOLI, G. (2010): The political economy of active labour market policy. In *Working Papers on the Reconciliation of Work and Welfare in Europe* (REC-WP 01/2010).

BORTZ, J.; DÖRING, N. (2006): Forschungsmethoden und Evaluation. Für Human- und Sozialwissenschaftler. 4., überarbeitete Auflage. Berlin, Heidelberg: Springer Medizin Verlag Heidelberg (Springer-11776 /Dig. Serial).

BOSCH, GERHARD; HENNICKE, PETER; HILBERT, JOSEF; KRISTOF, KORA; SCHERHORN, GERHARD (Eds.) (2002): Die Zukunft von Dienstleistungen. Ihre Auswirkung auf Arbeit, Umwelt und Lebensqualität. Frankfurt am Main u. a.: Campus Verl.

BOSSEL, H. (1999): Indicators for sustainable development. Theory, method, applications: a report to the Balaton Group. Winnipeg: International Institute for Sustainable Development/ Institut international du développement durable.

BOSSEL, H. (2007): Koexistenz von Natur- und Humansystemen: Zur Notwendigkeit einer Ethik der Nachhaltigkeit. In F. BECKENBACH (ED.): Soziale Nachhaltigkeit. Marburg: Metropolis-Verl. (Jahrbuch Ökologische Ökonomik, 5), pp. 73–98.

BOUIS, R.; CAUSA, O.; DEMMOU, L.; DUVAL, R.; ZDZIENICKA, A. (2012): The Short-Term Effects of Structural Reforms. An Empirical Analysis. In *OECD Economics Department Working Papers* (949).

BRAND, K.-W.; JOCHUM, G. (2000): Der Deutsche Diskurs zu Nachhaltiger Entwicklung. Abschlussbericht eines DFG-Projekts zum Thema „Sustainable Development/ Nachhaltige Entwicklung - Zur sozialen Konstruktion globaler Handlungskonzepte im Umweltdiskurs". MÜNCHNER PROJEKTGRUPPE FÜR SOZIALFORSCHUNG E.V. München (MPS-Texte, 1/2000). Available online at http://www.sozialforschung.org/de/literatur/deutscher_nachh_diskurs.pdf, checked on 5/20/2009.

BRAUN, S.; KAMIN, K.; MARTEN, M. K. (2014): Strategien für den Arbeitsmarkt der Zukunft: Die demografische Herausforderung meistern. In *Kiel Policy Brief* (72).

BRINKMANN, C. (2000): Zur Evaluation der aktiven Arbeitsförderung nach dem SGB III - Monitoring und Wirkungsforschung im Umbruch. In *MittAB* 33 (3), pp. 481–499.

BRINKMANN, C.; HUJER, R.; KOCH, S. (2006): Evaluation aktiver Arbeitsmarktpolitik in Deutschland. Eine Einführung. In *Zeitschrift für ArbeitsmarktForschung* 39 (3/4), pp. 319–327.

BRINKMANN, C.; WIEßNER, F. (2002): Zur Wirkungsforschung aktiver Arbeitsmarktpolitik - neue Herausforderungen für Monitoring und Evaluation. In G. KLEINHEINZ (ED.): IAB-Kompendium Arbeitsmarkt- und Berufsforschung. Nürnberg: Zentralamt der Bundesanst. für Arbeit (Beiträge zur Arbeitsmarkt- und Berufsforschung, 250).

BRINKMANN, U.; DÖRRE, K.; RÖBENACK, S.; KRAEMER, K.; SPEIDEL, F. (2006): Prekäre Arbeit. Ursachen, Ausmaß, soziale Folgen und subjektive Verarbeitungsformen unsicherer Beschäftigungsverhältnisse. Bonn: Friedrich-Ebert-Stiftung (Gesprächskreis Migration und Integration).

BROMLEY, D. W. (1990): The Ideology of Efficiency: Searching for a Theory of Policy Analysis. In *Journal of Environmental Economics and Management* (19), pp. 86–107.

BUJARD, M. (2013): Wie wirkt das Elterngeld? In *Analysen & Argumente der Konrad Adenauer Stiftung* (123).

BUNDESAGENTUR FÜR ARBEIT (2004): Begriff der Arbeitslosigkeit in der Statistik unter SGB II und SGB III. Grundlage für Statistik auf der Basis von Prozessdaten. In *Statistik der Bundesagentur für Arbeit*.

BUNDESAGENTUR FÜR ARBEIT (2014): Die Arbeitsmarktsituation von langzeitarbeitslosen Menschen. In *Arbeitsmarktberichterstattung: Der Arbeitsmarkt in Deutschland.*

BUNDESAGENTUR FÜR ARBEIT (2015): Arbeitsmarktpolitische Maßnahmen - Aktuelle Eckwerte April 2015. Edited by Arbeitsagentur. Available online at https://statistik.arbeitsagentur.de/Navigation/Statistik/Statistik-nach-Themen/Arbeitsmarktpolitische-Massnahmen/Arbeitsmarktpolitische-Massnahmen-Nav.html, checked on 5/20/2015.

BUNDESAGENTUR FÜR ARBEIT (2015): Der Arbeitsmarkt im April 2015. Available online at http://www.arbeitsagentur.de/web/content/DE/Presse/Presseinformationen/ArbeitsundAusbildungsmarkt/Detail/index.htm?dfContentId=L6019022DSTBAI745751, checked on 6/1/2015.

BUNDESREGIERUNG (2008): Fortschrittsbericht 2008 zur nachtionalen Nachhaltigkeitsstrategie. Für ein nachhaltiges Deutschland. Edited by Presse- und Informationsamt der Bundesregierung. Berlin. Available online at http://www.bundesregierung.de/Content/DE/_Anlagen/2008/05/2008-05-08-fortschritts bericht-2008.pdf?__blob=publicationFile&v=2, checked on 8/27/2013.

BUNDESREGIERUNG (2011): Gemeinsame Geschäftsordnung der Bundesministerien. GGO, revised. Rechtsstand 9/1/2011 (aktuelle Fassung)

BUNDESREGIERUNG (2011): Nationale Nachhaltigkeitsstrategie. Fortschrittsbericht 2012. Edited by Presse- und Informationsamt der Bundesregierung. Berlin. Available online at http://www.bundesregierung.de/Content/DE/Publikation/Bestellservice/2012-05-08-fort schritt sbericht-2012.pdf?__blob=publicationFile, updated on Oktober 2011, checked on 8/9/2013.

BUNDESZENTRALE FÜR POLITISCHE BILDUNG (Ed.) (2002): Die Diskussion um Nachhaltigkeit. Bonn.

BUSHNELL, P. (1998): Does Evaluation of Policies Matter? In *Evaluation* 4 (3), pp. 363–371.

CALIENDO, M.; STEINER, V. (2005): Aktive Arbeitsmarktpolitik in Deutschland: Bestandsaufnahme und Bewertung der mikroökonomischen Evaluationsergebnisse. In *Zeitschrift für ArbeitsmarktForschung* 38 (2/3), pp. 396–418.

CARROLL, A. B. (1991): The Pyramid of Corporate Social Responsibility: Toward the Moral Management of Organizational Stakeholders. In *Business Horizons* 34 (4), pp. 39–48.

CHARPE, M.; CORLEY-COULIBALY, M.; ERNST, E.; ESCUDERO, V.; HA, B.-J.; KHATIWADA, S. ET AL. (2011): Making recovery sustainable. Lessons from country innovations. Geneva: International Labour Organization, International Institute for Labour Studies (Studies on growth with equity).

CHELIMSKY, E. (1997): Thoughts for a New Evaluation Society. In *Evaluation* 3 (1), pp. 97–118.

COASE, R. H. (1937): The Nature of the Firm. In *Economica* (Vol. 4 No. 16), pp. 386–405.

CONSEIL D'ANALYSE ÉCONOMIQUE; SACHVERSTÄNDIGENRAT ZUR BEGUTACHTUNG DER GESAMTWIRTSCHAFTLICHEN ENTWICKLUNG (2011): Monitoring economic performance, quality of life and sustainability. Joint report as requested by the Franco-German Ministerial Council. 1. Aufl. Wiesbaden: Statistisches Bundesamt.

CONTANDRIOPOULOS, D.; BROUSSELLE, A. (2012): Evaluation models and evaluation use. In *Evaluation* 18 (1), pp. 61–77.

COSTANZA, R.; ALPEROVITZ, G.; DALY, H.; FARLEY, J.; FRANCO, C.; JACKSON, T. ET AL. (2012): Building a Sustainable and Desirable Economcy-in-Society-in-Nature. Edited by United Nations Division for Sustainable Development. New York. Available online at http://sustainabledevelopment.un.org/content/documents/Building_a_Sustainable_and_D esirable_Economy-in-Society-in-Nature.pdf, checked on 8/12/2013.

DALY, H. E. (Ed.) (2007): Ecological economics and sustainable development, selected essays of Herman Daly. Cheltenham, UK [etc.], Northampton, MA, USA: Edward Elgar.

DALY, H. E. (2007): Economics in a full world. Originally published in: Scientific American, September 2005, diagrams altered. In H. E. DALY (ED.): Ecological economics and sustainable development, selected essays of Herman Daly. Cheltenham, UK [etc.], Northampton, MA, USA: Edward Elgar.

DALY, H. E. (2007): Limits to growth. originally published in: Encyclopedia of Population, Paul Demeny and Geoffrey McNicoll, eds, Macmillan Co., 2003, pp. 602-3. In H. E. DALY (ED.): Ecological economics and sustainable development, selected essays of Herman Daly. Cheltenham, UK [etc.], Northampton, MA, USA: Edward Elgar, pp. 9–11.

DATTA, L.-E. (2000): Seriously Seeking Fairness: Strategies for Crafting Non-partisan Evaluations in a Partisan World. In *American Journal of Evaluation* 21 (1), pp. 1–14.

DATTA, L.-E. (2002): The Case of the Uncertain Bridge. In *American Journal of Evaluation* 23 (3), pp. 187–197.

DEININGER, K.; SQUIRE, L. (1996): A New Data Set Measuring Income Inequality. In *The World Bank Economic Review* 10 (3), pp. 565–592.

DEUTSCHER BUNDESTAG (1998): Konzept Nachhaltigkeit vom Leitbild zur Umsetzung. Abschlußbericht der Enquete-Kommission "Schutz des Menschen und der Umwelt - Ziele und Rahmenbedingungen einer nachhaltig zukunftsverträglichen Enwicklung". DEUTSCHER BUNDESTAG. Bonn (Drucksache 13/11200). Available online at http://dip21.bundestag.de/dip21/btd/13/112/1311200.pdf, checked on 12/19/2012.

DGB (2010): Gesundheitsrisiko Arbeitslosigkeit - Wissensstand, Praxis und Anforderungen an eine arbeitsmarktintegrative Gesundheitsförderung. Edited by Bereich Arbeitsmarktpolitik DGB Bundesvorstand. Berlin (09/2010).

DIEFENBACHER, H. (2001): Gerechtigkeit und Nachhaltigkeit. Zum Verhältnis von Ethik und Ökonomie. Darmstadt: Wiss. Buchges.

DIEFENBACHER, H.; PAQUÉ, K.-H. (2013): Pro & Contra. In *Wirtschaftsdienst* 93 (2), pp. 66–67. DOI: 10.1007/s10273-013-1487-3.

DIEFENBACHER, H.; TEICHERT, V.; WILHELMY, S. (2009): Leitfaden. Indikatoren im Rahmen einer lokalen Agenda 21. 4th ed. Heidelberg: LUBW.

DJSI (2010): Dow Jones Sustainability Indexes. Available online at http://www.sustainability-index.com/, checked on 3/26/2010.

DODGE, R.; DALY, A. P.; HUYTON, J.; SANDERS, L. D. (2012): The challenge of defining wellbeing. In *Journal of Wellbeing* (2 (3)), pp. 222–235.

DONALDSON, S. I.; GOOLER, L. E.; SCRIVEN, M. (2002): Strategies for Managing Evaluation Anxiety: Toward a Psychology of Program Evaluation. In *American Journal of Evaluation* 23 (3), pp. 261–274.

Drautz, Cordula (2011): Arbeit und Autonomie. Plädoyer für eine nachhaltige Arbeitspolitik. In: *Aus Politik und Zeitgeschichte* (15), S. 41–46.

DRESNER, S. (2008): The principles of sustainability. 2nd ed. London, Sterling, VA: Earthscan.

DULLIEN, S.; VAN TREECK, T. (2012): Ziele und Zielkonflikte der Wirtschaftspolitik und Ansätze für einen neuen sozial-ökologischen Regulierungsrahmen. Bonn: Friedrich-Ebert-Stiftung, Abt. Wirtschafts- und Sozialpolitik (Wiso-Diskurs - Expertisen und Dokumentationen zur Wirtschafts- und Sozialpolitik).

DYBE, G.; WEITH, T. (2004): Anspruch und Wirklichkeit von ökonomischen Nachhaltigkeitsindikatoren - Das Fallbeispiel Berlin. In *Vierteljahrshefte zur Wirtschaftsforschung* 73 (1), pp. 112–125.

EASTERLIN, R. A. (1974): Does economic growth improve the human lot? : some empirical evidence. In M. ABRAMOVITZ, P. A. DAVID, M. W. REDER (EDS.): Nations and households in economic growth. Essays in honor of Moses Abramovitz. New York: Academic Press, pp. 89–125.

EBRINGHOFF, J. (2005): Nachhaltige Lebensführung? Fähigkeit der Personen und Gestaltungsaufgabe einer subjektorientierten Arbeitskraftpolitik. In K. GROßMANN (ED.): Im Prinzip Nachhaltigkeit. Akteurskonstellationen und Handlungsmöglichkeiten in interdisziplinärer Betrachtung. 1. Aufl. München: Hampp, pp. 14–41.

EGGS, J.; TRAPPMANN, M.; UNGER, S. (2014): Grundsicherungsempfänger und Erwerbstätige im Vergleich. ALG-II-Bezieher schätzen ihre Gesundheit schlechter ein. In *IAB-Kurzbericht* (23).

EICHHORST, W. (2013): Wie weiter am deutschen Arbeitsmarkt? In *IZA Standpunkte* (61).

EICHHORST, W.; ZIMMERMANN, K. F. (2007): And Then There Were Four… How Many (and Which) Measures of Active Labor Market Policy Do We Still Need? Finding a Balance after the Evaluation of the Hartz Reforms in Germany. In *Applied Economics Quarterly* 53 (3), pp. 243–272.

EKARDT, F. (2005): Das Prinzip Nachhaltigkeit. Generationengerechtigkeit und globale Gerechtigkeit. München: Beck.

ELIASON, M.; STORRIE, D. (2009): Does Job Loss Shorten Life? In *The Journal of Human Resources* (Vol. 44, Issue 2), pp. 277–302.

ENDRES, A.; RADKE, V. (1998): Indikatoren einer nachhaltigen Entwicklung. Elemente ihrer wirtschaftstheoretischen Fundierung. Berlin: Duncker & Humblot (Volkswirtschaftliche Schriften, Heft 479).

ENQUETE-KOMMISSION (2013): Schlussbericht der Enquete-Kommission "Wachstum, Wohlstand, Lebensqualität - Wege zu nachhaltigem Wirtschaften und gesellschaftlichem Fortschritt in der sozialen Marktwirtschaft". Bonn: Bundeszentrale für politische Bildung (Schriftenreihe der BpB, 1419).

ESAW (2001): European statistics on accidents at work. Methodology. Luxembourg.

EUROPEAN AGENCY FOR OCCUPATIONAL SAFETY AND HEALTH AT WORK (1998): Annual Report. Bilbao: EASHW.

EUROPEAN COMMISSION (2007): The use of indicators in the European Commission. EUROPEAN COMMISSION, SUSTAINABLE DEVELOPMENT AND ECONOMIC ANALYSIS UNIT. Brussels. Available online at http://www.beyond-gdp.eu/download/bgdp-bp-white.pdf, checked on 8/6/2013.

EUROPEAN COMMISSION EQUAL (2008): EQUAL Community Initiative. EUROPEAN COMMISSION. Available online at http://ec.europa.eu/employment_social/equal_consolidated/, checked on 12/18/2014.

EUROPEAN COUNCIL (1994): European Council Meeting on 9 and 10 December 2004 in Essen. Precidency Conclusions. Brussels. Available online at http://www.europarl. europa.eu/summits/ess1_en.htm, checked on 5/28/2014.

EUROPEAN PARLIAMENT (2003): Working Time Directive. 2003/88/EC.

EUROSTAT (2012): Sustainable Development Indicators. Edited by Eurostat. Available online at http://epp.eurostat.ec.europa.eu/portal/page/portal/sdi/indicators, updated on 3/27/2014, checked on 04/17/2015.

EUROSTAT (2013): Sustainable Development Indicators. Edited by Eurostat. EUROPEAN COMMISSION. Luxembourg. Available online at http://epp.eurostat. ec.europa.eu/portal/page/portal/sdi/indicators, checked on 6/13/2014.

FALK, A. (2001): Homo Oeconomicus Versus Homo Reciprocans: Ansätze für ein Neues Wirtschaftspolitisches Leitbild? In *Institute for Empirical Research in Economics of the University of Zurich Working Paper Series* (Working Paper No. 79).

FENG, J.; NGUYEN, M. C. (2014): Relative versus absolute poverty headcount ratios: the full breakdown. Edited by The World Bank. Available online at http://blogs.worldbank.org/opendata/relative-versus-absolute-poverty-headcount-ratios-full-breakdown, checked on 6/1/2015.

FETTERMAN, D. M. (1994): Empowerment Evaluation. In *Evaluation Practice* 15 (1), pp. 1–15.

FISCHER-KOWALSKI, M.; HABERL, H.; PAYER, H.; STEURER, A. Z.-W. H. (1993): Das System verursacherbezogener Umweltindikatoren. Ein nicht-monetäres System für die ökologische Erweiterung der volkswirtschaftlichen Gesamtrechnung. Berlin (Schriftenreihe des IÖW, 64).

FISHER, A. C.; KRUTILLA, J. V.; CICCHETTI, C. J. (1972): The Economics of Environmental Preservation: A Theoretical and Empirical Analysis. In *American Economic Review* (Vol. 62), pp. 605–619.

FITZENBERGER, B.; SPECKESSER, S. (2000): Zur wissenschaftlichen Evaluation der aktiven Arbeitsmarktpolitik in Deutschland. Ein Überblick. Mannheim: ZEW (Discussion paper / ZEW, Zentrum für Europäische Wirtschaftsforschung GmbH Labour economics, human resources and social security, 00-06).

FORSA (2012): Nachhaltigkeit. Edited by Forsa Gesellschaft für Sozialforschung und statistische Analysen mbH. Available online at http://www.zukunftsprojekt-erde.de/ Auswertung-Nachhaltigkeit.pdf, checked on 3/21/2014.

FOSS HANSEN, H. (2005): Choosing Evaluation Models: A Discussion on Evaluation Design. In *Evaluation* 11 (4), pp. 447–462.

FREEDLAND, J. (2002): Greens don't need the US. In *The Guardian* 2002, 8/16/2002. Available online at http://www.theguardian.com/politics/2002/aug/16/environment.usa, checked on 11/19/2013.

FREEMAN, R. (2008): Labour Productivity Indicators. Comparison of two OECD databases. Productivity differentials & the Balassa-. Edited by OECD Statistics Directorate. Available online at http://www. oecd. org/dataoecd/57/15/41354425. pdf, checked on 6/3/2015.

FTSE (2011): FTSE4Good Index Inclusion Criteria. Thematic Criteria and Scoring Framework. London. Available online at http://www.ftse.com/Indices/FTSE4Good_Index_Series/Downloads/FTSE4Good_Inclusion_all_copy_Aug2013.pdf, checked on 12/11/2014.

FÜLLSACK, M. (2009): Arbeit. 1. Aufl. Wien: Facultas.wuv.

GABAGLIO, E. (2003): Europäische Gewerkschaften: Akteure für eine nachhaltige Entwicklung. In G. LINNE, M. SCHWARZ (EDS.): Handbuch Nachhaltige Entwicklung. Wie ist nachhaltiges Wirtschaften machbar? Opladen: Leske + Budrich (Handbücher Leske + Budrich), pp. 53–62.

GEBAUER, J.; GLAHE, J. (2011): Praxis der Nachhaltigkeitsberichterstattung in deutschen Großunternehmen. Befragungsergebnisse im Rahmen des iöw/future Rankings 2011. Edited by IÖW Diskussionspapier. Berlin.

GEYER-ALLÉLY, E.; EPPEL, J. (1998): Notwendiger Wandel der Konsum- und Produktionsstrukturen. In OECD (Ed.): Nachhaltige Entwicklung. Politikkonzepte der OECD für das 21. Jahrhundert. Paris, pp. 59–73.

GG (1949): Grundgesetz für die Bundesrepublik Deutschland in der im Bundesgesetzblatt Teil III, Gliederungsnummer 100-1. veröffentlichten bereinigten Fassung, das zuletzt durch Artikel 1 des Gesetzes vom 11. Juli 2012 (BGBI. I S. 1478) geändert worden ist. GG. Available online at http://www.gesetze-im-internet.de/bundesrecht/gg/gesamt.pdf, checked on 7/26/2013.

GIANNAKOURIS, K. (2008): Population and social conditions. In *eurostat statistics in focus* (72/2008). Available online at http://epp.eurostat.ec.europa.eu/portal/page/portal/product_details/publication?p_product_code=KS-SF-08-072, checked 4/2/2013.

GIMPELSON, V.; OSHCHEPKOV, A. (2012): Does more unemployment cause more fear of unemployment? In *IZA Journal of Labor & Development* (1:6).

GLOBAL FOOTPRINT NETWORK (2015): World Footprint: Do we fit on the planet? Available online at http://www.footprintnetwork.org/en/index.php/GFN/page/world_footprint/, updated on 3/12/2015, checked on 5/20/2015.

GLOBESCAN/SUSTAINABILITY (2012a): Collaborating for a sustainable future. Survey December 2012. Washington.

GLOBESCAN/SUSTAINABILITY (2012b): Global Public Opinion Report on the State of Sustainable Development. The Regeneration Roadmap. Washington.

GLOBESCAN/SUSTAINABILITY (2012c): Global Societal Trends on Sustainable Development Issues. The Regeneration Roadmap, December 2012. Washington.

GOODWIN, N. R. (2003): Five Kinds of Capital: Useful Concepts for Sustainable Development. Global Development and Environment Institute Working Paper No. 03-07. TUFTS UNIVERSITY, Medford. Available online at http://www.ase.tufts.edu/gdae/publications/working_papers/03-07sustainabledevelopment.PDF, checked on 8/2/2013.

GRABOW, B.; HENCKEL, D.; HOLLBACH-GRÖMIG, B. (1995): Weiche Standortfaktoren. Stuttgart, Berlin, Köln, Stuttgart, Berlin, Köln: Kohlhammer; Dt. Gemeindeverl (Schriften des Deutschen Instituts für Urbanistik, 89).

GRIEẞHAMMER, R.; JAHN, T.; KORBUN, T.; KRAEMER, A.; LEGGEWIE, C.; RENN, O. ET AL. (2012): Verstehen - Bewerten - Gestalten. Transdisziplinäres Wissen für eine nachhaltige Gesellschaft. Memorandum zur Weiterentwicklung der sozial-ökologischen Forschung in Deutschland anlässlich der BMBF-Agenda-Konferenz "Sozial-ökologische Forschung für eine zukunftsfähige Gesellschaft", Bonn, 19. und 20.März 2012. Edited by ISOE. Available online at http://www.isoe.de/fileadmin/redaktion/Downloads/Soziale_Oekologie/soef-memorandum-2012.pdf, checked on 8/21/2013.

GROBER, U. (2010): Die Entdeckung der Nachhaltigkeit. Kulturgeschichte eines Begriffs. München: Kunstmann.

GROßMANN, KATRIN (Ed.) (2005): Im Prinzip Nachhaltigkeit. Akteurskonstellationen und Handlungsmöglichkeiten in interdisziplinärer Betrachtung. 1. Aufl. München: Hampp. Available online at http://deposit.ddb.de/cgi-bin/dokserv?id=2681412&prov=M&dok_var=1&dok_ext=htm, checked on 10/29/2014.

GRUNWALD, A.; KOPFMÜLLER, J. (2006): Nachhaltigkeit. Frankfurt am Main: Campus-Verl. Available online at http://www.gbv.de/dms/hebis-darmstadt/toc/17671331X.pdf, checked 1/15/2014

GÜNTHER, E.; SCHUH, H. (2000): Definitionen, Konzepte, Kriterien und Indikatoren einer nachhaltigen Entwicklung. Eine Literaturstudie im Auftrag der Degussa-Hüls AG. In *Dresdner Beiträge zur Betriebswirtschaftslehre* (39/00).

GUTWALD, R.; LEßMANN, O.; MASSON, T.; RAUSCHMAYER, F. (2011): The Capability Approach to intergenerational justice. A survey. In *UFZ Discussion Papers* (8/2011). Available online at http://www.ufz.de/export/data/global/26149_DP_8_2011_GeNECA_ Gutwald.pdf, checked on 11/8/2013.

HABER, W. (2011): Die unbequemen Wahrheiten der Ökologie. Eine Nachhaltigkeitsperspektive für das 21. Jahrhundert ; [erste Carl-von-Carlowitz-Vorlesung des Rates für Nachhaltige Entwicklung anlässlich seiner 9. Jahreskonferenz in Berlin am 23. November 2009]. 2. Aufl. München: oekom-Verl. (Carl-von-Carlowitz-Reihe, 1).

HAGENAARS, A.; VOS, K. DE (1988): The Definition and Measurement of Poverty. In *The Journal of Human Resources* 23 (2), pp. 211–221.

HAGIST, C.; RAFFELHÜSCHEN, B.; WEDDIGE, O. (2006): Brandmelder der Zukunft - Die aktuelle Generationenbilanz. Edited by Stiftung Marktwirtschaft. Berlin (Argumente zu Marktwirtschaft und Politik, 97). Available online at http://www.stiftung-marktwirtschaft.de/fileadmin/user_upload/Generationenbilanz/Argument_097_Brandmelder_I_Generationenbilanz_2006_09.pdf, checked on 12/20/2011.

HAIPETER, T.; VOSS-DAHM, D. (2002): Nachhaltige Dienstleistungsarbeit? "Front-Line-Work" in der IT-Branche und in Banken. In G. BOSCH, P. HENNICKE, J. HILBERT, K. KRISTOF, G. SCHERHORN (EDS.): Die Zukunft von Dienstleistungen. Ihre Auswirkung auf Arbeit, Umwelt und Lebensqualität. Frankfurt am Main u. a.: Campus Verl., pp. 214–234.

HANBERGER, A. (2001): What is the Policy Problem?: Methodological Challenges in Policy Evaluation. In *Evaluation and Program Planning* 7 (1), pp. 45–62.

HARRISON, A. (2000): A Framework for measuring sustainable development. In OECD (Ed.): Frameworks to measure sustainable development. An OECD expert workshop. Paris: Organisation for Economic Co-operation and Development (Sustainable development), pp. 19–37.

HARTMUTH, G. (2004): Nachhaltige Entwicklung im lokalen Kontext. Schritte zur Entwicklung eines kommunalen Nachhaltigkeits-Indikatorensystems. Edited by UFZ-

Umweltforschungszentrum, Department Ökonomie, Soziologie und Recht. UFZ-UMWELTFORSCHUNGSZENTRUM. Leipzig (UFZ-Diskussionspapiere, 6/2004). Available online at http://www.ufz.de/export/data/1/29325_ufz_disk6_2004.pdf, checked on 9/10/2013.

HAUFF, M. VON (2007): Beschäftigung im Umweltschutzsektor. In K. D. JOHN (ED.): Arbeitslosigkeit in Europa. Neue Perspektiven durch die Vermarktung umweltfreundlicher Technologien? ; Beiträge zum 2. Chemnitzer Symposium "Europa und Umwelt". Aachen: Shaker (Schriftenreihe der Chemnitzer Wirtschaftswissenschaftlichen Gesellschaft, Bd. 8), pp. 15–31.

HAUFF, M. VON; JÖRG, A. (2013): Nachhaltiges Wachstum. München: Oldenbourg.

HAUFF, M. VON; KLEINE, A. (2009): Nachhaltige Entwicklung. Grundlagen und Umsetzung. München: Oldenbourg.

HAUFF, MICHAEL VON; NGUYEN, THUAN (Eds.) (2013): Nachhaltige Wirtschaftspolitik. 1. Aufl. Baden-Baden: Nomos (Bd. 5).

HAUFF, M. VON; SCHIFFER, H. (2013): Anforderungen des Paradigmas nachhaltiger Entwicklung. In M. VON HAUFF, T. NGUYEN (EDS.): Nachhaltige Wirtschaftspolitik. 1. Aufl. Baden-Baden: Nomos (Bd. 5), pp. 9–31.

HAYEK, F. A. (1973): Law, legislation and liberty. A new statement of the liberal principles of justice and political economy. Vol. 1, Rules and order. London: Routledge & Kegan Paul.

HAYEK, F. A.; CALDWELL, B. (1997): Socialism and war. Essays, documents, reviews. Chicago: University of Chicago Press (The collected works of F.A. Hayek, 10).

HECKMAN, J. J.; LALONDE, R. J.; SMITH, J. A. (1999): The Economics and Econometrics of Active Labor Market Programs. In O. ASHENFELTER, D. CARD (EDS.): Handbook of labor economics. Amsterdam: North-Holland (Handbooks in economics, 3), pp. 1865–2097.

HEDRICK, T. (1988): The interaction of politics and evaluation. In *Evaluation Practice* (9), pp. 5–14.

HEGELICH, S.; KNOLLMANN, D.; KUHLMANN, J. (2011): Agenda 2010. Strategien - Entscheidungen - Konsequenzen. 1. Aufl. Wiesbaden: Springer Fachmedien.

HEISTER, M. (2008): Aktuelle Erfahrungen mit der Evaluation von EQUAL-Projekten in Deutschland. In M. ANT (ED.): Nachhaltiger Mehrwert von Evaluation. Bielefeld: Bertelsmann-Verl., pp. 15–26.

HENSELING, C.; EBERLE, U.; GRIEẞHAMMER, R. (1999): Soziale und ökonomische Nachhaltigkeitsindikatoren. Freiburg im Breisgau: Eigenverlag; Öko-Inst.

HEYER, G. (2006): Zielsetzung und Struktur der "Hartz-Evaluation". In *Zeitschrift für ArbeitsmarktForschung* (3 und 4), pp. 467–476.

HILDEBRAND, E. (2003): Arbeit und Nachhaltigkeit. Wie geht das zusammen? In G. LINNE, M. SCHWARZ (EDS.): Handbuch Nachhaltige Entwicklung. Wie ist nachhaltiges Wirtschaften machbar? Opladen: Leske + Budrich (Handbücher Leske + Budrich), pp. 381–393.

HINTE, H.; RINNE, U.; ZIMMERMANN, K. F. (2011): Ein Punktesystem zur bedarfsorientierten Steuerung der Zuwanderung nach Deutschland. (erstellt für das Sächsische Staatsministerium für Wirtschaft, Arbeit und Verkehr). In *IZA Research Report* (35).

HOFSTEDE, G. (1984): The Cultural Relativity of the Quality of Life Concept. In *The Academy of Management Review* 9 (3), pp. 389–398.

HOLSTEIN, L. (2003): Nachhaltigkeit und neoklassische Ökonomik. Der homo oeconomicus und die Begründung intergenerationeller Gerechtigkeit. Univ., Diss.--Frankfurt am Main, 2003. Marburg: Metropolis-Verl. (Hochschulschriften, 83).

HOWLETT, M. (1991): Policy Instruments, Policy Styles, and Policy Implementation. National Approaches to Theories of Instrument Choice. In *Policy Studies Journal* Vol. 19 (2), pp. 1–21.

HUJER, R.; BELLMANN, L.; BRINKMANN, C. (2000): Evaluation aktiver Arbeitsmarktpolitik - Probleme und Perspektiven. Einführung in das Schwerpunktheft. In *MittAB* 33 (3), pp. 341–356.

HUJER, R.; FITZENBERGER, B. (2013): Stand und Perspektiven der Evaluation der aktiven Arbeitsmarktpolitik in Deutschland. In *ZEW Discussion Papers* (02-13).

IGES INSTITUT (2014): Belastung durch chronischen Stress. Sonderauswertung der Befragung der DAK - Gesundheit im Rahmen des Schwerpunktthemas 2014 -"Rushhour des Lebens". Berlin. Available online at http://www.dak.de/dak/download/Belastung_durch_chronischen_Stress_Sonderauswertungauswertung-1432950.pdf, checked on 2/5/2015.

ILLGE, L.; SCHWARZE, R. (2004): Messung von Nachhaltigkeit. In *Vierteljahrshefte zur Wirtschaftsforschung* (73/1), pp. 5–9.

ILO (1998): Statistics on occupational injuries resulting from accidents at work. Resolution adopted by the 16th International Conference of Labour Statisticians, Geneva, 6-15 October 1998. Geneva.

ILO (2014): Mission and objectives. Geneva. Available online at http://www.ilo.org/.

IMF (2013): World Economic Outlook Database 2013. IMF. Available online at http://www.imf.org/external/pubs/ft/weo/2013, checked on 3/20/2014.

IMF (2014): World Economic Outlook Databases. Available online at http://www.imf.org/external/pubs/ft/weo/2014/02/weodata/index.aspx, checked on 1/9/2015.

IMMERVOLL, H.; SCARPETTA, S. (2012): Activation and employment support policies in OECD countries. An overview of current approaches. In *IZA Journal of Labor Policy* (1:9). Available online at http://www.izajolp.com/content/pdf/2193-9004-1-9.pdf, checked on 10/25/2013.

JACKSON, T. (2011): Prosperity without growth. Economics for a finite planet. Paperback ed. London: Earthscan.

JACOBS, M. (1991): The green economy. Environment, sustainable development, and the politics of the future. London, Concord, Mass: Pluto Press.

JAHN, T. (2009): Understanding Social-Ecological Systems: Frontier Research for Sustainable Development. Implications for European Research Policy. ISOE. Brussels (sustainable development - a challenge for European research). Available online at http://www.isoe.de/fileadmin/redaktion/Downloads/Soziale_Oekologie/jahn-sust-dev-bruss-2009-en1.pdf, updated on 5/26/2009, checked on 8/21/2013.

JAHODA, M.; LAZARSFELD, P. F.; ZEISEL, H. (1960): Die Arbeitslosen von Marienthal: ein soziographischer Versuch über die Wirkungen langandauernder Arbeitslosigkeit, mit einem Anhang zur Geschichte der Soziographie. 1. Neuauflage. Allensbach: Verlag für Demoskopie (2).

JANN, W.; RÖBER, M.; WOLLMANN, H. (Eds.) (2006): Public Management - Grundlagen, Wirkungen, Kritik. Festschrift für Christoph Reichard zum 65. Geburtstag. Berlin: edition sigma.

JENKINS, S. (1991): The measurement of income inequality. In L. OSBERG (ED.): Economic inequality and poverty. International perspectives. Armonk: Sharpe, pp. 3–31.

JENSEN, M. C.; MECKLING, W. H. (1976): Agency Costs and the Theory of the Firm. In *Journal of Financial Economics* (3 (4)), pp. 305–360.

JOHN, KLAUS DIETER (Ed.) (2007): Arbeitslosigkeit in Europa. Neue Perspektiven durch die Vermarktung umweltfreundlicher Technologien? ; Beiträge zum 2. Chemnitzer Symposium "Europa und Umwelt". Aachen: Shaker (Schriftenreihe der Chemnitzer Wirtschaftswissenschaftlichen Gesellschaft, Bd. 8).

JOHN, K. D.; RÜBBELKE, D. T. (2007): Beschäftigung im Umweltsektor. In K. D. JOHN (ED.): Arbeitslosigkeit in Europa. Neue Perspektiven durch die Vermarktung umweltfreundlicher Technologien? ; Beiträge zum 2. Chemnitzer Symposium "Europa und Umwelt". Aachen: Shaker (Schriftenreihe der Chemnitzer Wirtschaftswissenschaftlichen Gesellschaft, Bd. 8), pp. 1–13.

JOHNSON, S. (2012): UNEP. The first 40 years : a narrative. Nairobi, [Kenya]: United Nations Environment Programme.

JÖRISSEN, J.; COENEN, R. (2003): Das integrative Nachhaltigkeitskonzept der HGF im Spiegel der Praxis. Einführung in den Schwerpunkt. In *Technikfolgenabschätzung Theorie und Praxis* 12 (3/4), pp. 5–9.

JÜDES, U. (1997): Nachhaltige Sprachverwirrung. Auf der Suche nach einer Theorie des Sustainable Development. In *Politische Ökologie* 15 (52), pp. 26–29.

KAS (2012): Corporate Social Responsitbility (CSR). KONRAD ADENAUER STIFTUNG. Available online at http://www.kas.de/wf/de/71.10174/, checked on 3/18/2014.

KHAKEE, A. (2003): The Emerging Gap between Evaluation Research and Practice. In *Evaluation* 9 (3), pp. 340–352.

KLEINE, A. (2009): Operationalisierung einer Nachhaltigkeitsstrategie. Ökologie, Ökonomie und Soziales integrieren. Wiesbaden: Gabler (Gabler Edition Wissenschaft).

KLEINHEINZ, GERHARD (Ed.) (2002): IAB-Kompendium Arbeitsmarkt- und Berufsforschung. INSTITUT FÜR ARBEITSMARKT- UND BERUFSFORSCHUNG <NÜRNBERG>. Nürnberg: Zentralamt der Bundesanst. für Arbeit (Beiträge zur Arbeitsmarkt- und Berufsforschung, 250).

KLINGER, S.; ROTHE, T.; WEBER, E. (2013): Makroökonomische Perspektive auf die Hartz-Reformen: Die Vorteile überwiegen. In *IAB-Kurzbericht* (11).

KLUVE, J. (2013): Aktive Arbeitsmaktpolitik: Maßnahmen, Zielsetzungen, Wirkungen. In *Arbeitspapier des Sachverständigenrates zur Begutachtung der Gesamtwirtschaftlichen Entwicklung* (7).

KOHLHAAS, M. (2005): Gesamtwirtschaftliche Effekte der ökologischen Steuerreform. Band II des Endberichts für das Vorhaben: "Quantifizierung der Effekte der Ökologischen Steuerreform auf Umwelt, Beschäftigung und Innovation". Edited by DIW. Berlin.

KOMAR, W. (2001): Beschäftigung im Umweltschutzsektor Ostdeutschlands - eine Analyse auf der Basis des IAB-Betriebspanels. In *Wirtschaft im Wandel* (13), pp. 320–325.

KOPFMÜLLER, J. (2011): Das Integrative Nachhaltigkeitskonzept der Helmholtz-Gemeinschaft. Idee - Anwendung - Perspektiven. Edited by KIT. Available online at http://www.mensch-und-technik.kit.edu/img/3_Kopfmueller_NeNa-Workshop_2011_-_Integratives__NH_Konzept.pdf, checked on 3/11/2014.

KRYSIAK, D. (2007): Nachhaltigkeit im Spannungsfeld von intra- und intergenerationeller Gerechtigkeit. In F. BECKENBACH (ED.): Soziale Nachhaltigkeit. Marburg: Metropolis-Verl. (Jahrbuch Ökologische Ökonomik, 5), pp. 129–155.

KUZNETS, S. (1955): Economic growth and income inequality. In *The American Economic Review* 45 (1), pp. 1–28.

LAMPERT, H.; ALTHAMMER, J.; (2001): Lehrbuch der Sozialpolitik. 6., überarb. Aufl. Berlin: Springer.

LAU, L. J.; JAMISON, D. T.; LOUAT, F. (1991): Education and Productivity in Developing Countries: An Aggregate Production Function Approach. In *World Bank Report* (WPS 612).

LEANA, C. R.; VAN BUREN, H. (1999): Organizational social capital and employment practices. In *Academy of Management Review* 24 (24), pp. 538–555.

LEÓN, C. D. (2005): Umweltindikatoren: Schlüssel zu einer nachhaltigen Entwicklung? In R. BÖCKER, C.-P. HUTTER (EDS.): Umweltindikatoren - Mythos oder Wirklichkeit? Was wissen wir wirklich über unsere Umwelt? Stuttgart: Wiss. Verl.-Ges. (Beiträge der Akademie für Natur- und Umweltschutz Baden-Württemberg, 39), pp. 45–61.

LINNE, GUDRUN; SCHWARZ, MICHAEL (Eds.) (2003): Handbuch Nachhaltige Entwicklung. Wie ist nachhaltiges Wirtschaften machbar? Opladen: Leske + Budrich (Handbücher Leske + Budrich).

LORENZEN, H.-P. (2008): Evaluationsstandards und ihre Umsetzung. In M. ANT (ED.): Nachhaltiger Mehrwert von Evaluation. Bielefeld: Bertelsmann-Verl., pp. 73–82.

LUDWIG, B. (2001): Begriff und Indikatoren nachhaltigen Wirtschaftens. In *Online Journal für Sozialwissenschaften und ihre Didaktik*, pp. 1–13. Available online at http://www.sowi-onlinejournal.de/nachhaltigkeit/ludwig.htm, checked on 4/1/2009.

LUSCHEI, F.; TRUBE, A. (2000): Evaluation und Qualitätsmanagement in der Arbeitsmarktpolitik - Einige systematische Vorüberlegungen und praktische Ansätze zur lokalen Umsetzung. In *MittAB* 33 (3), pp. 533–549.

MARTIN, J. P.; GRUBB, D. (2001): What works and for whom: a review of OECD countries' experiences with active labour market policies. In *Working Paper, IFAU - Institute for Labour Market Policy Evaluation* (14).

MASLOW, A. H. (1943): A Theory of Human Motivation. In *Psychological Review* (50 (4)), pp. 370–396.

MAYRING, P. (1990): Einführung in die qualitative Sozialforschung. Eine Anleitung zu qualitativem Denken. 1. Aufl. München: Psychologie-Verl.-Union (Kleine Bibliothek der Psychologie).

MCNALL, M.; FOSTER-FISHMAN, P. G. (2007): Methods of Rapid Evaluation, Assessment, and Appraisal. In *American Journal of Evaluation* 28 (3), pp. 151–168.

MEADOWS, D. H.; MEADOWS, D. L.; RANDERS, J.; BEHRENS, WILLIAM W. III. (1972): The limits to growth. A report for the Club of Rome's Project on the Predicament of Mankind. 5.th ed. New York: Universe Books.

MEIMETH, M. (2012): Introduction. In M. MEIMETH, J. D. ROBERTSON (EDS.): Sustainable Development - how to Bridge the Knowledge-Action Gap? Exploring the added value of social and cultural perspectives. 1. ed. Baden-Baden: Nomos (Denkart Europa. Schriften zur europäischen Politik, Wirtschaft und Kultur, 18), pp. 7–10.

MEIMETH, MICHAEL; ROBERTSON, JOHN D. (Eds.) (2012): Sustainable Development - how to Bridge the Knowledge-Action Gap? Exploring the added value of social and cultural perspectives. 1. ed. Baden-Baden: Nomos (Denkart Europa. Schriften zur europäischen Politik, Wirtschaft und Kultur, 18).

MIKL-HORKE, G. (1991): Industrie- und Arbeitssoziologie. München: Oldenbourg.

MITCHELL, G. (1996): Problems and Fundamentals of Sustainable Development Indicators. In *Sustainable Development* (Vol. 4), pp. 1–11.

MÖLLER, JOACHIM; WALWEI, ULRICH (Eds.) (2009): Handbuch Arbeitsmarkt 2009. Analysen, Daten, Fakten. Nürnberg: Institut für Arbeitsmarkt- und Berufsforschung (IAB-Bibliothek, 314).

MOOG, S.; RAFFELHÜSCHEN, B. (2013): Ehrbarer Staat? Die Generationenbilanz. Update 2013: Nachhaltigkeitsbilanz der Wahlprogramme. STIFTUNG MARKTWIRTSCHAFT (Argumente zu Marktwirtschaft und Politik, 121). Available online at http://www.stiftung-marktwirtschaft.de/uploads/tx_ttproducts/datasheet/Argument_121_Generationenbilanz_Update_2013_Wahlprogramme_2013_08.pdf, checked on 8/9/2014.

MORRIS, M. (2011): The Good, the Bad, and the Evaluator. 25 Years of AJE Ethics. In *American Journal of Evaluation* 32 (1), pp. 134–151.

MUTLAK, N.; SCHWARZE, R. (2007): Bausteine einer Theorie sozialer Nachhaltigkeit. Eine Bestandsaufnahme sozialwissenschaftlicher Ansätze und das Beispiel der sozialökologischen Risikoforschung. In F. BECKENBACH (ED.): Soziale Nachhaltigkeit. Marburg: Metropolis-Verl. (Jahrbuch Ökologische Ökonomik, 5), pp. 13–34.

MYERS, N.; KENT, J. (2008): The Citizen Is Willing, But Society Won't Deliver: The Problem Of Institutional Roadblocks. Winnipeg: IISD. Available online at http://www.iisd.org/pdf/2008/thecitizeniswilling.pdf, checked on 6/25/2014.

MYRDAL, G. (1973): Against the Stream: Critical Essays on Economics. New York: Pantheon Books.

NADLER, D. A.; LAWLER, EDWARD E. III (1983): Quality of Work Life: Perspectives and Directions. In *Organizational Dynamics* (Winter), pp. 20–30.

NEHRU, V.; SWANSON, E.; DUBEY, A. (1995): A New Data Base on Human Capital Stock: Sources, Methodology, and Results. In *Journal of Development Economics* 46 (2), pp. 379–401.

NETZWERK NACHHALTIGE ÖKONOMIE (2012): Kernaussagen der Nachhaltigen Ökonomie/Ökonomik. Langfassung vom 17.08.2012. Available online at http://nachhaltige-oekonomie.de/wp-content/uploads/2013/03/Langfassung_der_Kernaussagen-17-08-2012.pdf, checked on 10/11/2013.

NETZWERK NACHHALTIGE ÖKONOMIE (2012): Managementregeln. Edited by Netzwerk Nachhaltige Ökonomie. Available online at http://nachhaltige-oekonomie.de/?page_id=52, checked on 10/17/2013.

NEW ECONOMICS FOUNDATION (2012): The Happy Planet Index: 2012 Report. Edited by New Economics Foundation. London. Available online at http://www.happyplanetindex.org/assets/happy-planet-index-report.pdf, checked on 7/19/2013.

NISKANEN, W. A. (1968): The Peculiar Economics of Bureaucracy. In *American Economic Review* (Vol. 58 No. 2), pp. 293–305.

NORDHAUS, W. D. (1992): Lethal Model 2: The Limits to Growth Revisited. In *Brookings Papers on Economic Activity* 23 (2), pp. 1–60.

OBST, C. (2000): Report of the September 1999 OECD Expert Workshop on the Measurement of Sustainable Development. In OECD (Ed.): Frameworks to measure sustainable development. An OECD expert workshop. Paris: Organisation for Economic Co-operation and Development (Sustainable development), pp. 7–18.

OECD (Ed.) (1998): Nachhaltige Entwicklung. Politikkonzepte der OECD für das 21. Jahrhundert. Paris.

OECD (Ed.) (2000): Frameworks to measure sustainable development. An OECD expert workshop. Paris: Organisation for Economic Co-operation and Development (Sustainable development).

OECD (2002): Glossary of statistical terms. OECD. Available online at http://stats.oecd.org/glossary/detail.asp?ID=1163, checked on 6/1/2015.

OECD (2003): The Sources of Economic Growth. Washington: Organization for Economic Cooperation & Development.

OECD (2004): Environment and Employment: an Assessment. Edited by OECD Working Party on National Environmental Policy (ENV/EPOC/WPNEP(2003)11/FINAL).

OECD (2006): OECD Employment Outlook 2006: Boosting jobs and incomes. Paris: OECD Publishing.

OECD (2007): OECD Employment Outlook 2007. Paris: OECD Publishing.

OECD (2007): Society at a glance. OECD social indicators : Edition 2006. Paris: OECD Publishing.

OECD (2008): OECD Employment Outlook 2008. Paris: OECD Publishing.

OECD (2010): OECD Employment Outlook. Moving beyond the jobs crisis. Paris: OECD Publishing (OECD employment outlook, 2010).

OECD (2011): How's life? Measuring well-being (OECD better life initiative). Available online at http://dx.doi.org/10.1787/9789264121164-en, checked on 5/22/2015.

OECD (2012): The jobs potential of a shift towards a low-carbon economy. Final report for the european commission, DG employment. Edited by OECD Division for Employment Analysis and Policy. Paris.

OECD BETTER LIFE INITIATIVE (2011): Compendium of OECD well-being indicators. Edited by OECD. Paris. Available online at http://www.oecd.org/std/47917288.pdf.

OECD LEED (2012): Enabling Local Green Growth. Addressing Climate Change Effects on Employment and Local Development. Edited by OECD. Paris.

OESCH, D.; LIPPS, O. (2011): Does unemployment hurt less if there is more of it around? A panel analysis of life satisfaction in Germany and Switzerland. In *SOEPpapers* (393).

OLSON, M. (2002): The logic of collective action. Public goods and the theory of groups. 20. print. Cambridge, Mass: Harvard Univ. Pr (Harvard economic studies, 124).

OLTMANS, W.; CHOMSKY, N. (1976): Die Grenzen des Wachstums. Pro und contra : Interviews über die Zukunft mit Noam Chomsky et al. . Deutsche Erstausg., Reinbek bei Hamburg: Rowohlt (Rororo Sachbuch, 6879).

OSBERG, LARS (Ed.) (1991): Economic inequality and poverty. International perspectives. Armonk: Sharpe.

OTT, K.; DÖRING, R. (2007): Soziale Nachhaltigkeit: Suffizienz zwischen Lebensstilen und politischer Ökonomie. In F. BECKENBACH (ED.): Soziale Nachhaltigkeit. Marburg: Metropolis-Verl. (Jahrbuch Ökologische Ökonomik, 5), pp. 35–71.

PAECH, N.; PFRIEM, R. (2007): Wie kommt das Soziale in die Nachhaltigkeit? In F. BECKENBACH (ED.): Soziale Nachhaltigkeit. Marburg: Metropolis-Verl. (Jahrbuch Ökologische Ökonomik, 5), pp. 99–128.

PAGNATTARO, M. A. (2014): Labor rights are human rights: Sustainability initiatives and trade policy. In R. BIRD, D. R. CAHOY, J. D. PRENKERT (EDS.): Law, Business and Human Rights. Bridging the Gap. Cheltenham: Edward Elgar Publishing, pp. 143–170.

PALUMBO, D. J. (1987): Politics and Evaluation. In D. J. PALUMBO (ED.): The politics of program evaluation. Newbury Park: Sage Publ (Sage yearbooks in politics and public policy, 15), pp. 12–47.

PALUMBO, DENNIS J. (Ed.) (1987): The politics of program evaluation. Newbury Park: Sage Publ (Sage yearbooks in politics and public policy, 15).

PALUMBO, D. J.; HALLET, M. A. (1993): Conflict versus consensus models in policy evaluation and implementation. In *Evaluation and Program Planning* (16), pp. 11–23.

PATZELT, W. J. (2014): Transformationsprozesse: staatliche Statik vs. gesellschaftliche Dynamik. Welchen Beitrag leistet der evolutorische Institutionalismus zum Erklären eines funktionsfähigen Wettbewerbs? Beijing Humboldt Forum - Green Economy and Culture. Automobiles, Materials & Finance. Beijing, 2014.

PEARCE, D. W.; MARKANDYA, A.; BARBIER, E. (1989): For a Green economy. A report. London: Earthscan Publications.

PETSCHOW, U.; HÜBNER, K.; DRÖGE, S.; MEYERHOFF, J. (1998): Nachhaltigkeit und Globalisierung. Herausforderungen und Handlungsansätze ; mit 17 Tabellen. Berlin: Springer (Konzept Nachhaltigkeit).

PFISTER, G.; RENN, O. (1996): Ein Indikatorensystem zur Messung einer nachhaltigen Entwicklung in Baden-Württemberg. Stuttgart: Akad. für Technikfolgenabschätzung in Baden-Württemberg.

PICCIOTTO, R. (1999): Towards an Economics of Evaluation. In *Evaluation* 5 (1), pp. 7–22.

POLLARD, E. L.; LEE, P. D. (2003): Child Well-Being: A Systematic Review of the Literature. In *Social Indicators Research* (61 (1)), pp. 59–78.

POSCHEN, P.; ITURRIZA, A. L.; LI, X.; TOBIN, S.; DESSORS, E.; SAMAAN, D.; RENNER, M. (2012): Working towards sustainable development. Opportunities for decent work and social inclusion in a green economy. Geneva: International Labour Organisation.

POTIER, M. (1998): Integration von Umwelt und Wirtschaft. In OECD (Ed.): Nachhaltige Entwicklung. Politikkonzepte der OECD für das 21. Jahrhundert. Paris, pp. 17–30.

PREISENDÖRFER, P. (1999): Umwelteinstellungen und Umweltverhalten in Deutschland. Empirische Befunde und Analysen auf der Grundlage der Bevölkerungsumfragen "Umweltbewußtsein in Deutschland 1991-1998". Opladen: Leske + Budrich.

PSACHAROPOULOS, G.; ARRIAGADA, A. M. (1986): The Educational Composition of the Labor Force: An International Comparison. In *International Labor Review* 125 (5), pp. 561–574.

RABL, A. (1996): Discounting of Long Term Costs: What Would Future Generations Prefer Us to Do? In *Ecological Economics* (Vol. 17), pp. 137–145.

RADKE, V. (1999): Nachhaltige Entwicklung. Konzept und Indikatoren aus wirtschaftstheoretischer Sicht. Heidelberg: Physica-Verl (Umwelt und Ökonomie, Band 30).

RAFFELHÜSCHEN, B.; HAGIST, C.; HEIDLER, M.; SCHODER, J. (2007): Die Generationenbilanz - Brandmelder der Zukunft. Update 2007: Demografie trifft Konjunktur. Edited by Stiftung Marktwirtschaft Frankfurter Institut. Berlin (Argumente zu Marktwirtschaft und Politik, 100).

RANDERS, J. (2010): What was the message of the Limits to Growth? What did this little book from 1972 really say about the global future? In *Club of Rome*. Available online at www.clubofrome.org, checked on 5/6/2013.

RAT FÜR NACHHALTIGE ENTWICKLUNG (2009): Peer Review of Germany's Sustainability Policies (Info-News, 1). Available online at http://www.nachhaltigkeitsrat.de/de/projekte/eigene-projekte/peer-review-2009/?size= qpbjrunaujt, checked on 4/24/2009.

RAT FÜR NACHHALTIGE ENTWICKLUNG (2010): Bekanntheitsgrad des Leitbildes Nachhaltigkeit hat sich verdreifacht. Available online at http://www.nachhaltigkeitsrat.de/news-nachhaltigkeit/2010/2010-12-22/bekanntheitsgrad-des-leitbildes-nachhaltigkeit-hat-sich-verdreifacht/, checked on 10/25/2013.

RAT FÜR NACHHALTIGE ENTWICKLUNG (2013): Sustainability - Made in Germany. The Second Review by a Group of International Peers, comissioned by the German Federal Chancellery. Berlin.

RAWLS, J. (1971): A theory of justice. Orig. ed., reprint. Cambridge, MA: Belknap Press of Harvard University Press.

RENN, O.; DEUSCHLE, J.; JÄGER, A.; WEIMER-JEHLE, W. (2007): Leitbild Nachhaltigkeit. Eine normativ-funktionale Konzeption und ihre Umsetzung. Wiesbaden: VS Verlag für Sozialwissenschaften | GWV Fachverlage GmbH Wiesbaden.

REPUTATION INSTITUTE (2013): 2013 CSR RepTrak 100 Study. Available online at http://www.reputationinstitute.com/thought-leadership/csr-reptrak-100, checked on 3/18/2014.

RITT, T. (2007): Integrierter Umweltschutz und Beschäftigung - Ergebnisse von Erhebungen in fünf EU-Staaten. In K. D. JOHN (ED.): Arbeitslosigkeit in Europa. Neue Perspektiven durch die Vermarktung umweltfreundlicher Technologien? ; Beiträge zum 2. Chemnitzer Symposium "Europa und Umwelt". Aachen: Shaker (Schriftenreihe der Chemnitzer Wirtschaftswissenschaftlichen Gesellschaft, Bd. 8), pp. 69–129.

ROBINS, R. W.; BEER, J. S. (2001): Positive Illusions About the Self: Short-Term Benefits and Long-Term Costs. In *Journal of Personality and Social Psychology* (Vol. 80 No. 2), pp. 340–352.

ROCHEFORT, D. A.; COBB, R. W. (1993): Problem Definition, Agenda Access, and Policy Choice. In *Policy Studies Journal* (Vol. 21, No. 1), pp. 56–71.

ROGALL, H. (2007): Ökonomie der Nachhaltigkeit - Chancen für Beschäftigung und Umwelt. In K. D. JOHN (ED.): Arbeitslosigkeit in Europa. Neue Perspektiven durch die Vermarktung umweltfreundlicher Technologien? ; Beiträge zum 2. Chemnitzer Symposium "Europa und Umwelt". Aachen: Shaker (Schriftenreihe der Chemnitzer Wirtschaftswissenschaftlichen Gesellschaft, Bd. 8), pp. 33–67.

ROMER, CHRISTINA; ROMER, DAVID (Eds.) (1997): Reducing inflation. Motivation and strategy. Chicago: University of Chicago Press (Studies in business cycles, v. 30).

ROSS, S. A. (1973): The Economic Theory of Agency: The Principal's Problem. In *The American Economic Review* (Vol. 63 No. 2), pp. 134–139.

ROSSI, P. H.; FREEMAN, H. E. (1993): Evaluation. A systematic approach. 5.th ed. Beverly Hills: Sage.

SALOP, S. C. (1979): A Model of the Natural Rate of Unemployment. In *The American Economic Review* 69 (1), pp. 117–125.

Sauer, Dieter (2011): Von der "Humanisierung der Arbeit" zur "Guten Arbeit". In: *Aus Politik und Zeitgeschichte* (15), S. 18–24.

SCHAACK, D.; NIEMANN, H.; WARNKEN, T.; WÄGELI, S.; HAMM, U.; SANDERS, J. ET AL. (2013): Die Bio-Branche 2013. Zahlen - Daten - Fakten. Edited by Bund Ökologische Lebensmittelwirtschaft. Berlin.

SCHÄPKE, N.; RAUSCHMAYER, F. (2012): Addressing Sufficiency - Including altruistic motives in behavioural models for sustainability transitions. In *UFZ Discussion Papers* (17/2012). Available online at http://www.ufz.de/export/data/global/45182_17%202012%20Schaepke_Addressing%20Sufficiency_gesamt_internet.pdf, checked on 11/8/2013.

SCHEER, DIRK (Ed.) (2006): Governance und Nachhaltigkeit. Sondierung und Analyse beispielhafter sozial-ökologischer Steuerungsmuster. Schriftenreihe des IÖW (183/06). Heidelberg.

SCHMID, GÜNTHER (Ed.) (1997): International handbook of labour market policy and evaluation. Reprint., paperback ed. Cheltenham: Elgar.

SCHMID, G. (1997): The Evaluation of Labour Market Policy: Notes on the State of the Art. In *Evaluation and Program Planning* 3 (4), pp. 409–434.

SCHMID, G.; O'REILLY, J.; SCHÖMANN, K. (1997): Theory and Methodology of Labour Market Policy and Evaluation: An Introduction. In G. SCHMID (ED.): International handbook of labour market policy and evaluation. Reprint., paperback ed. Cheltenham: Elgar, pp. 1–33.

SCHMID, M. (2014): Legalität und Legitimität als Anforderung an die Economic Governance. Wittenberg (Economic Governance und Ordonomik), 5/21/2014.

SCHRAAD-TISCHLER, D. (2014): Nachhaltiges Regieren in der OECD und EU - Wo steht Deutschland? Sustainable Governance Indicators 2014 - Zukunftsfähigkeit im Vergleich. Edited by Bertelsmann Stiftung. Gütersloh.

SCHRADER, ULF; HANSEN, URSULA (Eds.) (2001): Nachhaltiger Konsum. Forschung und Praxis im Dialog. Frankfurt/Main, New York: Campus (Bd. 831).

SCHRÖDER, C.; RÖHL, K.-H. (2014): Die Kraft der Einkommen. Regionale Armut. In *iwd* (35), pp. 4–5.

SCHRÖTER, D. C. (2008): The logic and methodology of sustainability evaluation: a checklist approach. In M. ANT (ED.): Nachhaltiger Mehrwert von Evaluation. Bielefeld: Bertelsmann-Verl., pp. 217–236.

SCHWARTZ, M. S.; CARROLL, A. B. (2003): Corporate Social Responsibility: A Three-Domain Approach. In *Business Ethics Quarterly* (Vol. 13 No. 4), pp. 503–530.

SCRIVEN, M. (1997): Empowerment Evaluation Examined. In *American Journal of Evaluation* 18 (2), pp. 165–175.

SECRÉTARIAT DU CONSEIL DU TRÉSOR DU CANADA (2012): Theory-based approaches to evaluation: Concepts and practices. Concepts and practices. [Ottawa]: Treasury Board of Canada Secretariat.

SGB III (1997): Sozialgesetzbuch Drittes Buch - Arbeitsförderung, SGB III, revised zuletzt geändert am 8/11/2014 (BGBl. I S. 1348). In : BGBl- I S. 594.

SIMMONS, M. R. (2000): Revisiting The Limits to Growth: Could The Club of Rome Have Been Correct, After All? An Energy White Paper.

SINUS: Informationen zu den Sinus-Milieus 2015. Edited by Sinus Markt- und Sozialforschung. Heidelberg, Berlin. Available online at http://www.sinus-institut.de/loesungen/sinus-milieus.html.

SIRGY, M. J.; EFRATY, D.; SIEGEL, P.; LEE, D.-J. (2001): A new measure of quality of work life (QWL) based on need satisfaction and spillover theories. In *Social Indicators Research* (55), pp. 241–302.

SMITH, A. (1904): An Inquiry into the Nature and Causes of the Wealth of Nations. Facsimile of 1904 ed (16. Mai 2012). Chicago: University of Chicago Press.

SMITH, J. (2000): Evaluation aktiver Arbeitsmarktpolitik: Erfahrungen aus Nordamerika. In *MittAB* 33 (3), pp. 345–356.

SPANGENBERG, J. H. (2005): Die ökonomische Nachhaltigkeit der Wirtschaft. Theorien, Kriterien und Indikatoren. Univ., Diss.--Bremen, 2004. Berlin: edition sigma.

SPURGEON, A.; HARRINGTON, J. M.; COOPER, C. L. (1997): Health and safety problems associated with long working hours: a review of the current position. In *Occupational and Environmental Medicine* (54), pp. 367–375.

SRU (2002): Für eine neue Vorreiterrolle. Umweltgutachten 2002 des Rates von Sachverständigen für Umweltfragen. Edited by Deutscher Bundestag. Berlin (Drucksache 13/11200, 14/8792).

SRU (2011): Ökologische Leitplanken setzen, natürliche Lebensgrundlagen schützen. Empfehlungen zum Fortschrittsbericht 2012 zur nationalen Nachhaltigkeitsstrategie. Edited by Sachverständigenrat für Umweltfragen. Berlin (Kommentar zur Umweltpolitik, Nr. 9).

SRU (2012): Verantwortung in einer begrenzten Welt. Umweltgutachten 2012. Berlin: Schmidt (Umweltgutachten, 2012).

STABG (1967): Gesetz zur Förderung der Stabilität und des Wachstums der Wirtschaft vom 8. Juni 1967 (BGBI. I S. 582), das zuletzt durch Artikel 135 der Verordnung vom 31. Oktober 2006 (BGBI. I S. 2407) geändert worden ist. StabG. Available online at http://www.gesetze-im-internet.de/bundesrecht/stabg/gesamt.pdf, checked on 7/26/2013.

STAGL, S. (2004): Valuation for Sustainable Development - The Role of Multicriteria Evaluation. In *Vierteljahrshefte zur Wirtschaftsforschung* (73 (2004), 1), pp. 53–62.

STAIGER, D. O.; STOCK, J. H.; WATSON, M. W. (1997): How Precise Are Estimates of the Natural Rate of Unemployment? In C. ROMER, D. ROMER (EDS.): Reducing inflation. Motivation and strategy. Chicago: University of Chicago Press (Studies in business cycles, v. 30), pp. 195–246.

STAMM, M. (2008): Evaluation: Wirksame Wege zur Nutzung - Wege zur wirksamen Nutzung. In M. ANT (ED.): Nachhaltiger Mehrwert von Evaluation. Bielefeld: Bertelsmann-Verl., pp. 145–158.

STATISTISCHES BUNDESAMT (2008): Nachhaltige Entwicklung in Deutschland. Indikatorenbericht 2008. Edited by Statistisches Bundesamt. Wiesbaden. Available online at http://www.destatis.de/jetspeed/portal/cms/Sites/destatis/Internet/EN/Navigation/Statistics/TimeSeries/Indicators/SubstainableDevelopmentIndicators__nk.psml, checked on 1/8/2014.

STATISTISCHES BUNDESAMT (2010): Umweltökonomische Gesamtrechnungen. Nachhaltige Entwicklung in Deutschland - Indikatoren der deutschen Nachhaltigkeitsstrategie zu Umwelt und Ökonomie. Wiesbaden. Available online at http://www.destatis.de/jetspeed/portal/cms/Sites/destatis/Internet/DE/Content/Publikationen/ Fachveroeffentlichungen/UmweltoekonomischeGesamtrechnungen/Indikatoren2010,property=file.pdf, checked on 7/23/2014.

STATISTISCHES BUNDESAMT (2010): Nachhaltige Entwicklung in Deutschland. Indikatorenbericht 2010. Edited by Statistisches Bundesamt. Wiesbaden. Available online at http://www.destatis.de/jetspeed/portal/cms/Sites/destatis/Internet/DE/Content/Publikationen/Fachveroeffentlichungen/UmweltoekonomischeGesamtrechnungen/Indikatorenbericht2010,property=file.pdf, checked on 7/23/2014.

STATISTISCHES BUNDESAMT (2012): Sustainable development in Germany. Indicator Report 2012 of the Federal Statistical Office of Germany. Edited by Statistisches Bundesamt. Wiesbaden. Available online at https://www.destatis.de/EN/FactsFigures/Indicators/SustainableDevelopmentIndicators/SustainableDevelopmentIndicators.html, checked on 5/8/2014.

STATISTISCHES BUNDESAMT (2013): Nachhaltige Entwicklung in Deutschland. Indikatoren zu Umwelt und Ökonomie 2013. Edited by Statistisches Bundesamt. Wiesbaden (Umweltökonomische Gesamtrechnungen). Available online at https://www.destatis.de/DE/ZahlenFakten/Indikatoren/Nachhaltigkeitsindikatoren/Nachhaltigkeitsindikatoren.html, checked on 5/28/2014.

STAVINS, R. (1992): Comments on 'Lethal Model 2: The Limits to Growth Revisited' by William Nordhaus. In *Brookings Papers on Economic Activity* (2), pp. 44–50.

STEPHAN, G.; RÄSSLER, S.; SCHEWE, T. (2006): Das TrEffeR-Projekt der Bundesagentur für Arbeit: Die Wirkung von Maßnahmen aktiver Arbeitsmarktpolitik. In *Zeitschrift für ArbeitsmarktForschung* 39 (3/4), pp. 447–465.

STEURER, R. (2001): Paradigmen der Nachhaltigkeit. In *Zeitschrift für Umweltpolitik & Umweltrecht* (4), pp. 537–566.

STIGLITZ, J. E.; SEN, A.; FITOUSSI, J.-P. (2009): Report by the Commission on the Measurement of Economic Performance and Social Progress. Edited by Commission sur la Mesure de la Performance Économique et du Progrès Social. Paris. Available online at http://www.stiglitz-sen-fitoussi.fr/fr/, checked on 6/6/2014.

STOCKMANN, R. (2006): Evaluation in Deutschland. In R. STOCKMANN (ED.): Evaluationsforschung. Grundlagen und ausgewählte Forschungsfelder. 3. Aufl. Münster, New York, München, Wien: Waxmann (Sozialwissenschaftliche Evaluationsforschung, Bd. 1), pp. 15–46.

STOCKMANN, REINHARD (Ed.) (2006): Evaluationsforschung. Grundlagen und ausgewählte Forschungsfelder. 3. Aufl. Münster, New York, München, Wien: Waxmann (Sozialwissenschaftliche Evaluationsforschung, Bd. 1).

STUTZER, A.; FREY, B. S. (2008): Stress that Doesn't Pay: The Commuting Paradox. In *The Scandinavian Journal of Economics* 110 (2), pp. 339–366.

SYSTEM DYNAMICS SOCIETY (2013): The Field of System Dynamics. What is SD? SYSTEM DYNAMICS SOCIETY. Available online at http://www.systemdynamics.org/what-is-s/, checked on 11/13/2013.

TAKALA, J. (2002): Introductory Report: Decent Work - Safe Work. Paper presented at the 16th World Congess on Safety and Health on May 27, 2002. Vienna.

THE CLUB OF ROME (2013): About the Club of Rome. Available online at http://www.clubofrome.org/, checked on 10/25/2013.

THE WORLD BANK (2015): Data: Long-term unemployment. Available online at http://data.worldbank.org/indicator/SL.UEM.LTRM.ZS/countries, checked on 6/6/2015.

TIESSEN, J.; LEY, S.; ERNST, T.; JOBBERGER, L.; RIEDEL, H.; THODE, E. (2011): Leitfaden für Nachhaltigkeitsprüfungen im Rahmen von Gesetzesfolgenabschätzungen. Ein Projekt der Bertelsmann Stiftung mit Unterstützung durch die Prognos AG und die Pricewaterhouse-Coopers AG WPG. Edited by Bertelsmann Stiftung. Gütersloh.

TILS, R. (2005): Politische Strategieanalyse. Konzeptionelle Grundlagen und Anwendung in der Umwelt- und Nachhaltigkeitspolitik. 1. Aufl. Wiesbaden: VS Verl. für Sozialwiss.

TNS EMNID; BERTELSMANN STIFTUNG (2012): Kein Wachstum um jeden Preis. Kurzbericht. Edited by Bertelsmann Stiftung. Gütersloh. Available online at http://www.bertelsmann-stiftung.de/cps/rde/xbcr/SID-3294E172-05E4C265/bst/xcms_bst_dms_36359_36360_2.pdf, checked on 8/23/2013.

TREMMEL, J. (2003): Nachhaltigkeit als politische und analytische Kategorie. Der deutsche Diskurs um nachhaltige Entwicklung im Spiegel der Interessen der Akteure. Zugl.: Diplomarbeit. München: Ökom-Verl. (Hochschulschriften zur Nachhaltigkeit, 4).

TURNER, G. M. (2008): A comparison of the Limits to Growth with 30 years of reality. In *Global Environmental Change* (18), pp. 397–411.

TURPIN, A. (1989): Winner of the 1988 President's problem. In *Evaluation Practice* (10), pp. 53–57.

UN DESA (2002): Johannesburg Summit 2002. Key Outcomes of the Summit. UN DESA. Available online at http://www.unesco.org/education/tlsf/mods/theme_a/img/02_WSSD Outcomes.pdf, checked on 11/19/2013.

UN DESA (2003): Indicators of Sustainable Development: Guidelines and Methodologies - Methodology sheets. Available online at htt://www.un.org/esa/sustdev/natlinfo/indicators/ methodology_sheets.pdf, checked on 10/24/2014.

UN DESA (2004): Assessment Report on National Sustainable Development Strategies: The Global Picture 2003. Edited by UN DESA. Available online at http://www.un.org/esa/sustdev/natlinfo/nsds/assessmentreport_2003.pdf, checked on 8/16/2013.

UN DESA (2007): Indicators of sustainable development. Guidelines and methodologies. 3. ed. New York: United Nations (Economic & social affairs).

UN DESA (2012): Back to Our Common Future. Sustainable Development in the 21st century project. Summary for policymakers. New York: United Nations.

UN DESA (2012): Sustainable Development in the 21st Century. National Institutions for Sustainable Development. A preliminary review of the institutional literature. Draft. Edited by UN DESA. Available online at http://sustainabledevelopment.un.org/content/documents/ 1372Study2_final%20draft.pdf, checked on 8/16/2013.

UN General Assembly (1983): Process of preparation of the Environmental Perspective to the Year 2000 and Beyond. A/RES/38/161. A/RES/38/161. Available online at http://www.un.org/documents/ga/res/38/a38r161.htm, checked on 5/27/2010 .

UNCED (1992): Agenda 21. Available online at http://www.sustainabledevelopment.un.org/content/documents/Agenda21.pdf, checked on 5/27/2010.

UNCED (Ed.) (1992): Rio Declaration on Environment and Development. United Nations. Available online at http://www.unep.org/Documents.Multilingual/Default.Print.asp? documentid=78&articleid=1163, checked on 5/28/2013.

UNCHE (1972): Declaration of the United Nations Conference on the Human Environment. United Nations. Stockholm. Available online at http://www.unep.org/Documents.Multilingual/Default.Print.asp?DocumentID=97&ArticleID=1503&l=en, checked on 5/27/2010.

UNESCO (2015): Adult Secondary (Tertiary) Schooling Attainment Level. Online verfügbar unter http://www.un.org/esa/sustdev/natlinfo/indicators/methodology_sheets/education/adult_secondary_schooling.pdf.

UNFCCC (1999): Status of Ratification of the Kyoto Protocol. United Nations Framework Convention on Climate Change. Available online at http://unfccc.int/kyoto_protocol/status_of_ratification/items/2613.php, updated on 11/19/2013.

United Nations (1997): UN Conference on Environment and Development (1992). Available online at http://www.un.org/geninfo/bp/enviro.html, checked on 5/28/2013.

United Nation (2012): The future we want. A/RES/66/288. Edited by United Nations. New York. Available online at http://www.un.org/ga/search/view_doc.asp?symbol=A/RES/66/288&Lang=E, checked on 7/12/2013.

United Nations (2014): UN at a glance. Available online at http://un.org, checked on 7/25/2014.

Vandenberg, P. (2010): Impact of Labor Market Institutions on Unemployment: Results from a Global Panel. In *ADB Economics Working Paper Series* (219).

VIRTANEN, M.; SINGH-MANOUX, A.; FERRIE, J. E.; GIMENO, D.; MARMOT, M. G.; ELOVAINIO, M. ET AL. (2009): Long Working Hours and Cognitive Function. The Whitehall II Study. In *American Journal of Epidemiology* 169 (5), pp. 596–605.

VRING, T. VON DER (2007): Welche Politik schafft Arbeitsplätze? Eine empirische Überprüfung theoretischer Behauptungen. Marburg: Metropolis. Available online at http://www.gbv.de/dms/bs/toc/524641994.pdf.

WACKERNAGEL, M.; REES, W. E. (1997): Perceptual and structural barriers to investing in natural capital: Economics from an ecological footprint perspective. In *Ecological Economics* (20), pp. 3–24.

WAHEED, B.; KHAN, F.; VEITCH, B. (2009): Linkage-Based Frameworks for Sustainability Assessment: Making a Case for Driving Force-Pressure-State-Exposure-Effect-Action (DPSEEA) Frameworks. In *Sustainability* 1 (3), pp. 441–463.

WCED (1987): A/RES/42/187. Report of the UN World Commission on Environment and Development, General Assembly Resolution 42/187, 11. December 1987. UNITED NATIONS. Available online at http://www.un.org/documents/ga/res/42/ares42-187.htm, updated on 12/16/1999, checked on 4/7/2009.

WCED (1987): Our Common Future. Report of the World Commission on Environment and Development. With assistance of Gro Harlem Brundtland, Mansour Khalid. Edited by United Nations Organisation. Available online at http://www.un-documents.net/our-common-future.pdf, checked on 5/28/2013.

WEILAND, M. (2008): Arbeitsförderung für Ältere - Perspektive 50plus. In M. ANT (ED.): Nachhaltiger Mehrwert von Evaluation. Bielefeld: Bertelsmann-Verl., pp. 27–53.

WEINBERG, J. (1999): Neuere Arbeitsmarkttheorien zur Erklärung der Arbeitslosigkeit in Deutschland in kritischer Reflexion. Marburg: Tectum-Verl. (Wissenschaftliche Beiträge aus dem Tectum-Verlag Reihe Wirtschaftswissenschaften, 11).

WEINKOPF, C. (2002): Subventionierte Niedriglohnjobs - kein Königsweg zu mehr Beschäftigung. In G. BOSCH, P. HENNICKE, J. HILBERT, K. KRISTOF, G. SCHERHORN (EDS.): Die Zukunft von Dienstleistungen. Ihre Auswirkung auf Arbeit, Umwelt und Lebensqualität. Frankfurt am Main u. a.: Campus Verl., pp. 305–329.

WERLE, K. (2015): Königsklasse. Beste Arbeitgeber. In *manager magazin* (5), pp. 96–98

WETZEL, R. (2005): Hintergründe und Steuerungspotenziale der Nachhaltigkeit. ein systemtheoretischer Blick. In K. GROẞMANN (ED.): Im Prinzip Nachhaltigkeit. Akteurskonstellationen und Handlungsmöglichkeiten in interdisziplinärer Betrachtung. 1. Aufl. München: Hampp, pp. 189–210.

WGBU (2011): Welt im Wandel: Gesellschaftsvertrag für eine Große Transformation. [Hauptgutachten]. Berlin: Wiss. Beirat d. Bundesregierung Globale Umweltveränderungen (Welt im Wandel).

WIDMER, T. (2008): Qualitätsförderung und Qualitätssicherung mit Evaluationsstandards. In M. ANT (ED.): Nachhaltiger Mehrwert von Evaluation. Bielefeld: Bertelsmann-Verl., pp. 83–100.

WILLKE, G. (1999): Die Zukunft unserer Arbeit. Frankfurt am Main: Campus-Verl.

WOLFF, P. (2007): EU Sustainable Development Indicators. Monitoring the Sustainable Development Strategy. ESDN Workshop on Sustainable Development Indicators at the EU Level. ESDN. Cascais, 11/29/2007.

WOTTAWA, H.; THIERAU, H. (1998): Lehrbuch Evaluation. 2., vollst. überarb. Aufl. Bern: Huber.

WVS (2014): World Value Survey. Data files. Edited by WVS, checked on 1/9/2015.

ZIMMERMANN, K. F. (2014): Evidenzbasierte wissenschaftliche Politikberatung. In *IZA Standpunkte* (74).

ZINN, K. G. (2003): Nachhaltigkeit im Arbeitsleben. Hindernislauf gegen Unvernunft und Ideologie. In G. LINNE, M. SCHWARZ (EDS.): Handbuch Nachhaltige Entwicklung. Wie ist nachhaltiges Wirtschaften machbar? Opladen: Leske + Budrich (Handbücher Leske + Budrich), pp. 395–405.

MIX
Papier aus verantwortungsvollen Quellen
Paper from responsible sources
FSC® C105338

FSC
www.fsc.org

If you have any concerns about our products,
you can contact us on
ProductSafety@springernature.com

In case Publisher is established outside the EU,
the EU authorized representative is:
Springer Nature Customer Service Center GmbH
Europaplatz 3, 69115 Heidelberg, Germany

Printed by Libri Plureos GmbH
in Hamburg, Germany